The Rise and Fall of Keynesian Economics

The Rise and Fall of Keynesian Economics

An investigation of its contribution to capitalist development

MICHAEL BLEANEY

St. Martin's Press   New York

ISBN 0-312-68267-0

Library of Congress Cataloging in Publication Data

Bleaney, M. F.
   The rise and fall of Keynesian economics.

   Bibliography: p.
   Includes index.
   1. Keynesian economics.   2. Economic history –
1918-1945.   3. Economic history – 1945 –   . I. Title.
HB99.7.B55   1985   330.15'6   84–17746
ISBN 0-312-68267-0

Contents

Illustrations

vii

Tables

Preface

This book focuses on the practical achievements of Keynesian ideas. It is not a record of what government officials or academic economists thought at various times, but rather an attempt to assess what difference those thoughts and the policies which flowed from them have made to the economic history of the advanced capitalist world. This is a very big question – too big to be satisfactorily answered in one book – but also a very interesting one. It is one which is seldom addressed directly, although implicit answers to it underlie many deeply held opinions about macroeconomic problems. It raises major issues about the general pattern of capitalist development over the last half-century; the conclusions which I reach accordingly reflect much more than just a particular interpretation of Keynesian economics.

The book is structured as follows. Chapters 1 and 5 are theoretical. Chapter 1 reviews the whole debate about the Keynesian revolution, and Chapter 5 investigates how much is left of it after the Monetarist counter-attack. Those who feel they have had more than enough of such theoretical disputes may concentrate on the other chapters. Chapter 2 looks at the experience of four countries which employed fiscal measures to promote recovery in the 1930s, and draws some conclusions. Chapter 3 briefly describes the elevation of Keynesian thought into official orthodoxy in Britain and the USA during the war years. Chapter 4 investigates the contribution of Keynesian economics to the post-war boom, and Chapter 6 asks why it has slipped from official favour since that boom ended in the early 1970s.

Although the reader will find in this book much orthodox economic analysis, I would like to acknowledge my debt to writers in the Marxist tradition. The emphasis on class conflict, the insistence on the connections between economics and wider social developments, including politics, and the refusal to accept official formulations of economic problems at face value – all these have been consistent elements in the Marxist tradition and have powerfully influenced my own thinking. By contrast mainstream macroeconomics in the West, with the exception of a few individuals (amongst whom I would particularly like to single out Angus Maddison), has tended to remain trapped within the short-run perspectives of aggregate demand management or the abstractions of growth models, and has conspicuously failed to bring any sort of historical vision to current economic problems.

I would like to thank Sam Aaronovitch, Christine Ennew, Roger Middleton, Peter Morris and Jack Parkinson for their comments on chapters of this book in draft form. Any errors which remain are of course entirely my own responsibility.

M. F. B.

Abbreviations

EEC	European Economic Community
EFTA	European Free Trade Association
EO	OECD Economic Outlook
GDP	Gross Domestic Product
GNP	Gross National Product
OECD	Organisation for Economic Co-operation and Development
OEEC	Organisation for European Co-operation
TUC	Trades Union Congress
UN	United Nations

I
The Keynesian Revolution

In one sense the Keynesian revolution was purely the product of one person's mind. Others made a significant contribution, but if the mind of John Maynard Keynes had worked differently, *The General Theory of Employment Interest and Money* would have been a different book, or might never have been written at all. But in another, deeper sense, it was the product of the Great Depression, or rather of the crisis in economic theory produced by that Depression. The policy recommendations of the *General Theory* were, by the time it was published in 1936, fairly familiar (Davis, 1971; Garvy, 1975; Shackle, 1967), not least because of the use that had been made of them in several countries over the previous few years (see Chapter 2). Keynes's achievement was to bridge the gulf between these practical ideas and pure neoclassical theory; to root these thoughts in (as he conceived it) a new, general theory of economics.

The issues raised by this project have racked economic theory ever since, and have certainly not been resolved. Monetarists tend to attach no great significance to Keynes's book, except as a source of a number of influential but erroneous intellectual fads. 'Left Keynesians' see it as the foundation stone of an anti-neoclassical economics which should be linked to an earlier, classical tradition. And finally the textbook 'neoclassical synthesis' simply juxtaposes Keynesian macroeconomics and neo-classical microeconomics in the hope that no one will bother to ask any awkward questions.

None of these attitudes seems to me to be particularly useful in deciding what was truly novel in Keynes's theory. In this chapter I summarise the main arguments of the *General Theory*, and survey the debates which have subsequently developed over its relationship to the pre-existing neoclassical orthodoxy. My conclusion is that the *General Theory was* revolutionary in its analysis of the laws of motion of capitalist production, i.e. in its macroeconomic theory; but since it concentrates on short-run dynamics and makes certain simplifying assumptions it takes as given a large slice of economic life almost without inquiry. The book does not investigate the structure of twentieth-century capitalist economies; it simply takes over orthodox nineteenth century assumptions of competitive markets and carries on from there. As a work of criticism of received theory this is one of its main sources of strength, but the limitations to the theoretical innovations which result must be recognised. Keynes's remarks about future perspectives for the capitalist economies are interesting, but anecdotal and no more than suggestive. Lacking any historical theory of capitalist development, he has much less to say on these matters than the 'underworld writers', like Marx and Hobson, whom he commends for keeping alive the concept of effective demand.

In sum, the *General Theory* does not present its own distinctive *Weltanschauung*; there is nothing new in its underlying vision of the economic and social order. The great weakness of the 'left Keynesians' is that they have never absorbed the true significance of this point, a further reflection of which is the fact that there could be a Keynesian revolution in Marxian economics (Kalecki) as much as in neoclassical economics. But the Keynesian revolution certainly did alter our understanding of the dynamics of capitalist economies, and its subversive element lay in the challenge to the exaggerated notions of their stability characteristic of the neoclassical tradition (of which more below). Politically, this was a powder keg, and has led directly to Keynesianism being associated with a high degree of state intervention in economic life. Amongst non-economists, 'Keynesianism' is a term often used to summarise the entire ideology of post-war Welfare State capitalism, and in modern Monetarist ideology attacks on Keynesian macroeconomic theory run alongside a vigorous defence of the market mechanism. Such a politicisation of the debate about Keynes in fact rests more on an association of ideas than strict logic, but is none the less powerful for that.[1]

The claim that the *General Theory* was a revolutionary book was first made by Keynes himself in a famous letter to George Bernard Shaw,[2] and also in the first chapters of the book itself. But a theory can only be revolutionary by reference to pre-existing doctrine, so to judge this claim we must first build up some picture of orthodox neoclassical theory as it stood on the eve of the Great Depression.

The question which Keynes himself asked – and many others have asked since – is why the neoclassical tradition did not believe in the possibility of deficient effective demand and involuntary unemployment. The difficulty is that, in all the volumes of economic analysis which were produced over the years by this tradition, there is no direct answer to this question. This might seem peculiar, but the explanation is really quite simple: no one thought in terms of concepts such as effective demand. The mental habits of neoclassical economics were such that it never occurred to anyone that a question such as Keynes's could be a sensible one.[3] But why not? To understand that, which concerns the instinctive responses of the trained neoclassical mind to a macroeconomic problem, is the essential first step to understanding what the Keynesian revolution was about.

The Neoclassical Mind

The rise of neoclassical economics is usually dated from around 1870, although its roots can be traced much earlier. But this was the date when Walras, Menger and Jevons quite independently but virtually simultaneously presented theories of the distribution of consumer demand based on the principle of utility maximisation, and derived the proposition that marginal utilities would be proportional to price. This picture of the rational self-interested individual in the marketplace busily working out the optimum response to changing price signals is the essence of neoclassical economics. As originally presented, it related exclusively to the demand side and tended to suggest that demand was the sole determinant of price, but this bias was firmly corrected by Alfred Marshall, who demonstrated that equal attention needed to be paid to the supply side of the market.

The central point of early neoclassical writing, that high prices of a particular commodity would discourage consumption of that commodity, had not escaped Smith, Ricardo or other classical economists, but they were content to assume that this fact, in combination with the restless search of capital for the maximum profit, would always be driving market prices back to 'natural prices', which would just earn capital the same rate of return in each industry. For them the real issue was to ignore the day-to-day fluctuations of the marketplace and to understand the economic system on the assumption that all commodities traded at their natural prices. Just how many eggs and how much bread people chose to consume at these prices they did not regard as a very interesting question, and one relating more to the psychology of human taste than to economics.

However, to the neoclassical thinkers such interactions of prices and quantities were the nub of economic life. To comprehend the market mechanism in all its facets was the crux of the matter. Production created an interesting category of persons called entrepreneurs and a whole new set of markets for 'factors of production', but was of no deeper significance. Economic theory moved into a search for general laws of supply and demand. The analysis of the utility-maximising consumer immediately suggested that the demand curve should be downward-sloping in terms of price, and the most general form of the supply curve, allowing for the fact that some suppliers might be in a more favourable position than others, seemed to be upward-sloping. The natural conclusion from this was that in the typical market there would be a unique and stable equilibrium, where the supply and demand curves intersected. This conclusion rested on the assumption that prices of other commodities, consumers' incomes and the rate of profit prevailing in the rest of the economy could be taken as given.

The neoclassicals then went on to postulate the existence of a general equilibrium, with demand equal to supply in *every* market. In essence this was perhaps little more than their predecessors had envisaged in concentrating on the case where goods exchanged at their natural prices; but it quickly became imbued with all sorts of assumptions about its stability and the self-correcting powers of the free market that were neither seriously investigated nor, as Keynes was to show, justified. The assumptions necessary to the proof of stability in the individual market were invalid for the economy as a whole, and yet the results were unceremoniously translated from the particular to the general case without recognition of this point. Those who went in for the formal investigation of general equilibrium, notably Léon Walras, avoided the stability issue by the use of intellectual devices such as the 'auctioneer' or 'recontracting' (Edgeworth), both of which effectively meant that what occurred when the system was not at its equilibrium could be ignored. Those, such as Alfred Marshall and his followers, who tended to regard Walras's exercises as somewhat arid and meaningless were no better, for in their approach to macroeconomic issues they took the existence and stability of a general equilibrium entirely as a matter of course (Marshall does not even bother to discuss it in his *Principles*). As Stigler (1946, p. 244) has remarked, it was sixty years before anyone bothered to follow up Walras's investigations into the existence and uniqueness of general equilibria, let alone their stability.[4]

The concept of general equilibrium was essentially a long-run concept. Since the long run never arrived, the real world could be forgiven for being continually disturbed by technical changes, random events, financial crises and the oscillations of business and consumer expectations. These formed the subject matter of trade cycle theory – an attempt to explain the observed patterns of boom and slump, aspects of reality with which 'pure' theory did not have to bother. But the relationship of trade cycle theory to the pure theory out of which the concept of general equilibrium was generated was essentially subordinate. The raw material – the basic elements of economic analysis – may have been the same, but trade cycle theory was merely a study of the ripples on the surface of economic life, not an investigation of its innermost secrets. Because price changes were always occurring, there was a strong temptation to regard observed economic fluctuations as a manifestation of a human propensity towards an over-exuberant response to changing price signals. In other words, trade cycle theory necessarily included strong psychological elements which could be ignored in the luxurious environment of pure theoretical inquiry. Firmly based in reality and having to deal with tricky issues like expectations of the future, trade cycle theory found itself almost overwhelmed by the complexity of that reality and seemed unable to cut through it to offer simple explanations, whilst pure theory just inhabited a world of its own (an amusing description of this intellectual split may be found in Samuelson's (1968) recollections of what he was taught as a student).

This split need not have been so great, and perhaps need not have existed at all, if the pure theory of general equilibrium had been less blindly optimistic about the stabilising qualities of the free market mechanism or if it had been able to generate concepts useful to the study of economic fluctuations. Its great failure here was its dismissal of the concept resurrected with such effectiveness by Keynes, that of effective demand.

The fundamental problem was the obsession with relative price movements. The notion of general equilibrium immediately suggested the very static idea that if only all prices were at their equilibrium values, macroeconomic bliss would automatically follow. So macroeconomic disequilibria of any sort could be regarded as a problem of some prices being out of line with others, and the solution would lie in *relative price movements*. Commodities in excess supply should fall in price and those in excess demand should rise. But it was hard to make progress beyond this general statement: the infinite variety of possible relative price problems defeated further theoretical analysis. Any concept of real effective demand seemed to be ruled out by insoluble index number problems as prices of different commodities moved relative to one another (in any case how could *total* effective demand explain *relative* price problems?).

This last point probably explains the mystery about the quantity theory of money. The left-hand side of the quantity equation (MV–the volume of money multiplied by its velocity of circulation) is nothing less than the definition of total monetary effective demand, whilst the right-hand side (PT) is simply the monetary value of output. The equation was usually interpreted to mean that MV determines PT, so it is sufficient to postulate the short-run rigidity of the price level for it to become a theory of the determination of real output (T) by real effective demand (MV/P). That no one attempted to use the quantity theory in this manner reflected a combination of two strongly-held beliefs: that the price level maintained a considerable degree of flexibility, and that some prices were more flexible than others, so that relative price changes would inevitably occur, thereby demolishing the notion of real effective demand.

The notion of a flexible price level seemed to be supported by empirical observation. In the nineteenth century there had been lengthy periods of both rising and falling prices, with no obvious long-term trend in either direction. The First World War certainly produced a great inflation, but the subsequent slump had witnessed considerable falls in both prices and wages. It is true that in Britain during the rest of the 1920s money wages and prices demonstrated an obstinate refusal to fall very far despite high unemployment, but it was far from obvious that this difficulty was exportable to other countries with weaker trade unions and a shorter history of industrialism.

These, I think, are the reasons why the neoclassical tradition in pure theory never got an effective grip on macroeconomic questions. It was so impressed by the stabilising properties of the price mechanism (proved, as we have seen, only for the individual market) that it exuded a great optimism about the adaptability of a free market economy. The significance of 1929 and its aftermath was that it threw neoclassical economics for the first time into a major crisis. Explanations of a considerable degree of sophistication were of course offered, but how much was the economic theory worth which had to go through such contortions to explain a major economic catastrophe? It was the sense of the devalued reputation of economic theory in the world at large which made younger economists, in particular, sensitive to new thoughts on macroeconomic issues. The self-confidence of the neoclassical world was shattered, and Keynes's book had such an impact because it fulfilled a deep yearning for something meaningful, straightforward, relevant and yet still intellectually coherent at the highest level, to put in its place.

The General Theory

This, briefly, was the intellectual background to the *General Theory*. In the one-paragraph long first chapter of the book, Keynes states his main conclusion: that his is the *general* theory of output and employment, beside which neoclassical theory stands exposed as a *special case merely applicable to situations of full employment*. As we shall see, this dramatic claim has become the focus of all subsequent debate about the Keynesian revolution.

The first issue which Keynes raises is that of the labour market. The point which he wishes to make is that the problem cf deficient effective demand cannot readily be solved through adjustments in the market where the excess supply will manifest itself: the labour market. Lack of demand for goods will not result in an excess supply of goods, because firms will cut back production and sack workers, creating involuntary unemployment. The solution suggested by neoclassical theory would be that the excess supply of labour should be cured by a fall in its relative price, or in other words a fall in the real wage (whether economists did commonly argue for real wage cuts as a policy measure in the early 1930s I shall discuss later). But here Keynes explodes his first theoretical bombshell: that workers cannot easily effect a cut in their own real wage. Because their labour is exchanged for money and not directly for the products of their labour, workers can easily contrive a cut in their *money* wage, but in a competitive market (a standard neoclassical assumption) this will also tend to reduce goods prices by lowering marginal costs. To cut the money wage is simple; to cut the real wage is not. The obvious relative price adjustment, which neoclassical economics would prescribe, cannot be made.

Indeed Keynes went further than this. He argued that even if some fall in real wages resulted from this process, it would not raise the level of demand because of the adverse impact of falling prices on entrepreneurial expectations and the real burden of firms' debts. Price changes in the market where the symptoms of a demand deficiency appeared would not solve the problem.

This argument acts as a prelude to the formal introduction of the concept of effective demand. The relevance of the concept derives from the proposition that there is no intrinsic reason why the total demand in the system should equal the value of output at current prices in a state of full employment. Firms in the aggregate could find their production and employment constrained by a lack of sales. If we were talking about the market for one commodity alone, the neoclassical solution to this problem would be a fall in price. But for the economy as a whole this does not work. Falling wages and prices cut incomes and therefore expenditures; incomes chase prices downwards and the overall effect on real aggregate demand is unclear. There is no obvious solution to deficient effective demand through falls in price of either goods or labour.

Keynes's accusation is that the neoclassical tradition had evaded this difficulty by simply assuming that effective demand could never be deficient. It had never abandoned the early nineteenth-century idea known as Say's Law, that 'supply creates its own demand'. Originally based on a crude analogy of a monetary economy with a régime of barter, this argument proceeded along the lines that the value of output was always by definition equal to the value of incomes, and that all incomes are entirely spent in one form or another, since even savings are in reality lent at interest to other persons who spend them as additional consumption or investment. In the course of the nineteenth century, however, the doctrine had been rendered rather more sophisticated and more appealing to the neoclassical mentality by the appearance of 'abstinence' or 'waiting' theories of interest. These theories treated interest as providing an incentive to abstain from present consumption: at higher rates of interest a given rate of saving would yield a faster increase of wealth and therefore of future consuming power. In response to this incentive, savings could sensibly be regarded as an increasing function of the rate of interest. At the same time it was reasonable to assume that the amount of investment carried out with borrowed funds would fall as the cost of borrowing money rose: investment would be a decreasing function of the interest rate. Thus was constructed the notion of a *loanable funds* market functioning in a similar way to any other, with a downward-sloping demand curve intersecting an upward-sloping supply curve, investment being the demand for loanable funds, savings the supply and the rate of interest the price (Figure 1.1).

If then the rate of investment were to fall at any given interest rate, this would be interpreted as a downward shift in the demand schedule for loanable funds, from DD to $D'D'$, say. The market would find a new equilibrium at B, characterised by a lower interest rate and a lower rate of investment than at the original equilibrium A, but with a higher rate of consumption (i.e. a lower rate of saving). A tendency for investment to fall below saving at the original interest rate would thus be counteracted by a fall in interest rates sufficient to raise

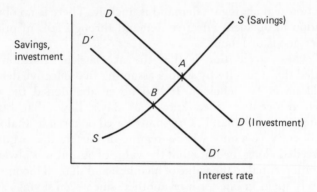

Figure 1.1   *Neoclassical analysis of the loanable funds market*

investment and consumption demand together *to the same level as before*. The normal adjustment mechanisms of the loanable funds market could therefore resolve any problem of deficient demand.

Keynes's objection to this analysis was that it examined the consequences of a fall in investment in only one of the two markets affected. An act of investment constituted a demand for goods as well as for loanable funds. But the consequences of the reduced demand for investment goods were ignored. Here Keynes made use of some ideas first presented by his Cambridge colleague, R. F. Kahn. The background to Kahn's (1931) article was the Treasury's argument, during the 1929 General Election, that public works schemes could not reduce unemployment because they would only siphon off savings that would otherwise be absorbed in private investment projects and would now be unavailable for private borrowers. Kahn's aim was to show that this was untrue: that extra public investment would in fact generate extra savings.

The idea was simple. The public works project would generate some extra employment. These people would then have higher incomes than before, so demand for consumer goods would be increased. This would generate a secondary expansion of employment in the consumption goods sector, yielding a yet further increase in demand, and so on. Kahn was able to show that the expansion in employment would continue until savings out of the extra incomes generated equalled the addition to investment. Kahn did not investigate the implications of this idea for pure theory, but it was clearly inconsistent with the loanable funds analysis, for it implied that should the government act to shift the *DD* curve to the right by undertaking investment projects of its own, the resulting increase in incomes would shift the *SS* curve to the right by the same amount. Savings, in other words, were a function of income as well as the interest rate, and since a change in investment would alter income through its impact in the goods market, the supply and demand curves in the loanable funds market could not be regarded as independent.

Keynes integrated this idea into his analysis with certain modifications. First of all he transformed Kahn's employment multiplier into an income multiplier, so that the multiplier became the ratio of the total change in income to the initial change in expenditure by the government (or whomever). Secondly he asserted a psychological law that people would save a certain fraction of any increase in income, which ensures that (in an elementary model) the multiplier would be greater than one but less than infinite. In combination with an assertion of the central importance of effective demand to employment fluctuations, this idea clearly added a whole new dimension to the government's budgetary decisions. Whereas the loanable funds analysis suggested that any change in effective demand would cause changes in the interest rate which would return effective demand to its full employment level, Keynes was arguing that not only the interest rate *but also real national income* would change.

Conviction of the correctness of his theory of effective demand caused Keynes to re-examine the neoclassical theory of interest.[5] The multiplier mechanism had simply introduced a second variable – income – to explain the reconciliation of planned investment and savings. Without something further, the theory would have been seriously incomplete. The question of to what degree it was changes in income rather than interest rates that brought planned savings and investment into equality would have reduced itself to a comparison of the relative speeds of adjustment of the money and goods markets. If the loanable funds market adjusted quickly, for example, as one might plausibly suggest, it could cut short the adjustment in income by causing quick offsetting changes in expenditure which would always tend to bring effective demand back towards its former level.

Keynes's new theory of interest, stated in the *General Theory*, essentially suggested that the interest rate was tied down by other forces, so that it could never adjust in such a way as to prevent the income changes from occurring. He objected to the notion of interest as the reward for 'waiting' on the grounds that savings could be held in a number of different forms, some of which – such as money – earned no interest at all. Interest, in Keynes's view, was the price of liquidity: the most liquid assets yielded no interest, whilst less liquid assets had to offer an interest rate in order to attract custom. This shifted the focus from the flow of new savings to the stock of wealth, the accumulated savings of past periods. The theory of interest was now to be based in the redistribution of this wealth between the various possible forms in which it could be held. Indeed the flow of new savings disappeared from Keynes's theory of interest altogether. By definition savings must always equal investment; the growth of demand for financial assets (new savings) would therefore always equal the growth of supply (new issues to finance investment), and consequently could play no part in the determination of the interest rate.

Since in this new theory interest was regarded as the price of money in relation to other financial assets, it was natural that it should be determined by the demand and supply of money (or of non-money financial assets – but since the sum of the two is the total stock of wealth and the new supply of financial assets must always equal the new demand, when one of these two markets is in equilibrium the other must be also). If the supply of money is under the control of the monetary authorities (i.e. they influence the ratio of money to non-money financial assets through open market operations) then the interest rate must be such as to make the public wish to hold that amount of money. In Keynes's new view only one part of the demand for money was a reflection of people's need to use it to make purchases, as in the traditional analysis. What was novel was his addition of a *speculative demand for money*, related principally to the current rate of interest. The essential idea was that money could be temporarily the best store of wealth, because alternative assets which on average earned a better return were expected to fall in price in the near future. In principle this could be applied to any asset, from company shares to works of art, but the main alternative to money which Keynes considered was government bonds. Since the price of a bond paying a specified monetary amount per time period varies inversely with the interest rate, expectations of a rise in interest rates amount to an expectation that bond prices will fall. Provided the expected capital loss outweighs the interest payments, it then makes sense to sell bonds and hold money until the expected fall in the bond price occurs. This is the speculative demand for money. It depends on people holding expectations of future interest rates which are not too heavily influenced by the present rate, but relatively independent of it – otherwise capital losses would only rarely be expected.

The interest rate is thus held where it is by wealth-holders' expectations of its future level. It is not free to move to equalise planned savings and investment, and most of the adjustment must come through changes in income. Since these changes in income will themselves affect the demand for money, they will disturb the equilibrium in the money market, thus causing some adjustment of interest rates. There are in fact two dependent variables, income and interest rates, whose movements interact, and which are determined simultaneously by the two equilibrium conditions: that planned investment equals planned saving and the demand for money equals the supply. This point was not entirely clear from Keynes's own exposition, and was first stressed by Hicks (1937). Such a modification does not however invalidate the fundamental point of Keynes's argument, that the interest rate *alone* cannot do the job which was expected of it in the loanable funds analysis.

I have already said that Keynes's theory had revolutionary implications for budgetary policy. But what did it imply about monetary policy? Through open market operations, monetary policy could disturb the equilibrium in the financial markets. If the authorities purchased bonds in the market, they would create an excess supply of money and a corresponding excess demand for bonds. For equilibrium to be re-established there would have to be a fall in the interest rate sufficient to cause the required switch from bonds into money. The switch would occur because the rise in bond prices would convince more people that their price was likely to fall in the near future. The fall in the interest rate would make some previously unattractive projects profitable, thus stimulating investment and effective demand. In

Keynes's analysis there was thus a monetary as well as a fiscal route to higher employment.

The mechanism just described implied that the effectiveness of monetary policy would depend on its ability to reduce interest rates. How much of a monetary expansion would be required to produce a given interest rate reduction would depend entirely upon how many people would choose to switch from bonds into money within the relevant range of bond prices. This would be determined by the similarity of people's expectations. If many people had similar expectations of future interest rates, they would all switch over more or less together, so that a sizeable increase in the quantity of money might only secure a small fall in interest rates.

For Keynes this was in fact a critical point in his doubts about the power of monetary policy to cure the Depression. There was no reason to believe that speculators would not have closely similar expectations of a 'normal' interest rate, but if they did a large increase in the quantity of money would be necessary. But such a policy could well create anxieties about financial stability which would act unfavourably on the rate of investment. It might undermine the state of confidence, 'a matter to which practical men always pay the closest and most anxious attention' (Keynes, 1936, p. 148).

Keynes's stress on the state of confidence is important to an understanding of his theory. The basis of it is our necessary ignorance about the future, which is such that we cannot sensibly even attach probabilities to the various possible outcomes. Thus decisions which necessarily incorporate expectations about the future, such as to purchase a new piece of capital equipment, must include a large element of conjecture and vaguely formulated feelings about what may happen. These conjectures will be strongly influenced by the one solid piece of information available: the facts of the present situation. Any developments which seem to hold portents for the future will receive close attention. The pattern of news will thus tend to create 'waves of optimism and pessimism', and in times of uncertainty these will cause serious fluctuations in investment demand. This implies two things. First, although these could be in principle offset by changes in the rate of interest, the changes required may be too great to be practicable. And secondly, the impact of a given set of policy measures on business confidence may turn out to be of more significance than other effects based on the assumption that the state of confidence remains unchanged. This is the basis of Keynes's doubts about monetary policy as a stabilising instrument. As we shall see, he applies the same reasoning with even greater force to a policy of money wage cuts.

Of some importance here, although much exaggerated by later writers, is the notion of a liquidity trap. This idea arises out of the analysis of the speculative demand for money. If the price of bonds reached such a level that *everyone* believed the short-run return on them to be negative, then they would all be willing to sell their stock to the government at the current price. Open market operations could not increase the bond price any further, so the demand for money would effectively be infinitely elastic at that interest rate (Figure 1.2), and monetary policy, however expansionary, would not be able to reduce the rate. And if at that interest rate the rate of investment was still too low to bring effective demand to its full employment level, monetary policy would be impotent to push it any closer. Keynes himself (1936, p. 207) did point out the possible existence of such a liquidity trap, but played down strongly its practical significance on the grounds that governments are too reluctant to be active enough in the bond market for it to be reached. Indeed none of his remarks about the limitations of monetary policy are based on it. Yet it has come to play a disproportionate and, as we shall see,

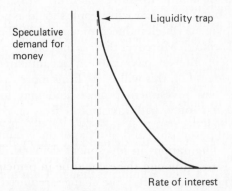

Figure 1.2   *The speculative demand for money*

quite inappropriate part in subsequent disputes about the revolutionary character of the Keynesian system.

Finally, it is appropriate to examine Keynes's more detailed discussion of the effects of falls in money wages. His initial point, it will be remembered, had been that this was not necessarily a very effective mechanism for effecting a cut in the *real* wage. But if involuntary unemployment existed, one could expect some downward pressure on the money wage, and it was important to examine whether this could provide a route for the return to full employment, whatever the precise effect on the real wage. In conformity with his model, Keynes argues that for a lasting effect on the volume of employment a fall in money wages must have significant repercussions on the propensity to consume, the expected rate of return on new investment projects or the interest rate. The redistribution of income towards those whose remuneration is fixed in money terms could change the propensity to consume, although because Keynes believes that the gainers will tend to be comfortable rentier elements, any such change is more likely to reduce demand than to increase it.

The effects on the expected return on investment depend on whether business expects the fall in money wages to continue or to be reversed. A falling price level implies that the real rate of interest (the money rate minus the rate of inflation) is above the money rate. This will discourage investment and also consumption (for similar reasons), if it is expected to continue. Only if money wages and prices are believed to have touched bottom and be about to move back up will investment be stimulated – but it is unclear why people should expect this when the unemployment which induced the original fall in wages and prices is still around. Moreover there is the consideration that the real burden of interest payments on accumulated debts will increase as prices fall; this will make firms more cautious about undertaking new investment projects and may force some of them into bankruptcy, with disastrous effects on confidence.

Keynes concludes that 'it is, therefore, on the effect of a falling wage- and price-level on the demand for money that those who believe in the self-adjusting quality of the economic system must rest the weight of their argument; though I am not aware that they have done so' (Keynes, 1936, p. 266). As the price level falls the demand for money for everyday transactions will fall with it, so that with a fixed money supply, only a rise in the speculative demand for money (i.e. a fall in the interest rate) can keep the money market in equilibrium. This is the same effect as can be achieved, when wages are constant, by expanding the supply of money, and it has the same limitations: that a small fall in money wages may have only a small effect on employment, whilst a large fall has such devastating effects on business confidence that it is likely to be counter-productive.

A Theoretical Revolution?

Keynes did not make any obvious departures from the neo-classical tradition in the assumptions around which his theory was built. Product markets were assumed to be competitive and firms profit-maximisers. Keynes was not therefore basing his argument (as he might well have done) on changes in the structure of the capitalist economy, such as the emergence of giant firms on the one hand and well-organised trade unions on the other, or the supposed dominance of a new managerial stratum. The liberating power of the *General Theory* lay in its production, out of the old assumptions, of a new or at least a discarded concept – that of effective demand – which was then wielded with great energy to demonstrate the lack of self-stabilising forces in the economic system. The stimulus given by the *General Thoery* to new departures in macroeconomics originated entirely from this concept. The seminal articles on trade cycle and growth theory by Samuelson (1939) and Harrod (1939) were distinctively Keynesian, not just in the use made of the multiplier, but in giving priority to the dynamics of real effective demand, with only minor attention being paid to movements in relative prices.

But to what exactly did Keynes's innovations amount? He seemed essentially to have done two things. First of all he had cleared the decks for the concept of effective demand by dismissing the likelihood of significant short-run movements in the *relative* (or even the absolute) prices of a typical package of consumer goods. Then he had produced a theory of the determinants of effective demand which effectively demolished the assumptions of Say's Law. But this left unclear the precise relationship between Keynesian and neoclassical theory.

Keynes's claim to have produced a more *general* theory was based on the idea that neoclassical theory could essentially only explain the distribution, amongst products and economic agents, of a *given* quantity of resources, and thereby implicitly assumed full employment, whereas his theory was the first to explain the level of output and employment. The implication, that his theory had encapsulated the previous orthodoxy as a limiting case, rather as Einstein's theory of relativity had incorporated Newtonian mechanics as a good approximation for objects whose velocities were low relative to the speed of light, was by no means universally accepted however. In fact the trend of mainstream theorising for the next three decades was to reject this view.

The basis of the neoclassical counter-attack was to pose the issue entirely in terms of long-run equilibria, whilst treating expectations as exogenous, as in Keynes's short-run model. In Keynes formal exposition he had treated the 'stage of long-term expectation', or in other words the state of business confidence, as given, so that the level of investment expenditure was a function of the rate of interest alone. The issue of the generality of Keynesian economics came to be posed in the following way: were the short-run unemployment equilibria which emerged from Keynes's model also long-run equilibria? In other words, did there exist a long-run equilibrium at less than full employment?

There is little doubt that such an interpretation did not conform to the spirit of Keynes's own thinking, which centred not around any abstract notion of long-run equilibrium but around the practical realities of the 1930s, that is how the short-run instabilities of the system could generate maladjustments which could subsequently prove extremely hard to correct. Apart from his famous comment that 'in the long run we are all dead', his remarks about the influence of waves of optimism and pessimism on the rate of investment, and about the limitations of monetary policy or wage cuts as a stabilising force as a consequence of fluctuations in business confidence all suggest that his concern was essentially with the short run. For in a long-run equilibrium expectations and the state of confidence are by definition no problem: everyone is completely confident that the existing state of affairs will continue for ever. So Keynes's verbal comments make it fairly clear that the exogenous 'state of long-term expectation' of the formal exposition was not true in anything other than the short run. How else can we interpret his view that expectations tend to be dominated by recent experience?

In the subsequent debate, this point was completely missed. The formal short-run model was taken over and its long-run properties investigated, on the assumption that wages and prices could now be treated as endogenous, but not expectations. I suspect that this development owed more to neoclassical habits of thought than to anything else. To write down a few equations, to ignore any complications arising from the expectations of economic agents and to regard the result as a statement about the long-run tendencies of the economy was a well-established procedure. This was exactly the treatment which the *General Theory* received.

The first important comparison of Keynesian and neoclassical theory which I shall examine is that of Modigliani (1944). This was by no means the first important commentary on the *General Theory*; it post-dates, for example, Hicks's famous clarification of the simultaneous determination of the two endogenous variables in Keynes's system, national income and the rate of interest, through his now very familiar IS/LM diagram (Hicks, 1937). Indeed it also post-dates, although only marginally, the article by Pigou to be discussed shortly. Its significance was that it examined at some length the conditions under which the Keynesian system would yield a long-run equilibrium at less than full employment.

What Modigliani sought to demonstrate was that, when the Keynesian system was reduced to a skeleton consisting of a few simple equations, a fall in investment would not in general produce a permanent state of unemployment if wages were forced down whilst unemployment persisted. The essential idea was that, since the transactions and precautionary demands for money were related to money income rather than real income, a fall in prices with real income constant would produce a fall in the demand for money, and therefore if the money supply remained constant the rate of interest would fall to compensate for this effect. This would stimulate investment. Wages and prices would continue to fall as long as unemployment persisted, so this mechanism would continue to work until full employment was reached once again. A fall in prices with money supply fixed would thus produce the same effect as an expansion of the money supply with prices fixed. The only case in which this would not work was the liquidity trap, where people were quite willing to increase their money holdings indefinitely in response to a small change in the rate of interest. The liquidity trap corresponded to the minimum attainable rate of interest, where bond prices were so high that all wealth would willingly be held in the form of money. If the rate of interest was already at this minimum, and investment was still insufficient for the economy to reach full employment, no increase in the money supply nor fall in prices would have any effect on employment. But with the exception of this special case, an unemployment equilibrium could only occur if money wages were inflexible in a downward direction.

Modigliani was effectively arguing that, in any situation where monetary policy alone would be sufficient to return the economy to full employment, the same result could be achieved by reductions in wages and prices which market forces would in any case tend to bring about. This was not a new argument: Keynes had made the same point explicitly in Chapter 19 of the *General Theory*. What was novel was the apparent conclusion that the downward inflexibility of money wages was in some sense critical to the assertions of Keynesian economics. Modigliani was translating Keynes's remarks about the self-stabilising character of a capitalist economic system into an assertion of the existence of a long-run equilibrium at less than full employment, and then demonstrating that (with the state of confidence exogenously fixed) unless the propensity to invest was so weak that even at the minimum rate of interest corresponding to the liquidity trap effective demand would be insufficient to purchase full employment output, this assertion depended on the assumption that wages would not fall in response to the existence of unemployment. Thus the Keynesian case that the system would not return to full employment was only true under one of two special assumptions: *either* the economy was caught in a liquidity trap, *or* wages were inflexible downwards.

It is symptomatic of this phase of the debate that Modigliani neglected a point relating to the adjustment of expectations to experience which would have strengthened his argument still further. For it makes little sense to talk about the liquidity trap in relation to long-run equilibrium, when the economy can only remain in the liquidity trap *so long as people's expectations of future interest rates are being continuously falsified.* In the liquidity trap everyone expects interest rates to rise; if they fail to do so for a long time, one must expect people to revise downwards their expectations of the normal level of interest rates. On this argument the speculative demand for money must be zero in long-run equilibrium, if this includes the reasonable requirement that no expectations are falsified by experience, as people will naturally take advantage of the interest to be earned on bonds. There can therefore be no liquidity trap at *any* positive interest rate. The neglect of this point (by Modigliani and subsequent writers) is, I think, testimony to the widespread failure to recognise the significance of expectations in Keynes's thinking.

But even before Modigliani's article was published, another and more powerful theoretical device had been wheeled out by the doyen of British economics, Cambridge professor and former pupil of Alfred Marshall, A. C. Pigou (1943). Pigou pointed out that, if wages and prices fell to one-hundredth of their former level, the real value of money holdings and other financial assets of unchanged money value would be multiplied by a hundred. As a result the population as a whole would feel much wealthier, and would consume more relative to its income. Making full allowance for this effect, one must come to the conclusion (argued Pigou) that there can be no long-run equilibrium at less than full employment, for the fall in wages and prices will always be working to raise real consumption demand.

Pigou's approach had the undoubted advantage over Modigliani's that it did not depend on the interest-elasticity of investment, or on interest rates continuing to fall as prices fell. It relied on a point explicitly made by Keynes himself, that increases in consumers' wealth would increase their propensity to consume. Keynes had argued that this was one of the more important causes of short-run shifts in the consumption function, but had neglected to mention it when considering the effects of falls in wages and prices. Pigou expressed no great faith in the practical usefulness of this effect, and put it forward only as a theoretical justification of the neoclassical assertion that the only possible state of long-run equilibrium was one of full employment. Indeed it was swiftly pointed out by Kalecki that the financial assets concerned could only be the liabilities of the government, and not all financial assets held by the private sector, since in the case of those which were liabilities of other parts of the private sector the effect would cancel itself out. This considerably narrowed the practical scope of the argument.

This idea of Pigou's could be expressed formally by making consumption an increasing function of real money balances (i.e. the ratio of the money supply to the price level) as well as of income. In this form it became the centre piece of the influential work of Don Patinkin (1956). With this weapon to hand Patinkin had no difficulty in reaching the unequivocal conclusion that a condition of insufficient effective demand could always be cured, in theory, by a sufficiently low price level, and a condition of excessive effective demand by a sufficiently high one. The only long-run equilibrium of a competitive capitalist economy with flexible money wages was full employment. Only on the assumption of downwardly inflexible money wages could a long-run equilibrium with less than full employment emerge.

Thus it seemed that the neoclassical belief in the self-equilibrating forces of a capitalist economy had not been overthrown by the Keynesian revolution. Keynes now appeared as the one who made special assumptions (rigid money wages); in the more general case, as Modigliani suggested, neoclassical theory was vindicated. Keynes's claim to have produced a 'general theory' thus came to be regarded as disproved. He was still accepted as having instituted a revolution in the theory of macroeconomic *policy*, since in practice wages were reluctant to fall and fiscal policy was proving to be a very useful tool of demand management. The 'neoclassical synthesis' was thus happy to grant to Keynes in the policy field what it denied him in theory. But he had not, after all, overthrown the formidable body of refined neoclassical thinking.

As I have emphasised above, this result was reached by a very specific intellectual process. Keynes's analytical scheme for portraying the short-run movements of the economic system, with the state of expectations taken as given, was written down as a series of equations; to this was added the presumption that involuntary unemployment would force money wages down, and prices with them; and finally, without regard to the impact of *this* on expectations, the equational system was solved. Clearly, only two possible conclusions could be reached. Either the deflation would bring about a return to full employment, or unemployment would persist and the price level would plummet indefinitely towards zero. Pigou, Modigliani and Patinkin had shown that the former was the more likely 'outcome'. But the question that was seldom asked – except by a few critical voices – was whether this was a reasonable test of the contribution of the *General Theory* to economic thought.

The Reappraisal of Keynes

By 1960 it therefore looked as if the neoclassicals had managed to refine their own doctrines enough to withstand the Keynesian theoretical attacks. The upstart had been confined to a box labelled 'wage and price rigidity' which could be accepted as his proper domain with a good grace. It could even be granted that much of the real world of the twentieth century inhabited this domain and required Keynesian policy measures for its proper management, now that the major theoretical issue of 'whose was the really general theory' was thought to have been decided in the neoclassicals' favour. Patinkin's contribution was the highpoint of this post-war reassessment.

The uncomfortable aspect of this conclusion was that it perpetuated the gulf between theory and the real world which had seemed to Keynesians to be the Achilles heel of the old orthodoxy. The general theory of macroeconomics had become, once again, the theory of long-run equilibria, offering little or no guidance on urgent policy questions – or so it seemed to those who instinctively responded to the immediacy and ready applicability of the Keynesian theory. Those whose spirits ran with Keynes could not easily swallow the Patinkin solution to the great debate.

In the late 1960s it began to seem as if a new generation of Keynesians had found a response. The work of Clower (1965) and Leijonhufvud (1968) offered a new interpretation of Keynesian economics as the economics of a world without a *deus ex machina* to impose the price changes necessary to maintain continuous full employment. The central idea was that when prices did not move instantaneously from one set of general equilibrium values to another, then there would be alterations in the quantities transacted in the various markets of the economy (for example, in the sales of goods or the employment of labour), producing situations resembling Keynes's unemployment equilibria. The argument was constructed around the theory of general equilibrium developed by the early neoclassical writers, particularly the French economist Léon Walras.

For Walras, the economy could be pictured as one vast marketplace, in which the representatives of all the various firms and households gathered to carry out transactions with others. At the moment of arrival no one knows what the prices are going to be; but they bring with them a large stock of commodities which they may wish to sell. There is a basic assumption that the amount of any commodity offered for sale will, like offers to purchase, vary according to its price. Moreover the demand and supply of any given commodity A will also be influenced by changes in the prices of commodities B, C, D, etc., because such changes will alter the incomes and expenditures of large numbers of economic units who may therefore be led to modify their sales or purchases of commodity A. Therefore the equilibrium price of commodity A cannot in general be established independently of all the other prices in the system. The general equilibrium set of prices, which equalises demand and supply in all markets simultaneously, can be deduced only from knowledge of the complete system.

It is easy enough to establish that, in a market for an individual commodity characterised by an infinite number of utility-maximising buyers and sellers whose incomes are assumed constant, there will be a stable equilibrium price towards which the actual market price should gravitate. This is much less obvious for the Walrasian general equilibrium system: because of the interdependence of prices and incomes, the fact that demand exceeds supply for commodity A at the current price is not sufficient to prove that the current price is below the general equilibrium price. How, then, does the market reach the general equilibrium set of prices? Walras overcomes this difficulty by inventing the theoretical device of an auctioneer, whose function it is to organise the market. The auctioneer starts the day by shouting out a set of prices which comes off the top of his head (since at this stage he lacks any information). The participants in the market *carry out no transactions at these prices*, but they tell the auctioneer exactly what they would have bought and sold if they had been allowed to, on the assumption that prices would remain constant in the future (thus eliminating the possibility of speculative transactions). The auctioneer collates this information, which tells him which commodities would be in excess demand and which in excess supply, and so gives him some idea of which prices should be moved up and which down. He then calls out a second set of prices, and the market participants once again inform him of their intended transactions. By this process of successive trial and error, or *tâtonnement*, the auctioneer feels his way towards the general equilibrium set of prices. Only when he has found it does he allow trading to proceed.

In Walras's model the market participants have no information about the state of the market as a whole. The auctioneer has such information, but only for those price sets for which he has obtained the data from the market participants by shouting out that particular set. In the standard neoclassical theory of the competitive market, embodying the assumptions known as *perfect competition*, there is no auctioneer but all the market participants are assumed to have complete information. Therefore they can be presumed to have worked out the general equilibrium price set for themselves, and a perfectly competitive system should move smoothly from one full employment equilibrium to another. But if one drops the obviously unrealistic assumption that all economic agents have complete information, then the situation of market participants in a competitive market is more akin to that of the traders in Walras's model, with the difference that in reality they would have no auctioneer to help them. In Walras's model, the economy is always at full employment equilibrium because no transactions are permitted before the general equilibrium set of prices is reached. In a Walrasian model with the auctioneer removed, individual sellers would be forced to resort to quoting their own prices and observing the state of the market at that price. In the absence of an auctioneer, many transactions would take place at *disequilibrium prices*.

Clower contends that Keynesian theory is intended to describe such a world in which transactions take place at disequilibrium prices. When the auctioneer shouts out a price set, the market participants inform him of their demands and supplies *on the assumption that they can buy and sell as much as they want to at that set of*

prices. But if transactions were allowed to take place at disequilibrium prices, then this assumption would be proved to be
false for at least some traders. In markets with excess demand
there would be frustrated buyers, and in those with excess supply
frustrated sellers. These traders would then revise their other
buying and selling decisions in the light of this unexpected
occurrence. Sellers left with unsold stocks of one commodity will
experience a reduction in income. They may be able to
counteract this to some extent by selling more of other commodities (if these are in excess demand), but they will almost
certainly have to cut their purchases, thus reducing the demand
for other commodities. Frustrated buyers will find themselves
with an unwanted stock of money. They may be able to purchase
other commodities (if these are in excess supply) but to some
degree at least they will tend to reduce their sales. The result of
trading at disequilibrium prices is therefore a reduction in the
quantity of transactions throughout the market compared with
what would have occurred at general equilibrium prices. In
Clower's terminology, *effective* demands and supplies, which take
account of these constraints, are less than the *notional* demands
and supplies originally expressed. In a production economy this
implies that output and employment would fall below the full
employment level.

This insight of Clower's is really very clever. Starting from the
neoclassical idea that general equilibrium, and therefore full
employment, is a matter of finding the right relative prices, he
has demonstrated that when the system is not in general
equilibrium, the result of frustrated transactions is a contraction
of the system through repercussions in other markets precisely
equivalent to the working of the Keynesian multiplier. If the
economy is suffering from an excess supply of labour, those who
cannot get jobs are constrained in their purchases of goods, with
adverse consequences for demand and employment in the
consumption goods industries.

In other words, trading at disequilibrium prices of the sort
which cause a deficiency in the effective demand for goods
produces a further reduction in income and output of a kind
which is already familiar from the Keynesian multiplier analysis.
But in a world of incomplete information with no auctioneer to
organise it, even a world characterised in all other respects by the

familiar assumptions of perfect competition, the economy has no mechanism for moving instantaneously from one general equilibrium price set to another, and so trading at disequilibrium prices is bound to occur. Such a world, according to Clower, is one in which there will be frequent departures from full employment through mechanisms of the type associated with the name of Keynes.

What Clower has done is to return the focus of attention to the short-run adjustments of the system, and to demonstrate that the economics of the interaction between markets out of general equilibrium is distinctively Keynesian. Since neoclassical theory had explicitly excluded these situations from analysis, its relevance is confined to a state of continuous full employment, as Keynes suggested. As soon as we depart from general equilibrium, Keynesian economics is required.

We may now see the general import of Clower's ideas. After this latest Keynesian thrust neoclassical economics appears as relevant only to the restrictive and patently unrealistic case of complete information (since in reality there are no auctioneers). Keynesian economics is required to deal with the more general case of incomplete information. Once again the mantle of greater generality has fallen on Keynes. At the same time the old argument which had seemed to emerge from Patinkin's work to the effect that Keynesian economics applied primarily to a world of institutional rigidities preventing wages and prices from making the necessary adjustments was pushed into the background; for with less than complete information available to economic agents, even in a competitive market it is implausible to suggest that in response to every disturbance the new equilibrium price will be found instantaneously. The market will have to feel its way there, making transactions at disequilibrium prices in the meantime.

The work of Leijonhufvud (1968) builds on Clower's ideas to undertake a fundamental re-reading of Keynes. It is a comparison of 'what Keynes really said' with the interpretation of him prevalent under the neoclassical synthesis, written with the intention of proving that there is a considerable gulf between the two. It is a much more broadly conceived work than Clower's, and it is unnecessary to discuss all of it here. But one point in particular is worth mentioning: the interpretation of Keynesian economics as a reversal of the neoclassical assumptions about the relative speeds of adjustment of prices and quantities. In Alfred Marshall's analytical system prices adjust instantaneously to clear markets, whilst the adjustment of quantities takes longer. In the *market period* Marshall assumes supply of goods unchanged; within the *short run* output can be varied within the limits of what may be produced with existing capital equipment; and in the *long run* supply can be altered without limit. But even in the shortest period the price mechanism is assumed to operate so as to clear the market. Leijonhufvud argues that the revolutionary element of the *General Theory* consists of making *prices* the fixed elements of short-run dynamics, and thus forcing quantities to make the adjustments required to produce a short-run equilibrium. The prices of capital assets may vary relative to consumer goods prices through alterations in the interest rate, but most other prices are fixed by Keynes's device of operating in wage units. 'The main innovation – and virtually the only major innovation – attempted in the *General Theory* was the effort to provide a systematic analysis of the behaviour of a system that reacts to disturbances through *quantity adjustments*, rather than through price-level or wage adjustments' (Leijonhufvud, 1968, p. 24).

Patinkin (1976) has taken issue with Leijonhufvud on this point, and suggested that the real distinction between Marshall and Keynes was the shift from micro- to macroeconomic concerns. If true, this would imply no necessary theoretical change of any consequence, merely a shift of focus. But it is hard to reconcile this view with the tradition of neoclassical monetary theory represented by Knut Wicksell or Keynes's own *Treatise on Money*. Though, like the *General Theory*, this tradition focused on the relationship between planned investment and planned saving in its macroeconomic analysis, a critical difference was precisely the assumption that these forces influenced *the price level but not real output*, which was assumed to remain at its full employment level. Leijonhufvud (1981) points out – and it is a highly significant point – that whereas price adjustments in response to a disequilibrating disturbance had always been reckoned, in this tradition, to operate to minimise the disturbance and to move the system back towards equilibrium, the quantity adjustments expounded in the *General Theory* were found to amplify any such disturbance (the multiplier effects). The neoclassical belief that the price mechanism was always manipulating the system back to equilibrium must surely be counted as central to their failure to investigate disequilibrium as a serious problem of pure theory.

The Clower–Leijonhufvud reappraisal of the whole debate about Keynes's theoretical achievement aimed to establish two fundamental points. First, the *General Theory* was about the short-run adjustments of the economic system to some disequilibrating disturbance, not about possible long-run equilibrium states. And secondly, the validity of the Keynesian revolution does not depend on the assumption of institutional rigidities in the price mechanism such as might be imposed by oligopolies, trade unions or governments, but simply on the highly realistic proposal that economic agents have less than complete information. As soon as perfect competition is less than perfect in an informational sense, a free market system will lack the mechanism for slipping instantaneously from one full employment equilibrium to another; transactions will take place at disequilibrium prices and quantity adjustments of the type first properly analysed in the *General Theory* will occur.

By returning to pure theory, this argument succeeds in linking the propositions of Keynesian economics with the neglected aspects of the neoclassical conception of general equilibrium. This was a necessary step, and illuminates the significant error in neoclassical thinking: the failure to consider the consequences of the interactions between markets when prices are not at their general equilibrium values. *Keynes's theories relate directly to the stability of a general equilibrium,* since this question cannot be investigated without considering what would happen if the system is nudged away from its equilibrium position. In this manner the Clower–Leijonhufvud approach brings the focus of debate back firmly to the short run, and can therefore integrate Keynes's verbal comments about expectations, referred to earlier, easily into its interpretation. It also recognises clearly that the fundamental assumptions employed by Keynes were no different from those of his neoclassical predecessors.

But if this view is correct – and I believe that fundamentally it is – then the Keynesian revolution is certainly a limited revolution. It overturns old views about the short-run dynamics of a capitalist economy, but not a great deal else. It does not imply a total reorganisation of our thinking about economic life in general. The *General Theory* does not add any new insights into the social nature of capitalism; this aspect is simply not discussed, nor do we get any systematic analysis of long-term historical trends in the world economy. When Keynes claimed that his new theory represented a definitive answer to Marxism, he could not mean that he had defeated the Marxists on their chosen intellectual territory, for he had not even ventured into it. What he meant was that his theory offered to intelligent governments the means to avoid major depressions and the apparent collapse of capitalism which Marxists were so fond of predicting. As a result the appeal of their ideas could be expected to recede.

Whether or not Keynes was right in this particular judgment, his book certainly stimulated a reassessment of a half-century of mainstream economic theorising. The suggestion that the neoclassical tradition, which had always prided itself on being technically much more sophisticated than its opponents, had made serious analytical mistakes or at least omissions which its critics had instinctively perceived was bound to be damaging. A certain *rapprochement* with the Marxist and underconsumptionist traditions occurred, and it became acceptable in academic circles to take their ideas seriously.

Reaction to the Keynesian revolution has taken broadly two forms. The majority response has been to continue to teach neoclassical microeconomics, up to and including the concept of general equilibrium, alongside Keynesian macroeconomics. This is the essence of the post-war 'neoclassical synthesis', and derives from a conviction that Keynes does not offer an alternative *Weltanschauung* to the traditional neoclassical one. The implicit assumption is that well-trained government officials can be relied on to minimise the economic instabilities of the private sector. The more radical view sees Keynesian theory as undermining the whole structure of neoclassical ideology and has attempted to connect it with an earlier, classical tradition. The crucial weakness in this 'left Keynesianism' is that, having shed its moorings in the neoclassical harbour, it has not been able to find a secure base in any alternative view of the world. It has never been able to embrace Marxism fully, and has found refuge in the rather formalistic propositions of the Sraffa interpretation of

Ricardo combined with a number of assertions about macro-economics which have seemed increasingly dogmatic with the passage of time. The strength of this tradition has been its acute awareness of the gap between neoclassical theory and reality, but it has never been able to reconcile itself to the absence of any alternative view of socio-economic life in Keynes's work.

The Policy Implications

The implications of the Keynesian revolution for economic policy are fairly well known and may be briefly summarised. The most important ones are:

(1) The balance of the government budget should be judged in relation to the state of demand in the economy and not according to rules of good housekeeping taken over from the private sector. In particular if the budget is in deficit at a time of large-scale unemployment then the appropriate response would be to *increase* the deficit and not to reduce it.
(2) Reducing the real or the money wage would not *necessarily* create more employment, and may have the opposite effect.
(3) Monetary policy may not always be capable of ending large-scale unemployment without the help of fiscal measures.

These conclusions could scarcely have been more topical. In the crisis years of 1929–33 there were few countries where the government had not at some stage reacted to the deficits created by the collapse of tax revenue by bringing in a package of expenditure cuts and/or tax increases. Such a package was usually justified by the need for the government to demonstrate an ability at least to maintain a degree of financial order in its own household, in the hope of reviving the battered climate of opinion in financial markets and in business circles generally. Some of these same governments (e.g. the USA) at other times tried to combat the Depression with public works programmes, which were seen, where they were not just a political gimmick, as measures to sustain demand. But this was not because anyone calculated the multiplier effects; they were essentially viewed as a way of operating on business psychology. And since business psychology was seen as the key to recovery, it was quite logical to introduce a *deflationary* fiscal package when business was in a state of jitters about the financial system. The revolutionary impact of Keynesian theory was to reorient policy thinking around the idea that employment was determined by effective demand rather than the state of confidence.

The one clearly formulated theoretical objection to deficit-financing as an employment-creating measure by a government of this time was the famous British White Paper, *Memoranda on Certain Proposals relating to Unemployment* (Cmnd 3331, 1929). This argued that public investment projects merely diverted investment expenditure away from the private sector and therefore created no extra employment at all. It is doubtful whether this hardline 'Treasury view' reflected the thinking of most governments of the time or even of the British government for more than a few years. It is safe to say, however, that a lot of people remained very sceptical of the employment-creating effects of public works programmes. As Pigou (1950, pp. 40–1) described it,

> there can be no doubt that in the period of the great slump many people did believe that thriftiness, or economy, would merely transfer employment from consumption to investment, thus not reducing it at the time and ultimately, in consequence of the contribution made to capital equipment, stimulating it. They believed this, not merely as regards periods of over-full employment, when, of course, it might be true, but also as regards periods of slump.

Neoclassical Economics and the Great Depression

In recent years research into what economists were actually writing and saying in the early 1930s has stimulated a 'revisionist' view of the relationship between Keynes and his neoclassical predecessors which in its extreme form reduces the novelty of the Keynesian revolution virtually to nothing. For example, in the Foreword to Davis (1971, p. xi), Gordon Tullock writes:

> granted the overwhelmingly 'Keynesian' view of American economists before the publication of the *General Theory*, it is not

exactly obvious why this book should be held to have been so influential. Davis demonstrates that there was really very little new in the book, and what there was that was new was largely in error.

This is a viewpoint which has become increasingly common in recent years (despite the fact that the extreme position just quoted is a considerable exaggeration of the implications of Davis's research). It has emerged as historical studies of economists' policy statements in the 1930s have demolished the simplistic mythology of the early post-Keynesian era. The mythology was essentially this: the policy errors of governments in the Great Depression were the result of bad advice by neoclassical economists, based on simple neoclassical theory, and it required the Keynesian revolution to bring about a decisive change in economic policy. This mythology rested less on detailed research than a diet of post-war textbooks combined with sketchy knowledge of the history of the 1929–33 period (that Keynes himself did not subscribe to so simple a story is indicated by a footnote to the *General Theory* (p. 20) in which he congratulates Professor Robbins for being one of the few to advocate policy measures consistent with his theory).

The recent research has proved beyond doubt that the history of economic thought at this time was not one of every economist seeking remedies for the Depression in the application of the simple neoclassical model, then in 1936 or somewhat later, reading Keynes's book, becoming convinced and advocating the opposite measures to those which they had previously urged. Many were partial to public works programmes and opposed to wage cuts (two policy issues which usually figure in the literature as the litmus test of a 'Keynesian' position) before 1936. A generally neglected issue in this body of research, however, is how Keynesian the thinking behind such policy views was. There is a widespread assumption that these policy positions represent fully-fledged Keynesian credentials. I want briefly to argue that this is a highly misleading view.

The crux of my argument is that such policy positions were not inconsistent with adherence to traditional neoclassical doctrine. The common view that a neoclassical policy would necessarily be one of real wage cuts and balanced budgets assumes an equilibrium interpretation of the Great Depression which was implausible and not generally accepted at the time. In the equilibrium interpretation, the central idea would be that real wages had been forced above their market-clearing level, so that output was constrained by the fact that the marginal product of additional employment was less than the real wage. But such an explanation was never really convincing. The collapse of world agricultural prices did mean that in many countries those who kept their jobs experienced a rise in living standards during the crisis years, but this was a reflection of the movement of the terms of trade against agriculture and not of a rise in money wages relative to industrial prices. The pattern was different in different countries, but in general the product wage in industry did not rise sharply after 1929, so it did not seem plausible that workers were suddenly pricing themselves out of the market. Indeed, far from being in a high-unemployment equilibrium with rigid real wages, the world economy exhibited all the symptoms of extreme disequilibrium – collapse of stock markets and financial institutions, disintegration of international trade, an agricultural crisis of the gravest proportions, etc. This was not a situation on which the static theory of long-run equilibria could find much purchase.

States of disequilibrium had been the subject matter of trade cycle theory. But this body of inquiry had not by 1930 achieved any broadly agreed theoretical approach – if anything, the tendency was in the opposite direction, towards an ever-increasing diversity of theories. There was scope for the advocacy of a wide variety of policy measures. If, in this confused situation, many observers offered support to policies which might be labelled 'Keynesian', to what extent was their underlying analysis Keynesian? Did they necessarily see the stimulation of effective demand as the centrepiece of recovery policy?

There is in fact nothing nonsensical about advocating either of the two policy measures principally regarded as Keynesian (public works and opposition to wage cuts) on the basis of the very un-Keynesian viewpoint that supply creates its own demand (i.e. Say's Law). Say's Law means that whatever business in the aggregate decides to produce it will find a market for. Output in the aggregate, and in a closed system, cannot be constrained by effective demand. But this is quite consistent with the recognition that each *individual* business may genuinely feel *its own output* to be limited by demand, even if this is untrue for business as a whole, because additional demand for firm A's output can only arise by the expansion of output of firms B, C, D, E. . . . . If each firm believes, in a state of mass unemployment, that such conditions are going to continue, then it will see no reason to increase output, and both output and demand in the aggregate will remain depressed. In other words it is quite possible, within the confines of Say's Law, to imagine the economy being stuck in a low-level equilibrium trap, where pessimistic expectations induce a low level of output, and hence a low level of effective demand, which in turn justifies the general pessimism about the future.

Now if it were possible, in such a situation, to bring together senior representatives of the vast majority of businesses in the country and to make them sign a solemn and binding agreement to increase output by 30 per cent in the next year, then according to Say's Law this would be the optimum solution – for demand would as a result increase by 30 per cent. Given, however, that this is generally impractical, then Say's Law would seem to suggest that government policy should be focused on improving the climate of business expectations. What this would imply depends on the precise state of the business mind at the time. At the beginning of a recession, for example, when the object is to offset fears of a serious decline, it would make sense for the government to try to suppress some of the most obvious symptoms of recession.

Because of the well-established (in 1930) tendency towards a pro-cyclical variation of prices, the government might try to prevent big business from cutting prices and wages. This was, for instance, one of President 'Hoover's first reactions to the crisis, and it was done for precisely this reason. Thus one could construct a perfectly respectable argument, based on Say's Law, *against* money wage cuts based on the need to maintain business confidence in the future price level. Indeed in the United States there seems to have been no great body of economic opinion advocating wage cuts, and the impact on business expectations did play a large part in the argument. In the more open economies of Europe wage cuts were advocated more frequently, in particular as a way of stimulating exports, but it is not certain to what degree the advocates of such a policy would have been in favour of them for the world as a whole, rather than just for their own nation relative to others.

Public works programmes could be justified in a similar manner. They would help to maintain demand in the investment goods industries, and for consumer goods by paying wages to people who would otherwise be unemployed. Since according to Say's Law any collective panic in the business community was liable to be self-fulfilling, prompt action by the government to sustain demand in certain critical areas could serve to prevent that. Moreover the very appearance that the government was acting, in these various ways, according to a coherent and purposeful anti-depression policy might reassure business that a serious depression could not occur. Thus the espousal by President Hoover, in 1930 and 1931, of a public works programme, and the widespread agitation for a bigger one than he was prepared to contemplate, are not necessarily inconsistent with Say's Law.

Yet by the end of 1931, President Hoover was bringing forward a massive package of tax increases in order to remedy the imbalance in the federal budget. And, in contrast to the great clamour for public works not long before (involving many economists), barely a voice was raised against it (Stein, 1969, pp. 32–3). Why the sudden turn-around in opinion, official and unofficial? I do not see how this can be explained if one assumes that people had already grasped the idea that the essence of an effective anti-depression policy was to stimulate demand. That analysis would have no difficulty in explaining their willingness to contemplate public works, but cannot begin to understand the swift return to budget-balancing with a massively deflationary fiscal package. It is true, as Stein notes, that this package *could* be given a justification in Keynesian terms, on the grounds that the effects on confidence of a continuation of high budget deficits and a rise in interest rates would be even more harmful; however I would argue that the absence of any challenge to this climate of opinion and the general failure to recognise the demand effects of the tax increase demonstrate how un-Keynesian the thought of the time was.

By contrast this apparent contradiction does seem comprehensible in the context of Say's Law. Since, according to Say's

Law, business confidence about the future will determine the level of output, it follows logically that the sound policy for the government is the one which the business community believes to be sound. It is immaterial whether these beliefs have any economic justification; all that matters is that they exist. Deflationary measures were taken, in the United States and almost always in other countries, at times when there were considerable worries about the state of the financial system and beliefs that large government borrowing could be the final straw for it, and would at the very least force up interest rates and inhibit private investment. The measures were not typically matters of blind prejudice but were taken in recognition of the psychological state of the business community – as Say's Law would suggest.

Thus it is of very limited use, in understanding the significance of the Keynesian revolution, to observe the policy recommendations of economists in the early 1930s if one does not simultaneously try to tease out the fundamental theoretical ideas behind them. For example, Britain was the home of the 'Treasury view', and also the place where Kahn's multiplier article in favour of public works was published, without apparently stimulating any serious outcry of protest from the body of trained economists. But this does not in the least mean that British economists, or indeed Kahn himself, had managed to fit his ideas into some consistent doctrine of pure theory. Indeed it must have been generally recognised that the received pure theory had little to say about economies outside the equilibrium state other than to imply that they were making their way back towards it, so that it could offer no straightforward recommendations for governments faced with a severe and prolonged disequilibrium. The neoclassical analytical tools could still be used, but seldom yielded clear-cut solutions. The situation cried out for a simple and yet convincing analysis of disequilibria, with unambiguous policy implications. Keynes's book captured the imaginations of so many young economists precisely because it met this need. It was a theoretically sophisticated exposure of the weaknesses of neoclassical pure theory, which by introducing the principle of effective demand yielded a very simple explanation of the problems of the Great Depression. It argued for policies which many people instinctively felt made sense, but could not be simply justified under the pre-existing theory, *and* it seemed to offer a coherent alternative general theory. Thus it was in all respects intellectually satisfying, a mirror image of the mental disarray which the Depression induced in neoclassical economics.

Conclusions

The Keynesian revolution represented a new view of the short-run dynamics of capitalism, not of its long-run tendencies, the structural differences in the economic environments of the nineteenth and twentieth centuries, or the relationships between classes in the production process. It broke open the neoclassical dogma of the strongly self-stabilising tendencies provided by the price mechanism, by examining the quantity adjustments created by the causal connections between events in different markets. In essence Keynes was examining what would happen if the economic system was pushed away from its general equilibrium – a question which neoclassical economics had systematically avoided. The key to Keynes's ability to do this and not to get mesmerised by myriad relative price movements was the concept of effective demand, whose validity ultimately rested on his convictions about the stickiness of money wages (for this was what rescued him from insoluble index number problems and allowed him to present his theory in terms of wage units).

In orthodox circles Keynesian theory encountered a neo-classical tradition suffering a crisis of self-confidence as a result of its inability to find an adequate response to the Depression. Since Keynes did not challenge any of the commonly accepted assumptions of economic theory (profit-maximising firms, utility-maximising consumers, competitive industries), his most striking ideas were fairly quickly absorbed into the mainstream of thought. Equally, there was nothing in the theory of effective demand that was inconsistent with a Marxian analysis of the 'laws of motion' of the capitalist mode of production – for Marx had after all denounced Say's Law as 'childish babble' and presented a theory of the trade cycle based on movements in investment, employment, the balance of power in the labour market and the rate of exploitation (Marx, 1954, Chapter 25), although, in general, Marxists were often hesitant about accepting Keynesian theory.

The main purpose of the rest of this book is to discover whether the theoretical tools offered to governments by the Keynesian revolution have in fact had any tangible impact on the economic development of the advanced capitalist countries. My broad conclusion is that they have, but that the recent disillusionment with them reflects a recognition of their limitations which has come all the harder for the exaggerated notions of their potential most apparent in the years around 1960.

Notes to Chapter 1

1. There is nothing in Keynes's theory of fiscal stimulation through the government budget which states that large budgets are preferable to small ones, or that expenditure increases are preferable to tax cuts. Conversely, Monetarist beliefs in curtailing the money supply do not necessarily entail low government expenditures. The links arise because Keynes is widely thought to have scientifically proved the necessity of state intervention to save capitalist economies from their own destabilising tendencies, thereby delivering a devastating blow to the whole 'free market' case.

2. His exact words were: 'I believe myself to be writing a book on economic theory which will largely revolutionise – not, I suppose, at once but in the course of the next ten years – the way the world thinks about economic problems' (Letter to George Bernard Shaw, 1 January 1935).

3. For a personal recollection of how difficult it was for someone trained in pre-Keynesian theory to absorb the notion of effective demand see Patinkin (1976, p. 83).

4. This omission cannot seriously be regarded as entirely innocent in a social science like economics. In the natural sciences the logical next step on from establishing the concept of an equilibrium is to consider what would happen if that equilibrium was disturbed. In this case, however, there were just too many ideological constructs at stake.

5. That this was indeed how his thought evolved is confirmed by a statement made in a subsequent article (Keynes, 1937, p. 250). It should however be noted that the essence of the speculative demand for money, as it appears in the *General Theory*, is already foreshadowed in the 'bull and bear markets' of the *Treatise on Money*.

2
Escaping from the Great Depression

The 1930s: a decade of depression, but not of stagnation in economic policy. When Keynes was writing his *General Theory*, there were already several countries which had, since 1933, experimented with unorthodox policies, including fiscal expansion. So when we consider the practical achievements of Keynesianism, it seems appropriate to start by assessing some of the experiences of that decade. The theory may not have been well understood (though this would be unfair in the case of Sweden) but the policies were applied nevertheless.

It is not worth discussing all the major countries, so I shall confine my attention to a few countries only: the United States, Sweden, France and Germany. These are all countries which in some measure, or at some stage, adopted unorthodox remedies for the Depression. In the United States, much the largest economy in the world, the New Deal strove by a variety of means, including fiscal expansion, to bring about a return to full employment, but with limited success. Sweden is commonly thought of as the prime example of a successful Keynesian recovery policy not based on rearmament. In France the economic programme of the Popular Front Government is a case of expansion against a background of political radicalism. And at the other end of the spectrum, Nazi Germany offers the spectacle of a remarkable recovery in a country which was very badly hit by the Depression. My treatment of all these countries is necessarily brief, but hopefully instructive.

The United States

The United States, generally regarded as the origin of the world slump, was also the worst victim, rivalled perhaps by Germany but by no other major country. The dramatic collapse of the stock market in October 1929 ruined many people who had borrowed in order to buy shares in the confident expectation of a capital gain, but it was not until late 1930 or even early 1931 that the recession revealed itself to be something seriously out of the ordinary. After dropping by 9.9 per cent in 1930, real GNP fell by a further 7.7 per cent in 1931 and by 14.8 per cent in 1932 (US Department of Commerce, 1975). By the spring of 1933 the country was in the grip of a severe banking crisis. One writer has described the situation on the inauguration of President Roosevelt as 'the most extreme prostration which any capitalist economy had ever experienced in peacetime' (Arndt, 1944).

One of the features of the Depression was a collapse of investment. Net investment became negative, and by 1933 gross expenditures on residential construction and on house repairs were each running at only a tenth of their 1928 level. Unemployment reached 25 per cent of the labour force, and in 1932 industrial production stood at only 53 per cent of its 1929 level (Lewis, 1949, p. 61). Many states had been forced to declare prolonged banking holidays in order to save local banks from collapse, and immediately after his inauguration Roosevelt declared a national banking holiday of indefinite length. Banks were to be allowed to reopen only after having shown proof of financial soundness. The situation clearly demanded a coherent policy for promoting recovery, and in his 'New Deal' Roosevelt sought to combine a dynamic and inventive approach to economic problems with the enactment of some overdue social reforms.

Before we discuss the New Deal in detail, the attempts of the outgoing President Hoover to grapple with the collapse deserve some attention. It should be borne in mind that in 1929 federal government expenditures represented only about 2.5 per cent of GNP, and federal purchases of goods and services about 1.3 per cent (Stein, 1969, p. 14). Hoover's reaction to the stock market crash was to open a campaign to persuade businesses to maintain wages and prices. The aim was to maintain confidence by preventing the falls in wage and price levels which were widely regarded as symptoms of recession. He also announced tax cuts for 1930, on the basis that the federal government anticipated a budget surplus in that year. This also was intended as a confidence-boosting measure, demonstrating a belief in the buoyancy of tax revenue. During 1930, he took steps to speed up investment spending by all levels of government and by public utilities – with some success, for such spending did increase by some 5 per cent (Stein, 1969, p. 22).

In 1931 a large fiscal stimulus was passed by Congress over the President's veto, in the form of a hand-out to war veterans. This reflected the veterans' political influence and the desire to relieve distress more than any economic theory. Veterans of the First World War had in any case been due to receive, by an act of 1924, certain payments in 1945, and the government had been putting money into a trust fund annually in preparation for this. The 1931 bill effectively provided for the immediate distribution of much of this money, which did not disturb the balance of the budget as normally framed, since the bulk of it came out of the trust fund.

Meanwhile tax receipts were falling sharply and for 1931 as a whole were barely more than half their 1929 level. In December Hoover asked for a large tax increase (this is the package which has since been so much criticised by Keynesians). Britain had gone off the gold standard in September, and since then the United States had experienced rapid outflows of gold, rising interest rates and a run on the banks. The Federal Reserve Board refused to expand the money supply. Hoover's package was designed to relieve the pressure on financial markets by reducing government borrowing (he stated that the federal budget would be balanced by fiscal year 1933). As emphasised by Brown (1956) this across-the-board increase in tax rates was a deflationary measure of major proportions, and yet it was passed by Congress (as the Revenue Act of 1932) without demur at the principle of increasing taxes at such a time; the debate was entirely about the composition of the increase.

In large part because of his failures on the economic front, Hoover lost the 1932 Presidential election to the Democratic Party candidate, Franklin Roosevelt, who during the campaign had paraded as the paragon of fiscal conservatism. But this was more a reflection of the attitudes of the electorate than of Roosevelt himself, whose true views were that decisive measures were required to end the Depression, and old dogmas should not rule out any experiments if they seemed to offer hope of a solution. Though he had no clear economic theory as to how to promote recovery, his promises of a New Deal and willingness to experiment marked a clear break with the conservatism of President Hoover.

As presented to the electorate, the New Deal did not consist of any very clearly formulated policies, and fiscal expansion was a relatively minor component of the initiatives taken by Roosevelt in his first term of office. In Stein's memorable phrase, fiscal policy was 'the ugly duckling of Roosevelt's 1933 barnyard'. Much more significance was attached to some of the other measures. These were:

(1) *Devaluation of the dollar.* As convertibility of dollars into gold had already been suspended as part of the measures to stem the banking crisis, the Roosevelt Administration took advantage of this to take the dollar off the gold standard, first permitting and then actively promoting a steady devaluation. The process was ended in January 1934 by fixing the gold price at $35 an ounce, representing a total devaluation of 41 per cent. The Administration anticipated that the devaluation would raise the internal price level substantially, thus relieving some of the burden of debt on industry and, in particular, agriculture. However this it did not do, for the United States was a relatively closed economy. But it did aid the US recovery in two ways. First of all, it encouraged exports and removed any possible balance of payments constraint on expansion, the dollar now being markedly undervalued. Secondly, by encouraging large flows of gold into the country it increased the liquidity of the banking system and made the pursuit of a cheap money policy that much easier.. But these gains for the United States of course increased the difficulties of other countries with their own balance of payments.

(2) *Low interest loans.* Roosevelt greatly enlarged the scope of the Reconstruction Finance Corporation, set up by Hoover in January 1932 as a source of cheap credit to financial institutions and railways, and which had been used largely to forestall

insolvency. After 1933 the RFC lent money at low rates of interest to a wide variety of businesses and even to local governments.

(3) *The National Industrial Recovery Act* (NRA) of June 1933. This was the most ambitious initiative of the New Deal. It empowered the President to regulate the whole of US industry through a series of codes which would determine its future conduct. It was intended to encourage investment by raising prices, and to encourage consumption by raising wages. The Act was welcomed by business (because it permitted collusion over prices), but at bottom it was a living contradiction: it was attempting simultaneously to stimulate business spending by reducing real wages, and to encourage workers' spending by raising them. In reality, real wages remained little changed and by the time the NRA was declared unconstitutional by the Supreme Court in May 1935, it was generally acknowledged not to have lived up to expectations.

(4) *The Agricultural Administration Act.* This was the agricultural counterpart to the NRA; it did have some success in reversing the catastrophic decline in agricultural prices (with some help from the dustbowl) and thus relieving the worst of the distress in agriculture. This was the main intention, but it is doubtful if it had much impact on aggregate demand, for the transfer of purchasing power to the farmers was at the expense of the rest of the population.

Roosevelt expected much more of the above initiatives than he did of public works, which he tended to regard as a sophisticated form of relief. Nevertheless in May 1933 he sent to Congress a $3300 million spending programme, the interest and amortisation of which were to be met out of new taxes. The Public Works Administration thus created was designed as a direct stimulus to heavy industry through large construction projects, of which the Tennessee Valley Authority became the most famous. This programme was supplemented by an Emergency Relief Administration, designed to channel federal money to the needy through the established institutions of state and municipal welfare, and a Civil Works Administration, a work creation project initiated in November 1933. In 1933 the effects of these measures were largely offset by a decline in state and local government spending, which since 1931 had been frantically chasing tax receipts downwards. It was not until 1934 that real spending on goods and services by all levels of government passed its 1931 peak, and in the meantime tax rates had been raised substantially by the 1932 Revenue Act.

But the recovery was certainly underway. Although the boomlet of the summer of 1933 petered out, real GNP rose by 9 per cent in 1934 and by another 10 per cent in 1935. With progress being made, Roosevelt did not feel inclined to push further down the road of deficit spending (a fuller assessment of Roosevelt's fiscal policy appears at the end of this section). For one thing, he remained personally sceptical throughout this period about the indirect or multiplier effects of these programmes; and for another he always felt under political pressure to be intending to balance the budget in the not too distant future. Excluding expenditures for veterans, federal expenditures in the fiscal years 1935 and 1936 remained close to their 1934 level, and although they rose by 15 per cent in 1937, this was largely the result of the new social security programme which was being financed by its own special taxes (Stein, 1969, p. 57). The one major fiscal stimulus of this period was a repeat of the 1931 payout to war veterans, once again passed over the President's veto. These two years, 1931 and 1936, were indeed the only two of the decade in which the federal full employment budget surplus was negative (Peppers, 1973) – and in both cases this was entirely because of the veterans' bonus which the President had resisted. Moreover, there was no move to reduce taxes, and the tax structure and rates laid down by the 1932 Revenue Act were retained.

Nevertheless the recovery continued. By 1937 real output had regained its 1929 level – although because of the growth in the labour force and in productivity unemployment remained a major problem. Straightforward interpolation between the peaks of 1929 and 1942 suggests a growth of potential output of about 3 per cent during this period, implying a potential output in 1937 some 25 per cent above 1929. However, both monetary and fiscal policy were becoming markedly more restrictive. In an effort to mop up the excess liquidity of the banking system the Federal Reserve Board decided to raise banks' reserve requirements by 50 per cent in July 1936, and it raised them again by a further one-third in two steps, on 1 March and 1 May 1937. As a result interest rates began to rise from their former very low levels. The federal deficit for 1937 was only about one-tenth of the figure for 1936, as a consequence of the new social security taxes (which initially raised far more revenue than was paid out in benefits) and the completion of the payments to veterans (Stein, 1969, p. 100). Roosevelt was promising a balanced budget for fiscal 1938.

In August the economy began to move sharply into recession, and at its trough in June 1938 industrial production was more than 30 per cent below what it had been a year earlier (Roose, 1954, p. 25). After some initial hesitation, Roosevelt decided on a spending programme. This was submitted to Congress in April 1938, and passed in June. The economy recovered rapidly, quickly reversing the decline. After the outbreak of war in Europe it was to be further stimulated by increased military expenditure. But in the spring of 1939 Congress had rejected a further spending programme which Roosevelt had proposed when he feared that the recovery might be faltering. The reasons for the rejection were various, but included the fact that the programme seemed to be extending federal intervention in the economy altogether too far (Stein, 1969, p. 122).

One possible conclusion from the 1937–8 recession, and one which the administration drew, was that the impact of fiscal policy on the economy could be very significant. But the recession also seemed to indicate that the US recovery was a fragile one. Indeed it seemed to many at the time, and subsequently, to prove the failure of the administration's recovery policy. A contrary argument has been put by Alvin Hansen. He points out that the recovery of 1933–7 had been exceptionally strong, that it was choked off largely by bad policy management, and that if it had been allowed to continue unchecked, the economy would have been close to full employment by 1940 (Hansen, 1963). This is an argument based essentially on statistical extrapolation. It may be correct, but what it seems to leave out of account is the sluggishness and fragility of the recovery in private sector investment. There is abundant evidence of a weak propensity to invest in the 1930s as compared with the later 1920s. Not only did investment recover much more slowly than output up to 1937; it also fell dramatically in 1938 and took another two years (more than a year longer than GNP) to return to its 1937 level.

Part of the problem was that residential investment remained exceptionally depressed in the 1930s. Unlike in Britain, where housebuilding was one of the motors of recovery, in the US it hobbled along at less than half of its late 1920s level. However since interest rates were generally low, the blame for this cannot easily be laid at the door of the federal government, and the explanation probably lies mainly in factors peculiar to the housebuilding industry, which shows evidence of cycles of about twenty years' duration (Matthews, 1959, Chapter 6).

But business fixed investment was also slow to recover. In 1937, when real GNP had more or less reached its 1929 level, non-residential investment measured at constant (1958) prices was still only 71 per cent of what it had been in 1929 (US Department of Commerce 1975). What was the reason for this? Since the Depression did not dramatically alter the relationship between output prices and costs of production in industry, this factor can be discounted. So also can arguments about the maturity of the US economy, which became fashionable around 1940, in view of the high rates of investment in the post-war period.

One possibility is that it was just the result of a much greater caution about expanding productive capacity after the traumatic shock of 1929–33. In the heady atmosphere of the late 1920s, few entrepreneurs can have imagined the possibility of the collapse of demand that was about to occur. They must have looked forward confidently to expanding markets. In the 1930s, that confidence had gone. The possibility that the recovery could peter out had to be seriously reckoned with, and indeed pessimistic views received emphatic confirmation in the recession of 1937–8. A reluctance to invest was a perfectly understandable reaction to an enormous negative demand shock.

But it has also been argued that the reformist policies of the New Deal actively discouraged investment. Vociferously expressed by business organisations after 1935, this position has been put most eloquently by Joseph Schumpeter (1939, pp. 1038–50). 'The year 1935 proved to be the pivot upon which the New Deal swung sharply towards reform, as if Roosevelt believed recovery assured, or thought it hopeless further to appease Big Business' (Wecter, 1948, p. 96). In addition to legislation on such matters as labour relations and social security, there were various tax changes. In June 1935 the President sent to Congress a set of tax proposals directed exclusively against the wealthy. The proposals included significant increases in tax rates on large personal incomes, higher tax rates on large corporations and a tax on inheritances. This 1935 Revenue Act was followed in 1936 by a proposal to institute a new tax on undistributed profits in place of the existing tax on corporate profits but designed to raise more revenue. This too was passed, with some amendments.

The economic argument was that in one way or another these changes imposed significant costs on business, and as a result, reduced the incentive to invest. A larger share of profits had to be handed over to the state; employers now had to make contributions to the social security fund; and various indirect costs arose out of new labour legislation. Individually, none of these measures could explain the sluggishness of investment, but in combination they amounted to a significant change in the relationship between business and the state. Moreover, Schumpeter argues, the situation was greatly exacerbated by the speed with which these changes came about and the 'Social Atmosphere' (Schumpeter's term) of hostility to the industrial bourgeoisie which lay behind them. Business found itself thrown on the defensive and became almost hysterically anxious about what the administration might next propose. On the other hand none of the measures actually taken was particularly radical by European standards, although they did represent a certain break with US tradition. Whether these sentiments did ultimately have any effect on investment decisions is extremely hard to judge.

To what extent did the federal government actually give a fiscal stimulus to the economy in the 1930s? Under Roosevelt there was certainly a rapid expansion of federal government spending, but there was also heavier taxation. Moreover, the economic impact of federal policy could easily be, and in many years was, dwarfed by the decisions of state and local governments, which might be motivated by entirely different considerations. Indeed in 1929 federal purchases of goods and services were less than 20 per cent of purchases made by state and local governments. This proportion changed rapidly in the 1930s, but the latent political resistance to such a dramatic growth of federal power was one of the factors which prevented the adoption of more vigorously expansionary budgetary policies.

The initial response of state and local governments to the Depression was relatively expansionary. Under encouragement from President Hoover they speeded up various public investments, and like the federal government they did not realise that their tax revenues were about to collapse. In conjunction with the veterans' bonus, this made 1931 a strongly expansionary year for fiscal policy. From 1931 to 1934 the impact of state and local government became heavily contractionary, as they cut back their expenditures and raised taxes in an effort to eradicate or reduce their deficits. Between 1930 and 1935 no fewer than twenty-one states introduced sales taxes, whilst by the end of the decade two-thirds of them had instituted some form of income tax (Wecter, 1948, p. 93). After 1934 the impact on demand of these lower levels of government was fairly neutral (Brown, 1956).

This influential article by Brown is largely responsible for the widespread impression that fiscal policy made little or no contribution to the US recovery. But this conclusion seems doubtful even on the basis of Brown's own figures, and is scarcely sustainable in the light of the further research by Peppers (1973). Brown poses the question in the following way: did the total spending and revenue-gathering activities of government in each year in the 1930s have a greater positive impact on aggregate demand than in 1929 (taken as the last year of full employment)? If so, then full employment could have been reached with a lower propensity to spend out of private disposable incomes than in 1929, and fiscal policy could be defined as expansionary. However this does not appear to me to be a good way of assessing the contribution of fiscal policy to the recovery. The exercise amounts to summing all the changes in fiscal policy between 1929 and the year in question and seeing whether the outcome is positive or negative. But when we are considering fiscal policy in 1935, say, we are no longer interested in what was done in 1931 or 1932. Those actions are past history and may be considered to have had their full impact. The question is what impact on demand the expenditure and tax changes *of 1935* will have. The appropriate figures are therefore not Brown's measures, but the *change* in those measures since the previous year.

This is even more clear if we consider the theory of 'pump-priming'. According to this theory, it is up to the government to give the first impetus to demand, but then the stimulus given by rising output to private sector investment will keep the ball rolling of its own accord. The government can sit back and watch its deficit being whittled away by rising tax revenues. It would be quite acceptable, according to this theory, to have a fiscal policy which is expansionary in the early phases of the recovery, but subsequently neutral, or even slightly contractionary if the recovery is strong. In this case Brown's approach of averaging over all years would give a highly misleading picture.

Looking at the *change* in Brown's measures of the shift in demand from year to year, we find that in 1934, the first full year of Roosevelt's public works and relief programmes, federal fiscal policy gave an expansionary impetus equivalent to about $1\frac{1}{2}$ per cent of full employment GNP (*before* multiplier effects), was roughly neutral in 1935, injected a further $\frac{1}{2}$ per cent in 1936 (because of the veterans' bonus payments) but was contractionary in 1937 to the tune of about $2\frac{1}{2}$ per cent of full employment GNP. About a third of the 1934 stimulus was offset by the contractionary stance of state and local governments, but the fiscal actions of these lower levels of government were slightly expansionary in both 1935 and 1936 (Brown, 1956, Table 1, Column 14).

Peppers (1973) offers some slightly more sophisticated estimates of the federal budget, measured at full employment, which are reproduced in Table 2.1. These indicate a first-round stimulus of 1.76 per cent of potential GNP in 1934 and a further stimulus of 1.33 per cent in 1936. At the actual levels of GNP then prevailing, 1935 fiscal policy was almost exactly neutral, although because of the new tax measures of that year, the budget surplus at full employment would have been significantly higher than in 1934. If we apply to this the multiplier estimated for the 1930s by Hickman and Coen (1976, p. 194) of 5.09 (which compares with an estimate of only 2.10 for the period 1951–65),[1] we can attribute to federal fiscal policy a large slice of the growth that occurred over the three years 1934–6 (Table 2.2). Since Peppers' estimates of the full employment budget surplus are unweighted, we may add in some balanced budget multiplier effects, so that in simple numerical terms fiscal policy could have been responsible for anything between 40 (Brown) and 70 per cent (Peppers) of the growth in real output over these three years.

Table 2.1 *Full employment budget surplus of the US Federal Government, 1929–39*

	Full employment surplus % of GNP	Difference from previous year
1929	+ 1.20	
1930	+0.90	−0.30
1931	−0.54	−1.44
1932	+0.87	+1.41
1933	+1.90	+1.03
1934	+0.14	−1.76
1935	+0.76	+0.62
1936	−0.57	−1.33
1937	+2.82	+3.39
1938	+2.92	+0.10
1939	+2.21	−0.71

SOURCE   Peppers (1973), Table 2.

Table 2.2 *Expansion in US demand attributable to fiscal policy 1934–6*

	Growth in real output	Growth attributable to fiscal policy	
		Peppers	Brown
1934	5.9	9.0	7.5
1935	7.0	0	−0.5
1936	10.4	6.8	3.0

All figures are expressed as percentages of potential GNP. Ratios of actual to potential GNP taken from Peppers (1973), actual GNP from US Department of Commerce (1975).

Since these were the critical early stages of the recovery, these figures certainly do not warrant Brown's conclusion that the fiscal policy weapon remained unused in the 1930s.

Nevertheless New Deal fiscal policy is open to substantial criticism, which is not surprising since the President regarded it more as a form of relief than as a demand-stimulating measure.

The tax increases of 1935 were deflationary and aroused the hostility of business unnecessarily; it would have been better to have eschewed them altogether or to have kept them in reserve in case the business community complained too loudly about the budget deficit. The 1936 stimulus was strongly influenced by the veterans' bonus, which was passed only over the President's veto, and the failure to offset the deflationary impact of the new social security system in 1937 was an error of major proportions. If fiscal policy contributed substantially to the early phases of the recovery, its contribution to the abrupt but temporary reversal of 1937–8 was even more clear. These weaknesses owed much to the strength of the ideology of budget-balancing in the country and Roosevelt's sense of his own vulnerability on this point. He was under continuous pressure to present budgets which would be back in balance within a year or two, and this consideration was a strong influence on his fiscal decisions.

Sweden

In September 1932 the Swedish electorate returned a Labour Government which quickly committed itself to a programme of public investment in order to revive the depressed economy. Although Sweden had not suffered as badly from the slump as many other countries (industrial production in 1932 stood at 89 per cent of its 1929 level; comparable figures for some other countries are: UK 84, France 72, USA and Germany 53 – Lewis 1949, p. 61), the effects were severe enough: the official unemployment figures increased from a monthly average of 14 000 in 1929 to a peak of 186 000 in March 1933. But the recovery was swift: by 1934 real output had regained its 1929 level and in 1935 was 7 per cent above it (Thomas, 1937, p. 221). The growth continued throughout the second half of the 1930s.

As a result of this impressive performance, Sweden has been claimed by some to be a shining example of how purposeful Keynesian measures could be used to overcome a depression, without resort to militarisation or excessive state control of the economy. The budget deficit was deliberately increased in a conscious effort by government to inject demand into the economy.

However, such discretionary action was not taken before the beginning of 1933. Up until 1932, the government then in power had not taken any active measures of fiscal policy to stem the Depression. If anything, its inclination had been to try to keep the budget in balance, and for this reason it raised the excise duties on alcoholic drinks sharply in 1932. Nevertheless it accepted a substantial deficit, and justified it by reference to the surpluses built up in previous years. The real turning point came with the September general election. The new Labour Finance Minister, Mr Wigforss, was quite happy to increase the deficit to give the economy some stimulus, on the assumption that the money could be recouped from tax revenues in the following boom.

In this he was greatly influenced by a group of Swedish economists whose thinking had been evolving in a Keynesian direction over a number of years. The most important of these, in this context, was Gunnar Myrdal. In an essay first published in 1931[2] Myrdal had introduced the simple but fundamental distinction between *ex ante* (intended) and *ex post* (realised) quantities, a proper appreciation of which would certainly have aided Keynes in writing his *General Theory*. A further significant feature of the book was the manner in which Myrdal unequivocally asserted that increased savings would exacerbate a depression, because of the impact on investment of reduced consumer demand. By 1933 Myrdal had become convinced of the desirability of balancing the budget over the economic cycle as a whole, incurring a deficit through public works expenditure in the depression, in an effort to promote industrial revival, and repaying the loans in the boom. This was the justification for the economic policy enshrined in the 1933 budget estimates, which were published together with a memorandum from Professor Myrdal on 'Budget Policy and the Trade Cycle'.

In his first budget estimate of January 1933 Wigforss decided to borrow 160 million kronor for public works expenditure, the interest and capital repayments being covered by increases in death duties estimated to raise 40 million kronor annually. In the Labour Government's second budget a year later, an extra 120 m kronor was to be borrowed for the same purpose. The repayment period was now extended to seven years, with extra revenue being generated by a new surtax on large properties and incomes, a stamp duty on estates and further increases in death duties. In each case the general principle was that additional taxation need only cover the interest payments on these loans.

The 1933 proposals were based on the assumption that there would be no significant improvement in the world economy and that Swedish recovery would come about only through effective government action. The proposals were passed with only minor amendments by Parliament, but much of the 1933 public works expenditure was delayed by a prolonged strike in the building industry. This strike lasted from April 1933 to February 1934 and brought construction work in the towns to a more or less complete standstill. Since the public works programme emphasised investment projects rather than relief of distress (unlike in the USA), it was quite severely affected, and unemployment did not start to fall quickly until the late spring of 1934. The improvement, once begun, was steady, and the 1935 budget proposals contained no provisions for extraordinary expenditures – all public works in the financial year 1935/6 were to be paid for out of current revenue – and by 1938 all the loans had been repaid out of budget surpluses.

There are two interesting features about this policy. First, the tax increases were carefully chosen to minimise the impact on consumption expenditures. Thus, the whole package reflected a coherent effort by the government to revive the economy by stimulating aggregate demand. Secondly, the theory was emphatically one of 'pump-priming' rather than sustained budget deficits. If the loans were to be repaid within seven years, then there would have to be budget surpluses in the latter part of this period. If the government measures stimulated a significant private sector revival, these surpluses would be generated automatically in the improving economic environment: this was the theory of pump-priming. If the private sector response was weak, then these loans would have failed to achieve their object and could only later be repaid either by taking out new ones or by cutting public expenditure and raising taxes. In the event the policy was highly successful.

In comparison to the USA, Sweden appears as a much more deliberate and purposeful example of pump-priming through active fiscal policy. The government had the theory of what it was doing quite clear in its own mind; it framed its programme so as to stimulate the most depressed industries rather than merely to relieve distress; and output quickly regained its 1929 level, so that within a few years the loans could be repaid. By contrast US government policy was much less clear-headed, less coherent and weakened by the prevalent ideology of balanced budgets and the small weight of the federal contribution to total state expenditure and revenue. But this comparison is in many ways an unfair one.

In the USA the unprecedented severity of the Depression damaged private sector investment prospects to a degree which would inevitably make recovery difficult. With industrial production falling back only to 89 per cent of its 1929 level, Sweden could be said to have experienced no more than a moderately serious recession. Moreover, world conditions were favourable to the recovery of her exports, always a significant factor in a relatively open economy. Indeed it was in the export industries that the first signs of revival were felt. In 1933, while the implementation of the public works programme was still seriously delayed, the volume of the country's staple exports was already significantly higher than in 1932. And this strong growth of foreign demand continued. The resurgence of exports was aided by a low exchange rate policy, but the main factor was a favourable commodity structure. Eighty per cent of total export receipts came from forest products, iron ore and iron and steel. These raw materials were little affected by the trend towards protectionism, and the demand for Swedish iron ore was greatly stimulated after 1934 by rearmament.

But the Swedish revival was, in fact, not simply a matter of export-led growth. Indeed, as a result of the general depression in world trade, exports were rather slower to return to their pre-Depression levels than other components of expenditure. The striking feature of the Swedish recovery was the buoyancy of investment, which grew by over 70 per cent in money terms and over 50 per cent in real terms over the three years 1934–6 (national income estimates for this period are given by Johannson (1967), who describes his constant price series as 'extremely doubtful'). By 1935 gross fixed investment was already some way above its 1929 level, and this was reflected in a strong recovery in the iron and steel industry.

The investment boom was certainly encouraged by the expansion in demand emanating from exports and the public sector, and the figures seem to indicate that of these the former was rather more significant. After allowance for the delays caused by the strike in the construction industry, fiscal policy was significantly expansionary only in the two years 1934 and 1935, whereas the growth of exports was much longer sustained and even in the years 1934–5 contributed about twice as large a demand stimulus as the public works policy (Jonung, 1979, Figure 3). Indeed in his memoirs Wigforss himself only attributed a minor part of the recovery to fiscal policy.

What this suggests is that, although in Sweden the commitment to an active fiscal policy was much clearer than in the USA, its contribution to the recovery was if anything rather smaller. Quite apart from the revival of exports, it was important that business confidence did not seem to have been severely damaged by a recession which was relatively mild by international standards, and that the financial community was not antagonistic to deficit-financing. Nevertheless there must have been other factors which were favourable to an investment boom in Sweden at this time, for the growth in investment spending is more than can be explained by the revival of demand alone.

France

The French economy experienced virtually no recovery in the 1930s and was actually in a weaker state at the end of the decade than the beginning. The index of industrial production (1928 = 100) stood at 83 in 1938, reaching 95 in the first seven months of 1939 under the stimulus of rearmament (Sauvy, 1967, p. 528). Although these figures are similar to those for the United States, the difference is that in the US they were the result of considerable recovery from an exceptionally severe Depression, with quite a margin of unemployed resources still available for use, whereas in France there had never been much of a recovery, and the experience of the Popular Front Government threw serious doubt on the degree of slack which in fact existed. It seemed as if the 1930s had been a decade of prolonged stagnation in potential as well as actual output.

This was despite the fact that France was hardly touched by the early phases of the Depression. Throughout the second half of

the 1920s the franc was undervalued, and although exports
began to fall in late 1929 under the impact of the world slump,
industrial production was not seriously affected until the middle
of 1931, and unemployment reached crisis proportions only in
1932. In that year industrial production stood 22 per cent below
its 1928 level – a good figure by North American or German
standards.

French difficulties really began, not with the slump itself, but
with the measures taken by other countries to cope with it. In
September 1931 sterling went off gold and was effectively
devalued by over 25 per cent. A number of other countries
followed suit, and by the end of 1932 no fewer than 32 countries
had depreciated their currencies in relation to gold. France,
however, remained on gold, and became the principal focus of a
European 'gold bloc' – countries which had neither devalued nor
imposed stringent exchange controls. Whilst such a position had
some claim to moral superiority, it left France at a serious
competitive disadvantage and opened the door to the international slump. Manufactured exports fell in volume by 30 per
cent between 1931 and 1932 (Sauvy, 1967, p. 562) and unemployment increased rapidly.

A balance of payments problem emerged, which was further
exacerbated by the US devaluation of 1933. The franc was now
clearly overvalued, and exports of gold in anticipation of a
devaluation became an increasing headache. The government
was confronted with a serious crisis involving a combination of a
severe depression, a budget deficit (caused by falling tax
revenue) and a balance of payments deficit. Devaluation was
rejected as a solution on the grounds that popular fears of
inflation made it politically suicidal. The government was
therefore forced to try the alternative route to international
competitiveness: deflation of internal wages and prices. This was
combined with a series of desperate attempts to bring the
government budget back into balance. This strategy was pursued
doggedly for half a decade and reached its high point under the
premiership of Laval in 1935. It did indeed have some success
in reducing the internal price level,[3] but its impact on public
opinion was demonstrated by the election, in June 1936, of a
Popular Front Government of Radicals and Socialists supported
in Parliament by the Communists, with a mandate to end the

deflation and go for expansion. The popular frustration with years of economic stagnation and wage cuts was demonstrated by the wave of strikes which accompanied the election of the new government. It is the policy of this government, led by Léon Blum, which interests us here.

The economic programme of the Popular Front, as elaborated before the election, was directed at stimulating effective demand by a combination of redistributive and spending measures. It was a strategy which reflected the concerns of organised labour, and might be described as Keynesianism with a left-wing slant. Its main features were:

(1) To raise consumer demand by increasing the purchasing power of the working class.

(2) To institute a programme of public works, to be financed by loans.

(3) To reduce working hours, in order to spread work.

It is worth examining the thinking behind this programme in a certain amount of detail.

The creation of demand by deficit-financing was straightforward enough, and by 1936 was already familiar from other countries' experience. But how precisely were points (1) and (3) to be combined to produce a similar effect? The policy proposal was extremely simple: working hours were to be reduced, without any reduction in money wages. Thus each fully-employed worker would earn as much as previously, but would have more hours of leisure. To produce the same output, employers would have to increase their workforce, thus soaking up some of the pool of unemployed. This was the work-sharing aspect. *Hourly* wages and labour costs would be higher than before, and so also would the total national wage-bill, since the same *weekly* wage was to be paid to a larger number of workers. *If prices remained the same*, a redistribution of income in the workers' favour would occur; the share of wages in value added would rise at the expense of the share of profits. It was assumed that capitalists saved much of their income, while newly employed workers would naturally spend most of theirs – so this redistribution would boost consumer demand. The essential idea was, therefore, that production of the same output would require more workers, but the redistribution would stimulate additional production, so that employment would be increased on two counts: the transfer of working hours from those already employed, and the stimulus to output from additional consumption demand.

This mechanism rested on the assumption that prices would remain unchanged. But if this was what occurred, it would reduce profits and might result in a cutback in investment, and if not, then the programme would be inflationary. These were dangers to which the right was not slow to point. It appears that when confronted with this problem, the architects of the Popular Front programme put their faith in the cost reductions that could be achieved with a higher rate of capacity utilisation. They hoped that most of the increase in labour costs would be absorbed by productivity gains. On reflection, however, it is clear that this argument is somewhat circular, for the stimulus to demand is supposed to come from additional employment, and any productivity increases will be reflected in lower numbers of the unemployed being offered work. In truth the Popular Front leaders never properly faced up to the fact that their economic programme, in so far as it was not just a sharing of work between the employed and the unemployed, rested on a redistribution from capital to labour. Thus they never committed themselves to a proper system of price controls, which were necessary to enforce that redistribution, nor did they formulate measures to deal with an investment strike in response to it. They simply hoped that capital could be reconciled to it.

What of the external constraints on the French economy, which had provided the rationale for the savage deflation of previous governments? Not surprisingly, devaluation was never suggested in public, whatever may have been contemplated in private, and the possibility of direct controls on the exchanges was very much played down. The *Programme du Rassemblement Populaire* of 10 January 1936 did advocate stringent controls on the export of capital, but events proved that this was to be too radical a step for the more moderate elements in the Popular Front coalition to contemplate, even when the haemorrhage of capital was reaching truly massive proportions.

Events never took the course envisaged in the Popular Front programme. As soon as the election result was announced, it sparked off a wave of strikes and factory occupations as workers celebrated the end of years of deflation. This movement had no clearly defined aim but it was a powerful one; and it posed problems for the government, which could scarcely afford to disillusion its main body of supporters so early in its term of office. It therefore pressed the employers to make concessions, even though the raising of wages was not a stated part of its economic programme. Blum met representatives of employers and trade unions on 7 June, and the so-called Matignon Agreements, signed the next day, represented a victory for the workers. Besides immediate wage increases averaging 12 per cent (15 per cent for the lowest paid; seven for the highest), the employers recognised the right to form trade unions and to designate trade union representatives in all enterprises with more than ten employees.

In his first speech to the Chamber of Deputies after the formation of his government, Blum went out of his way to rule out the possibility of devaluation. But he emphasised that his financial policy would be designed to promote expansion and recovery and argued that this would cut production costs. The same day he announced a series of bills which would come before the Chamber a mere three days later. This package included one bill establishing a working week of forty hours as a legal maximum, and another giving every employee the right to a minimum of two weeks' paid holiday per year. Since no reduction in weekly earnings was permitted, and the normal industrial working week was 48 hours, these two measures raised labour costs substantially. Allowing for a 20 per cent increase in hourly wages at a result of the forty-hours law, 4 per cent for the introduction of paid holidays and 12 per cent for the Matignon Agreements, it could be calculated that the measures taken in the very first days of the Popular Front Government would increase hourly wages by 40 per cent once fully implemented. Indeed this is an underestimate because wage increases in the summer of 1936 were if anything rather greater than 12 per cent.

These problems were compounded by foreign exchange difficulties. There had already been, long before the Popular Front Government was elected, a steady drain of capital abroad and a decline in the gold stocks held by the Bank of France, as a result of widely held expectations that sooner or later the French government would be forced to devalue the franc. The uncertainty created by the general election had stimulated ordinary citizens to buy gold, which reduced the Bank's gold holdings by 13 per cent in two months; but the stampede abated over the summer. The export of capital also declined in July, but it accelerated strongly in August, and in September was running at more than double the June rate (Sauvy, 1967, p. 221). In a bid to stop this outflow the Government raised interest rates from 3 to 5 per cent on the 24th. This move had little impact and on 26 September the franc was devalued.

The figures suggest that the tentative recovery in industrial production that had been taking place since the middle of 1935 had run out of steam by the middle of 1936. In September, industrial production was 7 per cent down on May and unemployment had increased; raw material imports were sharply reduced and the balance of trade in manufactured products had deteriorated. Consumer prices were 5 per cent higher than in May, as a result of an increased demand for agricultural products and increased costs of production in industry stimulated by the June events.

After devaluation there was a sharp change in trend, which suggests that shifts in the international competitiveness of France's exports were a major factor. Although the forty-hour week law did not come into force until the beginning of 1937, the Matignon Agreements in conjunction with paid holidays had already raised labour costs considerably by the autumn of 1936. After devaluation the franc was maintained within a band representing a fall of between 25 and 34 per cent with respect to its former parity, and although Holland and Switzerland followed suit, this was still enough to give France a certain competitive advantage in international markets. Industrial production revived strongly, recording a 12 per cent increase between September and December 1936, while unemployment fell. But one serious feature was an acceleration of inflation: consumer prices rose 12 per cent in three months, representing an annual rate of 60 per cent. At this pace the advantages of devaluation would be quickly eroded.

This autumn revival was not clearly perceived by the government, which was deceived in part by the failure of the unseasonally adjusted unemployment figures to fall. The budget for 1937 envisaged, as well as a deficit of some 5000 million francs on the ordinary account, extraordinary expenditures of F5000 m on public works and F9500 m on defence. This was a clear statement of intent to use deficit-financing to boost the economy, as promised in the election programme. The eventual impact of this deficit on real aggregate demand was diminished by inflation, but the additional measures nevertheless imparted an expansionary stimulus equivalent to about $2\frac{1}{2}$ per cent of national income (Arndt, 1944, p. 145).

The most dramatic social and economic change of early 1937, however, was undoubtedly the coming into force of the forty-hours law. The percentage of employees working forty hours or less shot up from 9.8 per cent in December to 64.4 per cent in January and 96.1 per cent in May (Sauvy, 1967, pp. 550–1. The figures refer only to establishments with more than 100 employees). This was the period when the intended demand-stimulating and work-sharing effects of this measure should have begun to make themselves felt. And indeed, the recovery continued throughout the winter.

But it did not last beyond the spring. Industrial production reached a peak in March. Recorded unemployment continued to fall, reaching 500 000 in June, but after March this represented no more than the normal seasonal influences. Moreover, all this time capital exports had been continuing at a damaging rate: devaluation had not succeeded in inducing a return of funds to France. The propertied classes were giving vivid expression to their fears about the economic and social policies of the Blum Government. In June the Government finally fell in the midst of a financial crisis: on the 14th the Bank of France raised interest rates by 2 per cent in an attempt to stem a flight from the franc which had become combined with a domestic scramble for gold, whilst the Government asked Parliament for emergency financial powers effective until 31 July. When on 22 June this was defeated in the Senate, the Government resigned.

Popular Front rule did not end immediately; indeed with two separate administrations led by Chautemps and then a second one led by Léon Blum, a government of the right did not return until the spring of 1938. But Blum's resignation did mark the end of bold initiatives in the field of economic policy. What, then, were the achievements of the 'Blum experiment'?

The experiment is usually regarded as a fairly heavy failure. Output did not rise by very much, and continued pretty flat through the remainder of Popular Front rule. So there was no dramatic recovery of the sort which the architects of its economic programme both intended and expected after years of deflation. Inflation was severe, and accentuated social divisions by harming the interests of salaried employees, pensioners and rentier elements, most of whom suffered a significant drop in real income. The distributional consequences of the Blum experiment have been analysed by Kalecki (1938). In the year to April 1937 *hourly* wages rose by about 60 per cent. Raw materials costs rose by a similar amount, but a 55 per cent rise in the price of industrial goods was sufficient to protect the share of profits. Agricultural prices rose by much less, and rents were frozen, so the rise in the cost of living amounted to only 27 per cent. Thus real hourly wages had risen substantially, but this was more or less exactly cancelled out by the enforced drop in working hours from 48 to 40. The employed worker's gain was therefore almost exclusively in the form of additional leisure time. Meanwhile the intended victims of the redistribution, industrial capital, were able to defend themselves quite effectively as inadequate control of prices enabled them to pass on the burden of rising costs to their customers.

It has been argued that the main weakness of the Blum experiment was the forty-hours law (Marjolin, 1938). Although industrial output had been stagnant for years, it was not the case that there was a large reserve of unemployed labour waiting for the chance to be drawn into production. The population census of March 1936 revealed unemployment of 823 000, or about 4 per cent of the working population. Unemployment had been kept down by a drift back to the countryside and a return of immigrant labour to its homelands. These were sources of supply which could only be tapped by a steady and sustained demand pressure in the labour market (as in the post-war period) and not by a sudden expansion. The full application of the forty-hours law therefore brought France close to full employment, and by the spring of 1937 many firms were reporting labour shortages. Since the legislation forbade overtime, the limits to supply started to become a serious obstacle to industrial production.

There is little doubt that in the circumstances the forty-hours law was an over-enthusiastic and inappropriate measure. Without it the inflation rate would have been lower (though not

zero), since industrialists would not have suffered the associated
20 per cent rise in labour costs. The competitive advantage
gained by devaluation, which had more or less disappeared by
the spring of 1937, would therefore have been retained for longer.
In addition, potential output would have been greater since it
would not have been subject to artificial legal limitations. But the
inflationary pressures set off by the Matignon Agreements would
have remained, and their effects on international competitiveness
and the absence of a strong policy for dealing with them were a
weakness which was apparent long before the forty-hours
legislation came into effect.

A more subtle factor in the fate of the Blum experiment was the
distrust of industrial and financial capital. This was reflected
most vividly in the continuous drain of capital overseas. Blum
refused to counter this by exchange control, as demanded by the
more left-wing elements within the Popular Front coalition and
by the Communist Party outside it. But even if he could have
done this effectively, it would not have solved the underlying
problem. First of all, there was the fear that if the Popular Front
programme proved successful and popular, it might be the
prelude to something yet more radical. Nothing that the leaders
of the Popular Front could have said could have removed this
fear. Secondly, capitalists greatly resented the industrial policy of
the Popular Front and the government's role in the Matignon
Agreements, and regarded it as altogether too sympathetic to the
trade unions. And thirdly, the size of the budget deficit and the
government's lack of concern about it were regarded as evidence
of financial irresponsibility, an attitude which was reinforced by
the high rate of inflation.

For all of these reasons, capitalists saw little future in tying up
large sums of money in new plant and machinery. Exchange
control could not have solved this problem; the most that could
have been achieved was to keep funds inside the country. But
then these funds would almost certainly have been directed into
speculative activity, seeking out the most suitable hedge against
inflation, rather than into purchases of new capital equipment.
Domestic interest rates might have been a bit lower as a result –
but then real interest rates were already strongly negative
because of inflation.

Thus a major difficulty behind the public works programme

and the attempt to stimulate aggregate demand was the reluctance of capitalists to invest. The government could meet this in two ways: it could either try to placate private capital, although this would have meant going back on the most popular measures of its programme; or it could devise means of forcing it to invest, a step which it was unwilling to take. The dilemma has been well expressed by H. W. Arndt (1944, pp. 149–50):

> *either* the Blum Government should have insisted on its radical policy, even if it meant forcing the capitalists into submission, by exchange control and more vigorous measures if necessary, *or* it should have provided the conditions in which the mainspring of the capitalist economy, the profit motive of entrepreneurs, would effectively function. In practice it wavered between these two policies – partly no doubt because it feared, rightly or wrongly, that either policy ruthlessly pursued might lead to civil discord which would weaken France still further in a menacing international situation: on the one hand, it pushed forward its radical social reforms and deficit public works expenditure regardless of their effect on 'business confidence', it brandished the weapons of socialism and refused to suppress the strikes with the vigour recommended by the Right; on the other hand, it refused to impose exchange control and take whatever other measures were necessary to ensure the success of its policy.

Germany

Adolf Hitler became Chancellor of Germany on 30 January 1933. At this time the country was still in the depths of a Depression which was more severe than any other in Europe and rivalled that of the USA. Officially registered unemployment stood at six million people. Net investment was negative. Industrial production was still nearly 40 per cent below the 1929 level, although there had been some slight recovery from the trough reached in the autumn of 1932. Yet within a few years productive resources were once again being fully utilised. By 1938 industrial production was 25 per cent above the 1929 level and unemployment had virtually disappeared.

There is little doubt that this was the result of vigorous policy action by the government. The main issue of debate has always been whether this can be regarded, at least in part, as a pre-eminently successful application of a Keynesian recovery programme, or whether it should merely be seen as an aspect of the conversion of the economy to a war footing, involving considerable supersession of the free market, half a decade in advance of the other major countries.

The history of the German Depression up until 1932 was a dismal one of deflation and financial crisis. As early as 1929, the deteriorating economic situation was already being reflected in declining tax revenues and rising unemployment. The foreign loans which had financed much public expenditure in previous years were now scarce, and the mounting deficit in the unemployment insurance fund was already worrying the government and causing it to consider rises in contributions and reductions in benefits. In March 1930 Heinrich Bruening became Chancellor and formed a Cabinet comprising a coalition of right-wing parties, and on 14 April a government bill to introduce high protective tariffs for the benefit of agriculture, combined with new duties on consumption goods and an increase in the turnover tax, was passed by the Reichstag with a small majority. But these measures were far from sufficient to balance the budget, and on 2 May the Minister of Finance announced that significant cuts in public expenditure would be necessary. Opposition in the Reichstag was overcome by the simple expedient of resorting to rule by emergency decree, thus inaugurating a presidential dictatorship which lasted until the Nazi takeover.

On 26 July President Hindenburg decreed a sizeable reduction in public expenditure; an increase in unemployment insurance contributions, in income tax and the tax on bachelors; and a special levy on all civil servants (Halperin, 1965, p. 433). It was also announced that in future the government would make up no more than 50 per cent of the deficit in the unemployment insurance fund. This set the pattern of deflation which was to last until mid-1932. Official salaries were reduced on more than one occasion, bringing the total reduction to 21 per cent by the end of 1931. Unemployment benefits were also reduced considerably, and taxes increased. By an Emergency Decree of 8 December

1931, described by the government as 'the final step' in the policy of deflation, all wages were reduced to the level of January 1927, implying a cut of 10 to 15 per cent (Guillebaud, 1939, p. 24); a wide range of prices was to be cut by 10 per cent, and interest rates on bonds were to fall by 2 per cent.

In May 1931 the financial system was rocked by the collapse of the Credit Anstalt, the most important Austrian Bank, which caused panic amongst Germany's foreign creditors and pre-cipitated a massive outflow of funds. The Reichsbank could not raise enough foreign funds to stem the flood, and was unable to prevent the closure of the Darmstaedter und National Bank. This caused a general run on all banks and savings institutions, and in July the Government closed the banks for several weeks. It also imposed foreign exchange controls.

As a result of the efforts to balance the budget and the drying up of the capital market which had financed many projects in the previous boom, total public expenditure fell from 20 900 m Reichsmarks in 1930 to RM14 500 m in 1932. In spite of the tax increases of 1930 and 1931, estimated by the Finance Ministry to bring in an extra RM 2 500 m in a normal year, revenue fell from RM19 900 m in 1930 to RM13 800 m in 1932 (Guillebaud, 1939, pp. 28–9).

The bottom of the slump was reached in August 1932. Shortly before that, the Government had changed tack and begun to move away from a policy of deflation. Papen, who had replaced Bruening as Chancellor in May, invented a device to improve business liquidity and confidence, without actually reducing current government revenue, in the form of tax remission certificates. These were issued to taxpayers according to their payments of certain taxes in the financial year 1932/3, and could be used to meet tax liabilities in any of the years 1934/5 to 1938/9, meanwhile earning interest at 4 per cent per annum. Their effect was to increase the wealth of taxpayers, and since they quickly established themselves as a short-term asset in the financial markets, they could be used by hard-pressed businesses to repay bank loans or build up working capital. The Finance Ministry was also empowered to issue these certificates at a specified rate to any employer who increased his or her labour force. In addition, Papen drew up programmes for the expenditure of RM740 m on housing, land improvement and capital investment by the Post

Office and the railways. To this was later added the Schleicher Government's RM500 m programme of public works expenditure, announced on 28 January 1933, just two days before Hitler became Chancellor.

It is clear from their first actions that the Nazis regarded the abolition of mass unemployment as a political priority to consolidate their position. Both the Papen and Schleicher expenditure programmes were retained, but in April 1933 the Papen programme (the bulk of which had consisted of subsidies to the private sector rather than direct public expenditure on goods and services) was redirected towards the public sector, and to stimulate the car industry, all taxes on new motor-cars were abolished. On 1 May Hitler announced his Four-Year Plan for abolishing unemployment. This combined measures designed to stimulate the demand for labour with ones aimed at reducing the supply. On the demand side there was the so-called 'Reinhardt Programme' of RM 1000 m of public works, to be financed by the issue of 'employment creation bills'. New public expenditure could not be financed by borrowing, since in the demoralised state of the capital market no one could be persuaded to lend long-term, even to the Government. But the Government was not legally permitted to borrow direct from the Reichsbank, and so resorted to the device of issuing bills which could then be discounted by the Reichsbank; the process was thus effectively a form of money creation. In September there followed the 'Second Reinhardt Programme' – a RM 500 m subsidy for repairs to houses and conversion into flats by private owners, on condition that receivers of the grant put up a similar sum from their own funds. In June 1933 a law was passed authorising a massive motorway construction programme at an estimated cost of RM3500 m. The importance of this in the early stages of the economic recovery has however been generally exaggerated, since only RM166 m was spent before the end of 1934 (Barkai, 1977).

These measures were complemented by a whole series of others designed to take people out of the main labour market. Labour service was made compulsory and the emergency relief work scheme was greatly extended: these forms of low-paid work occupied an additional 360 000 people in the last quarter of 1933 compared with a year earlier (Guillebaud, 1939, p. 41). There was a vigorous campaign against the employment of women, backed by interest-free marriage loans payable only on condition that the wife did not return to employment. An attempt was made to divert more of the female labour force into domestic service through more generous income tax allowances. Meanwhile large numbers were being absorbed into the state and party bureaucracy, and particularly after the introduction of conscription in 1935, into the army.

This programme was spectacularly successful, not only in reducing the unemployment figures but also in stimulating output. Registered unemployment fell by three million, from a yearly average of 5.6 million in 1932 to 2.7 million in 1934. By the end of 1934 industrial production was 30 per cent above its minimum, with the output of investment goods growing particularly fast. Private investment expenditure had more than doubled, albeit from a very low level.

There seems little doubt that the credit for this recovery must lie primarily with the government. There is no other obvious explanation, unless one is going to appeal to the natural forces of economic regeneration, and these were not evident in countries like France where deflation continued to be the order of the day. Moreover the programme was very deliberately conceived as an unemployment-reducing one, and the fiscal stimulus given to the economy in 1933 and 1934 was considerable. Compared to Roosevelt's New Deal, which began about the same time in a country in a similar state of prostration, the economic policy followed by the Nazis was more theoretically coherent and much more obviously successful.

By any means, 1934 was not the end of the recovery although there were some signs of a slowdown early in 1935. The expenditures of the government continued to be a major force in the growth of demand, but were increasingly dominated by military projects. Civilian public works expenditures were run down quite rapidly as unemployment fell. Table 2.3 presents a run of figures for some categories of government spending, although it should be emphasised that the military budget was kept secret and the numbers are a matter of some controversy. The table shows that military expenditure was beginning to take over the running from construction and work creation in 1935, and did so decisively in 1936. Other authors have judged that

Table 2.3   *Public expenditure in Germany by category 1932–8 (bn Reichsmarks)*

	Construction	Rearmament	Work creation
1932	0.9	0.7	0.2
1933	1.7	1.8	1.5
1934	3.5	3.0	2.5
1935	4.9	5.4	0.8
1936	5.4	10.2	—
1937	6.1	10.9	—
1938	7.9	17.2	—

SOURCE   Overy (1982), Table XIII.

almost all the new spending programmes authorised after the spring of 1935 were essentially military (Barkai, 1977; Guillebaud, 1939).

Thus from 1936 onwards the German experience ceases to be of great theoretical interest. By June 1936 unemployment was down to 1.3 million, including a strong regional component, and by October a shortage of labour was making itself felt in many industries, and hours of work were being increased (Guillebaud, 1939). The problems from then on were essentially those of a war economy: how to make room for additional military expenditure when resources were already fully employed. The recovery was to all intents and purposes complete.

There were two major, and not entirely independent, potential difficulties in this recovery programme, both of which began to make themselves felt during 1934. First of all there was the possibility that some of the expansionary momentum might be dissipated in inflation. This danger was enhanced by the fact that part of the strategy to relieve the distress in the countryside was to raise agricultural prices, as well as by the increase in the money supply which was the only practical method of financing. However one of the first steps of the Nazi Government was to abolish the trade unions and to transfer all their funds to a new organisation called the German Labour Front, which embraced employers as well as employees. Meanwhile the power to set wages was vested in the Ministry of Labour, whose aim was essentially to keep wage rates stable. Thus the problem of wage militancy, which might well have emerged as unemployment fell,

was solved by state regulation and the elimination of independent workers' organisations. During 1934 there was a
marked tendency towards a rise in prices, which was brought
under control by a series of decrees requiring all cartel price
increases to be notified to and approved by the Price
Commissioner. This was a reasonably effective solution, because
the government was able to establish strong control over labour
and raw materials costs.

The other difficulty was the balance of payments. After 1929
the German balance of trade moved into a strong and continuing
surplus, an effect of improving terms of trade as the world price of
raw materials collapsed and of the exceptional severity of the
German Depression. The surplus survived both the 1930
Hawley–Smoot tariff in the United States and the sterling
devaluation of 1931, and only disappeared when expansion was
well under way in 1934. Like the Bruening Government in 1931,
the Nazis chose not to devalue. Devaluation would have pushed
up production costs and excited popular fears of inflation, and
the government decided that it was preferable to maintain an
overvalued currency and to restrict imports artificially. Thus the
'New Plan' for foreign trade of September 1934 made it
obligatory to obtain a foreign exchange certificate before any
goods could be imported. Though this solved the payments
problem, it created a scarcity of raw materials which did, in
certain cases, interrupt the growth of production and required a
rigid system of rationing to prevent prices from being pulled up
by excess demand.

One of the important factors in the recovery was the support of
the business community. Despite interference in the investment
and pricing decisions of individual firms and periodic 'requests'
for funds from the local Party apparatus, the Nazis were
committed to the health of private enterprise and sought only to
harness it to national ends. Under their rule the share of profits
increased significantly as recovery raised capacity utilisation
levels, whilst their much publicised militarism and aggressive
nationalism seemed to offer the possibility of richer pickings in
the future, particularly for the investment goods industries. In
addition, business was grateful for the elimination of the trade
unions, and relieved that the polarisation of politics in the
Depression had ended in victory for the right rather than the left.

Big business therefore had little cause for complaint about the Nazi regime.

In sum, the German experience comes across, after 1932, as an overwhelmingly successful example of a Keynesian response to the Depression (before that it was the classic example of persistent deflation). The government ceased to be afraid of budget deficits and was prepared to finance them by the creation of money, countering the possibility of inflation with a barrage of wage and price controls. In the first stage of the recovery programme, the emphasis was on civilian projects; it was only after the end of 1934 that military expenditures came to predominate.

The interesting question about the German recovery concerns the part played by the politics of the Nazis. Would a traditional conservative or centrist government have been able to achieve as much? The general attitude of Hitler was to treat the economic system as a means to his political objectives: if something was politically desirable, it was up to his subordinates to make it economically feasible. This liberated his recovery policy from the paralysis of fear: about inflation, the balance of payments, the budget deficit, etc. Having decided that a strong recovery was vital both to consolidate the Nazis in political power and to achieve their wider ambitions, his response to the problems, as they arose, was to create new forms of state bureaucracy to solve them. Hence the controls on prices, on foreign trade, and the increasing state direction of private investment. These controls did what was required of them quite effectively.

But these were the benefits of regarding economic life as a servant of the state, rather than the state as the guardian of a free economic system. A more traditional government would have been hampered first of all by the fact that there was no means of financing the budget deficit other than the creation of money. The sum total of tax concessions and expenditure measures decided upon by the Nazis in 1933 was far greater than the Papen and Schleicher programmes. Even if such an expansion of the money supply could be risked initially, the appearance of inflationary pressures (which might have occurred even earlier in the recovery with the trade unions still intact) would have aroused immense fears about the soundness of the budget deficit – a legacy of the terrible experiences of 1922–4. The deterioration in the balance of payments as expansion sucked in imports would have caused similar problems. It is very difficult to see that any of the governments which had existed up until 1932 would have kept up their expenditure programmes in the face of these pressures, rather than cutting back and hoping that the private sector would take up the running; and the result would almost certainly have been a petering out of the recovery. Thus I would conclude that the establishment of an authoritarian government with an essentially military approach to economic problems was critical to overcoming the Depression in Germany. The methods were essentially Keynesian, but they could be ruthlessly pursued only because the motivation to restore German greatness overrode every other consideration.

Conclusion

All the major countries responded to the Great Depression with some degree of deflation, in some cases prolonged. Yet in all of the four countries discussed in this chapter serious attempts were made to use deficit spending to stimulate recovery, before the economic theory of such a policy was clearly established in academic terms, and in particular before Keynes's book was published.

This may seem surprising, since it suggests, quite contrary to Keynes's famous dictum, that economic policy was actually in advance of theory. The reasons were essentially political. The spending measures were undertaken by people who had been in opposition through the worst of the crisis, and who were acutely conscious of having been brought to power by a wave of popular revulsion against the policies of deflation. They were well aware that their political futures hung on finding a way out of the Depression, and not having been associated with earlier policy failures gave them greater freedom of action. Moreover public works had a lot of political advantages: they looked positive and dynamic to the public eye, they could be directed to the most urgent needs and the most depressed sectors of the economy, they took people directly out of the dole queue and were of obvious benefit to some individuals.

As far as President Roosevelt was concerned in 1933, this was about the sum total of the appeal of work creation programmes.

He was deeply sceptical about the multiplier effects of such spending at that time. Consequently in the United States priority was given to other measures and the work creation programmes themselves were directed much more to the relief of human distress than the stimulation of depressed industries. It was only after the recession of 1937–8 that this attitude began to change.

Subtle ideas of economic theory played equally little part in the mentality of the Nazis, who were carried forward by an ideology of the subjection of society to the state and a sense of historical mission. The vigour of their recovery policies reflected this vision, backed up by common sense and a refusal to be inhibited by potential difficulties such as inflation or balance of payments deficits. In economic terms their early measures added up to a well-conceived package, certainly the most impressive of the decade, but the strategy as a whole could be pursued effectively only by an authoritarian right-wing government which could solve problems by price controls, import controls and the abolition of trade unions, and still retain the confidence of big business.

In the other two cases, there was somewhat more theoretical influence. In France the economic programme of the Popular Front reflected the traditions of working-class under-consumptionism, supplemented by public works, but some of the potential problems of such a programme were never adequately confronted. It was only in Sweden that the idea of deliberately counter-cyclical use of the public sector's impact on effective demand was the major intellectual influence.

What conclusions can we draw from the results of these diverse experiments? The discussions of the effectiveness of fiscal policy that appear in macroeconomic textbooks certainly give us little guidance, since they ignore any influences on investment other than the rate of interest; and whatever the precise reasons for the collapse of investment over the years 1929–33, the rate of interest was not one of them. The theory of pump-priming suggests that if government spending gives the initial impetus to get the recovery going, private spending could then keep up the momentum so as to return the economy to full employment and the government budget to balance within a reasonable period of time. In terms of modern trade cycle theory based on the interaction of the multiplier and accelerator mechanisms, the initial push off the 'floor' will keep consumption and investment expanding until the economy reaches the 'ceiling' of full employment of resources, rather like someone jumping inside a spacecraft in orbit. If we can assume the consumption multiplier to be reasonably reliable, the key to the success of pump-priming will lie with the accelerator coefficient, i.e. the responsiveness of investment to the expansion in demand.

But there seems little justification for regarding the accelerator coefficient as some kind of predetermined variable, especially in conditions of widespread excess capacity. Investment decisions necessarily depend on expectations about the future, and since such expectations are seldom quantifiable in probabilistic terms, matters such as the general state of 'business confidence' or industrialists' and financiers' perceptions of the overall 'soundness' of government policy are likely to play an influential part (particularly because of the possibility of delaying investment decisions without shelving them altogether). And this is indeed what seems to emerge from our study.

In the two more successful examples of expansionary fiscal policy, Sweden and Germany, there was never any real problem about business confidence in government policy. In Sweden expansionary fiscal measures were put in train by a government of the left, but not one which aroused any great anxieties in business circles, and the idea of deficit financing seemed to be accepted fairly easily. In fact government stimulation of demand was of secondary importance to the recovery of exports; investment responded strongly and Sweden's relatively mild Depression was swiftly overcome. After a couple of years the government could end its extraordinary expenditures and enjoy an increasing budget surplus.

In Germany the key to the situation lay in the political crisis of the Weimar Republic. By 1932 the Social-Democratic Party was the only one actually to support the existing political system. With the situation of the masses becoming increasingly desperate, the Nazis were accepted by business as infinitely preferable to revolution, a faith which they promptly justified by the abolition of trade unions and all other political parties. Increasing state controls and direction of investment were accepted as the price of the preservation of private enterprise, particularly as profits increased quite markedly in the course of the recovery. Military expenditures were not of great significance in the early part of the recovery, but the whole Nazi conception was essentially military: their political project demanded the rapid growth of output, and potential obstacles were met by new forms of state control of the sort normally familiar to capitalist economies only in wartime. This was acceptable to private capital only because it was based on the decisive political defeat of the left. In a more normal, democratic political atmosphere, private business would have resisted bitterly such enormous state intervention, even under a government of the right, because if there was a successful recovery on such a basis it would shift public opinion massively in favour of state intervention and it would be the left which would reap the political benefits. Thus a democratic government of the right or the centre would not have been able to use the same weapons to deal with the problems of inflation and the balance of payments, and its expansionary programme would have had to have been infinitely more cautious.

In France the hostility of private capital to the Popular Front's economic programme was absolutely clear. Major social reforms, including mandatory paid holidays and the right to organise in trade unions, were imposed on employers, and the government's economic programme centred on the redistribution of income from profits to wages through reductions in working hours without loss of pay. Moreover there was a fear that if successful, the Popular Front's programme could shift the political atmosphere markedly to the left, so that even though nationalisation scarcely figured in it in 1936, all sorts of more radical measures might be seriously contemplated within a few years. On top of this, any anxieties that the reversal of deflationary policies would be inflationary and undermine the competitiveness of French exports seemed to find confirmation in the Matignon Agreements, in the negotiations for which governmental pressure was exerted principally against the employers rather than the trade unions. In view of all this, it is not surprising that capital was unwilling to respond by increasing investment, despite the fact that profits were quite effectively protected through price increases.

The weakness of the Popular Front Government was that it never properly faced up to these issues. It did not seriously consider the possibility that private capital's zeal for social reform failed to match up to its own, and that it might perceive in the Popular Front's release of the energies and enthusiasm of the workers a threat to its own power and freedom of action. Controls on the export of capital, demanded by the left, were unpalatable to the moderate elements in the coalition, though to make its programme work a much more energetic approach was required. First of all it was necessary to introduce an effective system of price controls, to make sure that the redistribution of income was indeed at the expense of profits, as intended, rather than those whose incomes for one reason or another failed to keep pace with inflation. And secondly, this needed to be backed up by a series of sanctions against private companies that refused to invest, or were found guilty of trying to export capital. If these measures had been tried, they would no doubt have set off a prolonged and bitter social conflict, but they would at least have amounted to a recognition of a basic fact of life in a capitalist economy: that if you are not prepared to pander to the power of private capital, as the Popular Front was not, then you have to be prepared to confront it.

In the United States the recovery from 1933 to 1937 was essentially consumption-led. Investment of all kinds recovered less strongly than output. To business the Depression had been a severe psychological shock, and it is not surprising that companies were rather more wary about authorising new investment than before. High levels of investment in the 1920s had reduced the pressure to replace obsolescent equipment, whilst excess capacity and fears about the resilience of the recovery inhibited installation of new production facilities. Moreover, unlike in Sweden and Germany, the government did not direct its extra expenditures primarily towards the capital goods and construction industries. Its programmes were aimed much more at lifting the incomes of destitute households.

From 1935 onwards big business started to become worried about the trend of thinking in the Roosevelt Administration. However, by and large the social reforms being hatched did not go beyond what had been accepted for some years in the more advanced countries of Europe, and which seemed fairly natural in a rich country like the United States. Writers like Schumpeter acknowledge these points, but stress instead the speed of the change, the sudden shift in social ideology and the tactlessness of officials as sources of business disquiet. However, there was certainly no threat to private enterprise in the sense that there could be said to be in France, where the Popular Front Government relied on the Parliamentary support of the Communist Party and had aroused almost revolutionary enthusiasm amongst the industrial workers. On balance it is doubtful whether one needs to fall back on these slightly nebulous factors to explain the weakness of investment spending in the USA.

On a broader scale, however, one can certainly maintain that the conservative ideology of the country, of which business hostility to social reform was one manifestation, inhibited the recovery because Roosevelt always had the balanced budget school breathing down his neck. Even though he was sceptical about deficit-financing as a measure to stimulate recovery, it is likely that he would have been rather less anxious to reduce the budget deficit in the years 1935–7 if he had not felt that it was an issue on which he was politically vulnerable. Fiscal policy must undoubtedly bear a major responsibility for the 1937–8 recession, but it was also largely responsible for ending it, and given all the circumstances, it contributed a surprising amount to the early stages of the recovery. Nevertheless, the New Deal was never as successful as recovery policy in Sweden and Germany.

Our survey indicates that in dealing with a major depression, the success of fiscal policy in the 1930s did not depend on the degree of 'crowding out' of private investment by high interest rates, as macroeconomic textbooks tend to suggest. This was a negligible factor, largely because of expansionary monetary policies. Of much greater significance were other influences on the rate of investment often summarised as the general state of business confidence. When output is seriously depressed, governments cannot expect to regain high levels of employment by the multiplier effects of their own additional expenditures alone, so the impact on private sector investment becomes critical. Moreover a fiscal expansion entails enlarging a budget deficit which is already in all probability large by historical standards. The examples of the 1930s indicate that such a policy can meet two quite separate sets of difficulties: fears that it is unsound in an economic sense, and fears that it is unsound (i.e. threatening to the existing order) in a political sense.

Objections to deficit-financing based on economic considerations can be met in a variety of ways, most of which were used in
the 1930s: by reference to the relationship between tax revenues
and national income, which could imply that the deficit would
disappear in more 'normal' circumstances; or by analogy with
private sector investment financed by borrowing, perhaps with
additional taxes being raised specifically to cover the interest
payments (as in Sweden); or of course by presenting the
theoretical arguments why it is a sound policy. If the government
expresses the theory behind its policy clearly, these objections can
usually be countered without too much difficulty, provided they
do not have a deeper political foundation. The strength of
hostility to budget deficits in the United States, for example,
derives not from a special propensity to intellectual backwardness
but from a widespread suspicion of federal government officials,
who are believed by many to come from alien social strata in
privileged parts of the country, and need to be restrained by rigid
curbs on federal activity. Such animosity towards the power of
central government is much less significant in the smaller, less
diverse and more centralised nations of Europe.

On the other hand, in some European countries historical
experience has created deep-rooted fears of inflation. If such fears
are *exceptionally* strong, and the capital markets in such a state that
money creation is the only possible way of financing a deficit, as
was the case in Germany in the 1930s, then inhibitions about
expansionary fiscal measures can be considerable. The Nazis got
around this problem only by very stringent price and wage
controls and political censorship, which prevented such fears
from being articulated. French governments up to 1936 never did
get around it; they were convinced that an expansionary policy
would represent political suicide, although the Popular Front's
election victory must raise a question mark over this judgment.

But if the centre and right of the political spectrum are
committed to a policy of deflation, the advocacy of vigorous fiscal
action may fall to a left whose economic programme has been
radicalised by the crisis. This is what happened in France, and in
a very muted form in the USA. This raises a whole new set of
political problems which have economic repercussions. Fixed
capital is immobile, long-lived and vulnerable to expropriation.
Private business is unwilling to make new investments in an

uncertain political situation, especially one in which there is significant pressure for radical change. An economic programme which offers no political guarantees to private capital (as the Nazis effectively did) yet imposes considerable restrictions on its freedom of action is liable to meet hostility and in all probability some form of investment strike. This introduces a new dimension: the government has to confront not only the 'normal' relationship between economic aggregates but the domination of the economy by private interests. To take in possible solutions to this problem is far beyond the scope of this book, but we should note its relevance to some of the 'alternative economic strategies' proposed in the current recession.

Notes to Chapter 2

1. This assumes that the change in the full employment budget surplus can be attributed to changes in spending on goods and services rather than transfers less taxes, in which case the appropriate multiplier would be 4.09. In this period of strong expansion of federal purchases of goods and services, the larger multiplier seems appropriate.
2. An English translation appeared as *Monetary Equilibrium* (London: William Hodge, 1939). This was a translation of the German text *Der Gleichgewichtsbegriff als Instrument der Geldtheoretischen Analyse,* which was an extended version of the original Om Penningteoretisk Jaemvikt (*Ekonomisk Tidskrift,* 1931). For a discussion of Myrdal's theoretical contribution see Shackle (1967), Chapter 10.
3. Marjolin (1938) estimates French prices to have been only about 9 per cent above foreign prices in July 1935, though this estimate may well be over-optimistic (see the comments in Sauvy, 1967, p. 508). By this time consumer prices were about 20 per cent lower than in 1931.

3
The Impact of the War

The Second World War brought the era of the Depression to a sudden and dramatic end, as the entire resources of the major countries were absorbed in the military struggle. With the outbreak of hostilities, full employment was fairly swiftly achieved everywhere. There was a massive increase in real output: in Britain by 31 per cent in four years from 1938 to 1942 and in the United States by 50 per cent in three years from 1939 to 1942. In Britain employment increased by nearly 20 per cent from 1939 to 1943 (Beveridge, 1944, pp. 113, 120). Even after allowance had been made for exceptional expansion in the supply of paid labour because of wartime conditions, this still represented a dramatic illustration of just how many additional resources could be mobilised under the influence of buoyant demand. Recognition of this fact stiffened the popular resolve to ensure the maintenance of high employment conditions when peace returned.

Once the military advance of the Axis powers had been halted and their ultimate defeat assured, post-war arrangements became one of the major topics of public discussion. In Britain this debate was greatly stimulated by the publication on 1 December 1942 of the Beveridge Report, which described itself as a plan to establish social security for all from the cradle to the grave. The Report was received with great enthusiasm, and an opinion poll found 86 per cent in favour of its adoption, with only 6 per cent against (Addison, 1977, p. 217). What this enthusiasm for social security reflected was an intense desire to end the scourge of poverty and want which had been such a prominent feature of the pre-war world. The advanced countries were now rich enough for this objective to be achieved, provided society made it one of its priorities. This was a fact which sunk deep into the popular consciousness.

Inter-war experience suggested that the greatest threat to this aspiration was mass unemployment. People remembered that the end of the First World War had been accompanied, after a brief boom, by a very severe slump. And then, of course, there had been the 1930s, a whole decade of depression. There was thus a very widespread sense that, unless governments were actively committed to preventing it, large-scale unemployment would once again rear its ugly head when peace returned.

It is difficult to generalise, but in much of Europe, in particular, the war generated a significant popular radicalism. In countries which had been under German occupation, the prestige of the left in general and of Communist Parties in particular was raised by the part they played in the resistance. In Britain and the United States, the sense of national emergency and unity of purpose contributed to an atmosphere in which the pursuit of private profit seemed strangely antiquated and immoral. Moreover, in many European countries there was a sense that the old ruling classes, or sections of them, had discredited themselves through collaboration, appeasement or incompetence. The whole political situation was characterised by a marked shift to the left.

At the same time it was appreciated everywhere that the end of the war created an unparalleled opportunity for a fresh start, in which the traditions and assumptions of the pre-war period might be re-established but could equally well be laid quietly to rest. In countries which had been under foreign occupation, these feelings were bound up with the recovery of national self-respect. In countries which had not, they expressed themselves in a deep determination not to return to the 1930s. In these countries the intervention of the state in economic life had grown to an unprecedented degree during the war, generally success-fully and with broad support across the political spectrum. But if the state could sort out the problems of wartime planning, surely it could also plan the peace. The prestige of state intervention and the belief that it could be used to prevent the return of economic disasters in peacetime were enormously encouraged by this experience.

Given the immediate pre-war experience, it is not surprising that popular aspirations focused first of all on the elusive goal of full employment. This is where Keynesian economics came into its own. During the war its influence grew steadily in both academic and policy-making circles to the point where one could say that, in 1945, it had more or less established itself as the new orthodoxy. Six years before, its challenge had only just been gathering momentum. The tremendous theoretical advantage of Keynesian economics in the context of planning for peace was, of course, that it offered a relatively simple theory of how governments could use their own expenditure and revenue decisions to keep the economy close to full employment. It was a natural tool for post-war employment policy.

In terms of the internal development of Keynesian theory, probably the most significant novelty of the war was the emergence of the notion of continuous government management of the natural fluctuations of the private sector through budgetary measures. The appropriate counter-cyclical expenditure and tax decisions could in principle be used to iron out the trade cycle or, in a phrase coined later, to fine-tune the economy. Thus Keynesian economics was beginning to be conceived not just as an emergency weapon, which might be kept in the government's policy cupboard until a depression threatened, but as a tool for stabilisation of the economic system by continuous, even though possibly quite minor, adjustments of the budgetary stance.

A significant step here was made by Keynes himself, drafted back into the Treasury with the onset of war. His small book on *How to Pay for the War* was published in 1940, though the essential ideas were already contained in three articles published in *The Times* in November 1939. The Keynesian principle of effective demand was now being applied, for the first time, to a situation of excess demand rather than depression. However the situation was more complex than any peacetime state of excess demand, because the demands of the war meant that no significant cuts in government expenditure could be contemplated. The policy problem was therefore, according to Keynes, to reduce private consumer demand to a level just sufficient to buy the supply of consumer goods which was to be permitted at current prices. Unless consumer demand could be suppressed in this way, the massive increase in government expenditure would inevitably mean inflation. Inflation would also be a solution to the problem of excess demand in the sense that it would temporarily reduce the demand to match the supply by cutting real wages and inflating profits, which were more likely to be saved. But Keynes argued, by reference to the experience of the First World War, that workers would soon get wise to this and the time-lag between price increases and the compensating wage increases would shorten. The consequence was that for any given pressure of excess demand, the inflation was likely to accelerate. Keynes's preferred solution was that a certain proportion of people's pay should be deferred until after the war, as if a certain proportion of their income had been paid into a blocked account where it could only accumulate as money balances.

In practice, 'deferred pay' played a relatively minor role in British war finance and there was much more widespread use of the ration card than Keynes thought desirable. Nevertheless the essential theoretical point that policy should aim to control effective demand for consumer goods rather than the quantity of money was universally accepted. Since if expenditure was effectively controlled, surplus money balances could not exert any inflationary pressure, the interest rate could be maintained at a markedly lower level than during the First World War (Harrod, 1952, p. 493). This sort of approach to war finance had not even been suggested in the earlier conflict (Keynes, 1940, p. 70).

In Britain Keynesian ideas became fully accepted in the economic establishment and the Treasury, and were at the centre of discussions about the future conduct of macroeconomic policy in peacetime. In May 1944 the Government published a White Paper[1] on *Employment Policy* (Cmnd 6527) which began:

> The Government accept as one of their primary aims and responsibilities the maintenance of a high and stable level of employment after the war. This Paper outlines the policy which they propose to pursue in pursuit of that aim.

It argued that under modern conditions the natural process of recovery from a trade recession was slow and sometimes ineffective. A graph of unemployment since 1858 was included to illustrate the apparent regularity of such recessions in the absence of a systematic policy to counteract them. The most volatile items of national expenditure were stated to be exports and private investment, and since they were difficult to control the Government would need to follow a policy designed to offset the fluctuations in these items. Having argued that monetary policy would eventually have a role to play in influencing investment expenditure through adjustments in the rate of interest, the White Paper stated that the Government would supplement this by counter-cyclical timing of public sector capital expenditures, and was also optimistic about the possibility of encouraging large private companies to follow a similar policy. The other prong of demand management was to be the manipulation of consumption via tax rates and social insurance contributions. Whilst making it clear that the Government retained an open mind on this issue, the White Paper stated a preference for adjustments in social insurance contributions to counter fluctuations in consumers' expenditure. Finally, it pledged the Government to develop a much more comprehensive set of statistics on the current state of the economy and movements in the various components of national expenditure, and to set up a small central staff to analyse economic trends and to give economic advice to Ministers. In Britain as elsewhere, the new ambitions in stabilisation policy were recognised to require a vast development in the collection and analysis of economic statistics.

Fifteen years before, proposals in this spirit had been in the forefront of the Liberal General Election campaign at a time of high unemployment, but had been rejected by the two major parties. The Conservatives had clung to the Treasury view whilst Labour regarded public works schemes as a diversion from the struggle to achieve its nebulous and illusory version of socialism (Skidelsky, 1967). The transformation of opinion is indicated by the fact that the 1944 White Paper was brought out by a Coalition Government dominated by the Conservatives. In the 1945 General Election all parties supported it. Nevertheless it is interesting to note that the White Paper went out of its way to stress the fundamental soundness of the budgetary policy which it outlined. It stated that the Government would keep in mind the problem of the National Debt, which had grown extremely large as a result of two world wars, as well as the state of the economy. Indeed the whole section on 'Central Finance' began with the patently dishonest statement that 'none of the main proposals contained in this Paper involves deliberate planning for a deficit in the National Budget in years of sub-normal trade activity'. Given that at the end of the same paragraph we read that severe depressions are normally characterised by budget deficits, and all the proposed policy measures implied deliberate increases in the deficit in such a situation, this sentence can only be construed as a ritual genuflection to fundamentalist beliefs in the inherent virtues of balanced budgets. As we shall shortly see, in some other countries (notably the United States) such beliefs retained a rather stronger hold on public opinion than in Britain.

A striking feature of all the discussions about employment policy at this time is the recognition that, if successful, it could have a profound impact on the labour market and might create a new problem of inflation. The White Paper states for perhaps the first time what has become one of the stock official phrases of the post-war period: 'Increases in the general level of wage rates must be related to increased productivity due to increased efficiency and effort'. William Beveridge, already a national hero for his Report on Social Insurance, had meanwhile been hatching his own private work on the problem of full employment. This emerged later in 1944 as a substantial book entitled *Full Employment in a Free Society*, and included a chapter on 'the internal implications of full employment'. A large part of this chapter was concerned with the implications of a changed balance of demand and supply in the labour market. Beveridge did not expect a serious decline in industrial discipline, even though pre-war statistics did show a procyclical fluctuation in the incidence of bad timekeeping and certain other measures of industrial misconduct. He was much more guarded, however, about the possibility of inflation. He accepted that the practice of sectional wage bargaining could lead to 'a vicious spiral of inflation, with money wages chasing prices and without any gain in real wages for the working class as a whole' (Beveridge, 1944, p. 199). To counter this he advocated a greater role for the TUC as a co-ordinator of wage claims, and provision for resort to an independent arbitrator as a means of resolving industrial disputes. But for Beveridge the proof of the pudding would clearly be in the eating.

This anxiety about inflation was equally apparent in academic circles. Indeed it is not possible to find a serious study of the economics of full employment written at this time which does not confront this issue. The most common conclusion was that there was no historical experience that could offer much guidance on the likely outcome for money wages and prices of continuous full employment, but many writers were quite prepared to accept a mild inflation as the price of full employment.

In the United States public opinion was flowing as strongly in favour of full employment as in Britain. The contrast between the experience of the 1930s and the 1940s was so vivid, not just in terms of numbers employed but also as measured by workers' standards of living, that the maintenance of such strong demand for labour in peacetime inevitably stood out as the most important single contribution that the government could make to popular wellbeing. In 1944 a prize-essay contest on the subject of post-war employment attracted nearly 36 000 manuscripts (Bailey, 1950, p. 9). Much as in Britain, it came to be regarded as political suicide to swim against the tide. But then during the war words were still cheap: the hard practical decisions did not yet have to be taken.

In the war the idol of the balanced budget, which Roosevelt had been obliged to worship, perhaps not entirely unwillingly, on so many occasions, was brutally pushed aside by the simple fact that the burden of taxation required to cover the federal government's expenditures was too enormous to contemplate. The removal of this obstacle created a golden opportunity for the development of Keynesian techniques within government, along the lines suggested by Keynes's *How to Pay for the War*. The relatively technical problem of to what degree the war should be financed by taxation and to what degree by borrowing never emerged as a serious political question. So the substantial body of economists newly employed in Washington were left relatively free to pursue their own methods of approaching the problem. They chose the effective demand technique of Keynes, which acquired the name of 'gap analysis' as a reflection of the procedure of calculating the gap between effective demand and full employment supply at current prices which had to be closed by taxation in order to avoid inflation (for a description of the procedure see Stein, 1969, p. 192). The economists' advice was not necessarily followed, but awareness that such techniques had been developed and could equally be applied to peacetime economic management was a significant factor behind the Full Employment Bill which was placed before Congress in 1945 and eventually passed, in amended form, as the Employment Act of 1946.

The Full Employment Bill first saw the light of day on 18 December 1944, when it was included in a *Year-End Report* on 'Legislation for Reconversion and Full Employment' submitted by Senator Murray to the Senate Committee on Military Affairs. In this initial version the Bill asserted the right to a useful job for everyone able and willing to work, and 'the responsibility of the Government to guarantee that right by assuring continuing full employment'. It further committed the Government to transmit to Congress an annual forecast of the gross national product and its main component parts, together with a statement of how far this fell short of what the GNP would be in a state of full employment. The President was then required to set forth in this so-called 'National Production and Employment Budget' the measures which he proposed to take to stimulate non-Federal investment and expenditure, and also to include a programme of Federal expenditures of an amount sufficient to bring GNP up to the full employment level (the full text of the original Bill is given in Bailey, 1950, Appendix A). The Bill clearly embodied the principle that full employment was the overriding objective of fiscal policy and the balance of the budget merely a means to achieving that end. This was fundamentally the same idea as that presented in the British Government's White Paper earlier in the year.

The publication of the *Report* stimulated considerable press comment, most of it hostile. Editorials in the *New York Times* and the *Wall Street Journal* condemned it as a deficit-financing measure (Bailey, 1950, p. 54). The prospect of budget deficits obviously touched a raw nerve in the American psyche in a manner which was not mirrored on the other side of the Atlantic. Not only staunch conservatives but a range of middling opinion had serious doubts about the Bill. If it was going to be passed, it was likely to have to be seriously amended.

The process of amendment had already begun by the time the Bill was introduced into the Senate on 22 January 1945. To forestall any attempt to portray the Bill as rampant New Dealism prominent references were made to the objective of fostering and strengthening competitive private enterprise. There were various other amendments, but the essence of the original remained (the full set of changes is listed in Bailey, 1950, pp. 57–9). Although this version of the Bill was passed by the Senate virtually unamended, it ran into trouble in the more conservative House of Representatives. Of a number of possible House Committees to which it might have been referred, it was sent to the Committee on Expenditures in the Executive Departments, which was dominated by conservatives. Personal pressure from President Truman made sure that the Committee did not reject the Bill altogether, but he could not prevent substantial modifications. The new, substitute Bill which emerged from the Committee aimed only at 'high' rather than 'full' employment, and instead of the 'National Production and Employment Budget' it required the President to produce a general report on economic conditions with no specific requirements attached to it. It retained the notion of a counter-cyclical public works programme, and provided for the establishment of a Council of Economic Advisers. The purpose of the change was to remove any suggestion that everyone had a right to a job at federal expense, which was the conservative interpretation of what the original Bill had implied (Bailey, 1950, Chapter 8).

This watered-down version was passed by the House, and was of course inconsistent with what had been passed by the Senate. The standard constitutional procedure was now to set up a Conference to thrash out a compromise acceptable to both sides. This compromise, which became the Employment Act of 1946, this time set the objective as 'maximum' employment, production and purchasing power. It required of the President an annual Economic Report, together with a programme for achieving the aims of economic policy specified in the Act. It established a Joint Committee of Congress to consider the Report, and also the Council of Economic Advisers, to be appointed by the President. The Act was entirely concerned with these administrative changes, and did not commit the federal government to any specific policy measures for promoting maximum employment. The opponents of the original Bill had thus succeeded in cutting out any reference to full employment or to federal investment as an employment-creating measure, so that no future government need realistically fear that its economic policy would be constrained in any way by this Act.

What the struggle over the Full Employment Bill demonstrated was the continuing strength of the notion of a balanced budget in US politics. But this was in the context of a Bill designed to lay down the general principles of economic policy for the future. That the House of Representatives was not prepared to pass the original Bill does not necessarily imply that when a recession seemed to be on the horizon, those same individuals would definitely reject a fiscal expansion as a means of meeting that threat, despite the rise in the budget deficit that would be involved. Congress had indeed already shown itself willing to pass spending measures in such circumstances in 1938. In other words the episode did not represent a rejection of Keynesian techniques for counter-cyclical purposes – this matter would be tested on other occasions. But it did demonstrate the continuing suspicion in which rural and small-town United States held the federal government, and the determination of these layers of society not to give any sort of a blank cheque to Washington.

I have taken the example of only two countries, albeit two major ones. Nevertheless they are sufficient to demonstrate some characteristics of the period which were felt to a greater or lesser extent in all the major capitalist nations. First the transformation of the labour market demonstrated just how disastrous the economic conditions of the 1930s had been, a fact which had been apparent at the time but which lost some of its political force out of sheer familiarity. The war ended the demoralisation induced by the Depression and created a steely determination not to relive the past. This was the political background to the unprecedented public interest in peacetime employment policy. Meanwhile Keynesian techniques of economic analysis conquered the academic world and became familiar in government circles, and seemed ideal for the new requirements of economic management. With the help of wartime experience, Keynesianism ceased to be depression economics and became a central tool of stabilisation policy.

To many economists, the world in 1945 seemed for these reasons to be on the threshold of a new era in economic history. The old *laissez-faire* attitudes to economic fluctuations were now politically unacceptable. A capitalism with continuous full employment, if it could be achieved at all, could prove to be a very different animal with some entirely new characteristics. The record of the post-war economy, and the contribution of Keynesianism towards that, form the subject matter of the next chapter.

Note to Chapter 3

1. Similar White Papers were also published in Australia and Canada around this time. For a comparison see D. H. Merry and G. R. Bruns, 'Full Employment: the British, Canadian and Australian White Papers', *Economic Record*, XXI (1945), 223–35.

4
The Post-War Boom

After the devastation of war, the quarter century or so that followed was for the advanced capitalist countries a period of exceptional economic dynamism, innovation and structural change. Moreover by historical standards the progress was extremely smooth, with recessions representing only small dents or mere decelerations in the upward path of output (Table 4.3). The contrast with the depressed 1930s could scarcely have been greater.

One of the most obvious indicators of improved economic conditions was the state of the labour market (Table 4.1). The post-war period emerges from these figures as strongly superior to 1913–50, when the unemployment rate was on average more than twice as high (despite the fact that this period includes two major wars). The post-war unemployment rate is also well below that for the period before 1914, when governments certainly did not accept any responsibility for reducing unemployment (as

Table 4.1 *Unemployment in the advanced capitalist countries*

	Average percentage rate
1870–1913	5.7
1913–50	7.3
1950–70	3.1

Source Maddison (1977).

Stedman Jones, 1971, shows, the term did not even enter the English language until the 1880s).

Of course this comparison would not be quite so favourable if the post-war figures were extended to the present day – but that would bring in the issue of why the boom broke down, which I shall be treating in Chapter 6. In this chapter I investigate how much the superlative economic performance of the 1950s and 1960s reflected the contribution of Keynesian ideas and Keynesian techniques of economic management.

Since full employment became a near-universal objective of economic policy in this period, I shall look first at the unemployment record. The average figures for unemployment quoted in Table 4.1 represent a blend of a considerable variety of experience across countries. In some full employment was already established in the 1950s. Such was the case in France, the UK and a number of smaller European countries such as Sweden and the Netherlands. Moreover some of these, like Britain and Sweden, were generally regarded as having governments committed to counter-cyclical budgetary policies, so that it was tempting to claim the outcome as proof of the success of Keynesian ideas. But there were also important countries where the employment experience of the 1950s left something to be desired. In the United States the Eisenhower Administration's concern about rising prices caused an upward drift in unemployment towards the end of the decade which took some years to disappear, despite President Kennedy's public commitment to fiscal expansion. In West Germany a rapid economic expansion was presided over by a government committed to monetary conservatism and free market principles; the unemployment associated with the immense influx of expellees and refugees was not absorbed until the end of the decade. In Italy the brilliant export-led growth performance of the north of the country was still insufficient to absorb all the surplus labour of the less developed *Mezzogiorno*, and unemployment remained significant throughout the 1950s.

It is not really until the middle of the 1960s that employment could definitely be said to have been acceptably close to its maximum throughout the developed capitalist world. The United States economy turned upwards in 1961, and under the stimulus of tax cuts and additional government expenditures (associated in the later stages with the Vietnam War) the expansion continued for an unprecedented eight years. Both Italy and West Germany averaged much lower unemployment rates in the 1960s than in the 1950s. The Belgian economy, whose growth had been sluggish up until 1960 with significant unemployment in the older industrial areas, managed to move into a higher gear. By contrast there were no countries which experienced a serious deterioration in their employment record. Table 4.2 illustrates this. For North America the 1950s average was boosted by the Korean War, and so to give a truer picture I have included the officially recorded unemployment rate (as a percentage of the civilian labour force) for the years 1958–61.

Table 4.2   *Unemployment in selected countries, 1950–73* (%)

	1950–60	1958–61	1962–73
Belgium	5.4		2.1*
France	1.3		2.2
West Germany	4.1		0.6
Italy	7.9		3.5
Norway	2.0		2.0
Sweden	1.7		2.1
United Kingdom	2.5		3.1
Canada	4.4	6.8	5.1
United States	4.5	6.1	4.6

NOTES: With the exception of the figure for Belgium marked*, national figures have been adjusted where necessary to make them comparable with other countries.
SOURCES   Maddison (1964), Table II–1; OECD; *Main Economic Indicators*; OECD, *Economic Outlook* No. 21, July 1977.

It would be facile to attribute this success on the employment front to official conversion to Keynesian doctrine without further investigation. Effective demand may grow because of increased public expenditure or increased private expenditure, and there are many causes of changes in private expenditure other than tax policy. *A priori* one can envisage various possibilities. If it emerged that the primary source of additional demand (compared with pre-war) was government budgetary policy, this would create a strong *prima facie* case that official conversion to Keynesianism *had* been the major factor in the better employment performance.

The burden would then rest on the opponents of this argument to show that the more expansionary budgetary stance had been the fortunate result of other, unrelated factors, such as the high military expenditure induced by the political atmosphere of the Cold War.

If, on the other hand, the stimulus to effective demand had come from private expenditure, without cuts in taxation, then we would need to inquire why this had occurred. We already know that the theory of pump-priming saw a government injection of demand primarily as a way of unleashing the accelerator mechanism and reviving private investment. By an analogous argument, if investment was maintained in part by a belief that an incipient depression would be met by prompt and vigorous stimulation of demand from the government, thus reducing the risk of catastrophic losses to business, then the official embrace of Keynesian doctrine could be said to have given significant indirect support to demand.

This suggests that a number of questions needs to be investigated. Was a changed stance of budgetary policy responsible for the much higher employment levels of the post-war period relative to the 1930s? Was budgetary policy used as a counter-cyclical device, in contrast to the pro-cyclical stance implied by the balanced budget doctrine? Did governments create the impression that they would be prepared to contemplate budget deficits to avoid a major depression? Did any of these factors significantly alter the spending propensities of the private sector?

Before tackling these questions, we should note that for the advanced capitalist world as a whole the outstanding characteristic of the post-war period has been not so much its approach to full employment as its general economic dynamism. Maddison's figures for his sixteen countries demonstrate this eloquently (Table 4.3). These figures show a very marked acceleration in the growth of output, and even more so for output per head and the stock of fixed capital, as compared with any previous historical period, accompanied by recessions so mild as to represent merely an interruption of growth rather than a serious retreat.

It is fairly safe to say that these growth rates were not anticipated. One authoritative book on French economic growth written at the beginning of the 1970s states categorically that 'even amongst the greatest optimists, no one dared hope, after the

Table 4.3   *Cyclical and growth characteristics of different periods. (Arithmetic average of figures for sixteen advanced countries)*

Time period	Annual average percentage growth rate in			Percentage maximum fall in GDP
	Output	Output per head of population	Non-residential capital stock	
1870–1913	2.5	1.5	2.8	−6.7
1913–50	1.9	1.1	1.6	−13.1
1950–70	4.9	3.8	5.6	+0.3

SOURCE   Maddison (1977), Tables 6 and 7.

war, that the pace of French expansion could be maintained for so long at such a high level' (Carré *et al.*, 1972, p. 9). The same could be said for most of Western Europe and Japan. Growth rates fell significantly below this international average over the whole period only for the major Anglo-Saxon countries (United States, Canada, Britain). Other countries, such as Belgium and Denmark, which had experienced sluggish growth in the 1950s acclerated to join the pack in the 1960s.

This fact can be related to the observation that, on the whole, the notion that the economic successes of post-war are fundamentally attributable to improved demand management has been accepted in a much more straightforward fashion amongst the intelligentsia of the English-speaking countries than elsewhere. For it is precisely in these countries that the acceleration in economic growth has been least marked, and the contrast with the 1930s has shown itself most obviously in labour market conditions. In continental Western Europe and Japan productivity growth has been running at roughly twice the rate of any earlier historical period, whereas in North America and Britain it has accelerated only slightly and has remained below 3 per cent per annum. For these countries it would be perfectly plausible to argue that there has been no break in the historical trend, but a slight improvement in the average because growth had not been punctuated by a serious recession.

The Sources of Demand

The figures given in Table 4.3 for the growth in capital stock immediately suggest that there has been a pronounced improvement in the propensity to invest in the advanced capitalist world. A higher rate of investment means a major injection of demand which would help to explain the much higher levels of employment in the post-war period, but the question is: what brought about this investment boom? It may of course have been a response to a much more expansionary budgetary stance than in the 1930s, or it may have been the result of other factors, so that governments have been able to maintain their commitment to full employment without having to put their beliefs in deficit budgeting to a really searching test. For many countries lack of data or boundary changes preclude an answer to this question, but for a few a reasonable attempt can be made. I shall look at three examples: Britain, France and the USA.

Britain

In a well-known article, Matthews (1968) examined British national income statistics for five years representing peaks in the trade cycle: 1929 and 1937 for inter-war; 1955, 1960 and 1964 for post-war. Taking a simple Keynesian model, in which investment, exports and net property income from abroad are assumed to be exogenous, while savings and imports are treated as proportional functions of income, he investigated movements in the ratio of actual to potential income in terms of changes in the savings and import propensities and changes in the exogenous variables (as a proportion of potential GDP). What emerges from this analysis is that the deflationary impact (amounting to about 3 per cent of potential GDP, including multiplier effects) of the loss of overseas property income through the enforced sale of assets during the war has been more than offset by the dramatic rise in investment, from 9–10 per cent of potential GDP before the war to over 15 per cent in 1955 and over 18 per cent in 1964.

Matthews takes output to have stood at 91 per cent of potential in 1929 and 1937, 100 per cent in 1955, and 99 per cent in 1960 and 1964. In judging the role of fiscal policy, he notes first of all that the total (i.e. central plus local) government surplus on *current account* (excluding capital expenditures) was about 3 per cent of national income in the post-war period; in 1937 it was zero. But such a simple comparison is not an adequate measure of the change in the stance of fiscal policy. If full employment had prevailed in 1937 the budget would have been in substantial surplus on current account, since output and income would have been 10 per cent higher; moreover there are also the balanced budget multiplier effects of the growth of the government sector between 1937 and 1955. So Matthews proceeds in the following way: he inquires what the impact on effective demand would have been if, in 1937, tax rates and government expenditures had been at their 1964 level. His simple model answers that national income would have been 1 per cent *less* than it actually was. This is a striking conclusion, suggesting that post-war fiscal policy made a negative contribution to closing the gap between actual and potential output which had existed in the inter-war period.

There are several grounds for arguing that Matthews's procedure is likely to bias the estimated impact of fiscal policy in a deflationary direction. One is that he does not appear to have allowed for the fact that, at 1937 levels of unemployment, 1964 expenditures would have been boosted by additional unemployment benefits. A second is that in a progressive tax system tax revenue would decline more than in proportion as income declines, so that his procedure probably overestimates the tax revenue that would have been received, had 1964 tax rates applied in 1937.

Slightly more serious than either of these adjustments is the objection that the capital expenditures of government might reasonably be included. Capital formation of central and local government represented 3.7 per cent of actual GDP (3.4 per cent of potential) in 1937, 4.5 per cent in 1955, 3.8 per cent in 1960 and 4.8 per cent in 1964 (Feinstein, 1972, Tables 1 and 39). This represents, on average, an increase of about 1 per cent of GDP between the inter-war and post-war periods, before multiplier effects. Inclusion of this (and is there a good reason for excluding it?) suggests a reversal of Matthews's conclusion with regard to the *direction* of the impact of fiscal policy: that the budget did exert a slight stimulus in 1964 compared with 1937. However it does not invalidate his main point, which is that any such budgetary stimulus to demand was certainly small compared with the impact of the big spurt in non-government fixed investment.

This type of analysis refers only to the proximate causes of a shift in aggregate demand, so that it cannot take into account any of the myriad possible ways in which government policy might have influenced the rate of investment in the private sector. Nevertheless within these limitations Matthews has certainly demonstrated that fiscal policy played no more than at most a minor *direct* role in explaining the higher employment levels of the post-war period in Britain.

France

A similar study for France has been carried out by Carré *et al.* (1972, pp. 320–5). They analyse the factors influencing the movement of total demand between the benchmark years of 1938 and 1951, 1951 and 1957, and 1957 and 1963. Rather than express their results as a proportion of national income (potential or actual) they give the absolute changes in constant (1959) prices. Thus we are told, for example, that exports gave an additional stimulus of F11 500 m in 1951 as compared with 1938 (before multiplier effects); of only F2100 m in 1957 as compared with 1951; and of F18 700 m in 1963 as compared with 1957. For the 1938/51 comparison, what emerges is a tremendous increase in tax revenues, without any significant increase in government expenditure; the deflationary impact on demand was, however, more than offset by a big growth in private sector investment and exports. In 1938 the budget had been in deficit, in part because of rearmament; in the late 1940s a tremendous effort had been made to get it back into balance as part of the stabilisation programme to stem the post-war inflation, and the buoyancy of investment and export demand had permitted this posture to be continued into the early 1950s without ill-effects.

From 1951 to 1957, the growth of government expenditure was the main expansionary force in the economy, divided about 2 : 1 between current and capital accounts. Much of the growth in current expenditure was associated with colonial wars in Indo-China and Algeria; but the growth in capital expenditure reflected a commitment to the objective of economic growth. There was only a very mild deflationary influence from increased taxation, so that the overall budgetary stance was strongly expansionary, resulting in an overheating of the economy and (eventually) the devaluations of 1957 and 1958. From 1957 to

1963 the major stimulus came from exports, reflecting increased competitiveness after the devaluations, though the propensity to import also increased with trade liberalisation and the creation of the EEC. The expansionary effect of further growth in government expenditure was largely offset by increased taxation, but company investment once again increased significantly. Overall, the main forces of expansion in the post-war years relative to 1938 were foreign trade and investment (both public and private). Exports were stimulated by the removal of trade barriers but a worsening of the terms of trade meant that their volume had to expand faster than imports to avoid sizeable balance of payments deficits. The budgetary stance emerges in this analysis as strongly deflationary relative to 1938 even in the 1960s – with the important proviso that the authors do not make any adjustment for changes in the ratio of actual to potential GDP.[1]

The United States

For the United States – undoubtedly the most interesting case because of its weight in the world economy – I know of no published work summarising the results of an exercise similar to the above, but the material is certainly available. There already exist estimates of the full employment budget surplus for a run of inter-war and of post-war years, and although these are not completely satisfactory from our point of view because they take no account of any balanced-budget multiplier effects, appropriate adjustments can be made for this.

For the 1930s, Peppers (1973) has estimated the federal full employment surplus for the last pre-war peak year (1937) at 2.8 per cent of potential GNP, actual output at this time being about 25 per cent below Peppers' estimate of potential. This figure may be compared with some post-war estimates calculated by Teeters (1965), using a similar procedure (neither Peppers nor Teeters apply any system of weights to the different forms of expenditure and revenue to allow for differential impact on aggregate demand; but Okun and Teeters, 1970 demonstrate that application of a weighting procedure makes little difference to the time profile of *movements* in the full employment surplus – for the period since 1955, at least). In 1956, when the US economy was close to its conventionally accepted measure of potential GNP (an unemployment rate of 4 per cent), the full employment surplus comes out at 1.5 per cent of potential GNP. According to this measure, therefore, fiscal policy was less restrictive in 1956 than in 1937, by 1.3 per cent of potential GNP. Applying to this the multiplier for the United States calculated by Hansen (1969) of 2.12, this gives us a demand stimulus of 2.7 per cent of potential GNP, whereas the gap to be explained is of the order of 25 per cent. Clearly, the change in the full employment surplus is insufficient to explain the much closer approach to full employment after the war.

However, as the second row of Table 4.4 shows, the balanced budget multiplier effects of the greatly swollen activities of government as a purchaser of goods and services were of considerable significance. Largely because of much higher defence spending, total government spending on goods and services increased by nearly 9 per cent of potential GNP. Assuming a balanced budget multiplier of one (a point which has been disputed – see Ward and Neild, 1978, who argue that it should be zero), this yields a total positive impact of government fiscal activities in 1956 as compared with 1937 of $11\frac{1}{2}$ per cent of potential GNP – a far from negligible amount. But this is still

Table 4.4 *The sources of demand growth in the United States, 1937–56. Percentage of Potential GNP*

	(A) 1937	(B) 1956	(C) (B)−(A)	(D) Multiplier	Demand effect ((C) × (D))
Full employment surplus	2.8	1.5	−1.3	−2.12	2.7
G	9.9	18.75	8.85	1	8.85
I (non-residential)	6.1	10.4	4.3	2.12	9.1
I (residential)	1.6	6.3	4.7	2.12	10.0
Change in average propensity to consume			−1.2	2.12	−2.5
actual GNP	75	99	24		

G – Total government purchases of goods and services.
I – Private fixed investment.
SOURCES Rows 1 and 6 – see text; rows 2, 3, 4 – US Department of Commerce (1975); row 5 – Table 4.5.

smaller than the combined effects of the expansion in residential and non-residential private investment, although it is larger than either of these taken separately.

But the demand effects of a boom in residential building need to be considered a little further. The boom was sustained throughout the 1950s and 1960s; it could not have been sustained without consumers spending much more, relatively, on housing than in the 1930s. Housing, however, is treated differently from other consumer durables in the national income statistics: whereas they are regarded as consumption expenditure, housing is treated as a consumer investment. Such a housing boom by definition therefore absorbs a large quantity of household savings. But did this represent a diversion of savings from other assets, or a reduction in other forms of consumer spending? The answer is critical in assessing the demand effect of the housing boom, because if it replaced other consumer spending, the extra residential investment would have been offset by a reduction in autonomous consumption.

Fortunately, the national income statistics permit us to estimate the size of this change. By applying the 1937 average propensity to consume (APC) to 1956 household incomes, and comparing it with actual consumers' expenditure in 1956, we can estimate directly the impact in 1956 of the reduction in APC relative to 1937 (Table 4.5). This impact is then multiplied in normal fashion, with the results shown in Table 4.4. The result indicates a negative but relatively small impact on aggregate demand.

Table 4.5   *Changes in the US average propensity to consume, 1937–56*

	1937	1956
(A) Personal disposable income ($bn)	71.2	293.2
(B) Personal outlay ($bn)	67.4	272.6
(C) APC (%) ((B)/(A))	94.7	93.0
(D) 1956 Personal outlay at APC of 94.7%		277.65
(E) Change in autonomous consumption 1937–56 ((B)−(D))		−5.05
(F) (E) as percentage of potential GNP		−1.2

SOURCE   US Department of Commerce (1975).

These exercises, necessarily approximate, seem to demonstrate that whereas in Britain and France, and probably most other European countries, the direct impact of the stance of fiscal policy on demand was only a small (and quite possibly a negative) factor in explaining the much higher levels of demand in the post-war period, in the United States fiscal policy was of considerable significance, even though still secondary to the boom in private investment spending.

But because the United States was such a pre-eminent force in the world economy in the 1950s, this raises the issue of whether Europe imported a demand stimulus from the US: was a more relaxed stance of budgetary policy in Europe rendered unnecessary by the US government's policy? Here the observation that most of the expansionary impact of US fiscal policy came through the expanded size of the government sector (the balanced budget multiplier) rather than a change in the (unweighted) full employment surplus is of relevance. Statistically a 1 per cent growth in GNP is a 1 per cent growth in demand whichever method of fiscal policy is used to achieve it. But this obscures the differential impact of the two methods on the private sector. A discretionary increase in government expenditure, with no increase in taxation, would stimulate consumption demand and raise capacity utilisation throughout the consumer goods industries, with possible induced effects on investment. It would impart a *generalised stimulus* to the economy. By contrast a similar increase in GNP achieved through the balanced budget multiplier would have only a *localised impact*. Let us assume that the government spends more on the military, since this is in fact what explains, to a very large degree, the increased weight of US government purchases of goods and services in the post-war period as compared with the 1930s. Here the secondary impact on consumption of extra defence expenditure is exactly offset, in the elementary model, by the effects of the higher taxes imposed to pay for it. The consumption goods industries experience no stimulus, and the rise in GNP is precisely equal to the value of additional military goods and services demanded. This implies that the stimulus to imports will be very limited. The import content of the services provided by a soldier is necessarily zero, and there is an understandable strategic bias towards the home product in purchases of military equipment.

The stimulus to imports would therefore have been largely confined to two sources: the stationing of units overseas, and purchases of raw materials which could not be obtained in the United States. Moreover it should be remembered that these raw materials came mostly from outside Europe, and the exporting countries would therefore have spent a fair slice of their extra dollars on US rather than European products. Thus we are left with the expenditure on overseas military bases. In some cases this made a significant contribution to the host country's balance of payments, but can hardly explain the surge in investment which was characteristic of these economies after the war.

The above analysis suggests several conclusions.

(1) If the arms bill had been smaller and taxes correspondingly lower, then without a compensating rise in other expenditures the United States would have fallen significantly short of full employment throughout the period. With military expenditure at 5 per cent of GNP (still much above the 1930s ratio but close to European standards), national income would have been 5.9 per cent less in 1955, 4.7 per cent less in 1960 and 3.1 per cent less in 1965. To compensate for this through an expansionary fiscal policy would have required acceptance of sizeable budget deficits. Even the full employment balance would have been persistently negative. To what extent this would have been accepted by the public is extremely hard to say. At any rate the experience of the years of slack around 1960 suggest that there is little reason to suppose that a fiscal stimulus would have been rendered unnecessary by a further jump in investment.

(2) The direct demand impact of the change in the stance of US budgetary policy in 1956 relative to 1937 fell overwhelmingly in the military sector, with only a limited spillover to other parts of the economy. This *direct* effect cannot therefore explain the greatly increased propensity to invest across the whole spectrum of output (possible indirect effects, such as technological spin-off, I discuss below).

(3) United States fiscal policy did not act as an engine of growth for the whole world. Although high US demand certainly attracted exports from European countries, the role of US fiscal policy in this was limited.

The Sources of Dynamism

If fiscal policy did not directly create the high employment levels of the post-war period by and large, was the apparent connection of this achievement with the official acceptance of the Keynesian revolution largely a coincidence? Not necessarily, because we have not yet inquired into the causes of the investment boom. Macroeconomic policy might have fuelled that boom either by giving evidence of a new competence in combating recessions, or in issuing strong signals that it would undertake emergency spending programmes or tax cuts if a serious recession threatened, or by a combination of both. This could have reduced the perceived risk in business minds of a collapse in aggregate demand, with its associated falls in capacity utilisation and profitability. I shall review later both the stated positions of the governments of some major countries and their record in stabilising their economies. But first it is useful to ask whether there were any special features of the period which were unusually favourable to investment. From this we may be able to judge whether the achievement of the policy-makers was one of *creating* the right environment for an investment boom, or the more passive one of preventing it from being cut short by serious policy errors.

I consider that there were several factors which were unusually favourable to growth and investment in the advanced capitalist countries at this time. The first (and one which has been somewhat neglected) is the transformation in international politics. The strategic configuration of the post-war scene has become so settled that it is not easy to imagine the consequences of anything different. Yet it is sufficient to cast one's mind back to the 1930s to recognise that the war brought fundamental changes in international relations. A major effect of this was to create an unusual and historically unprecedented political solidarity within the advanced capitalist world, under the leadership of the United States.

This was essentially the result of the combined weight of two largely independent forces: the new power of socialism in Europe and the upsurge of nationalism in the colonies. Before 1939 subject peoples had not achieved any significant victories against a colonial power, despite in some cases having built up a considerable popular movement, whilst the Soviet Union was more important as a symbol of revolution and a social experiment than as a world power. The Bolsheviks had only just survived the Civil War, and throughout the period seemed more concerned with defence against capitalist encirclement than the export of revolution.

The Second World War changed all this. The USSR emerged with considerable economic damage but militarily strong, its army having liberated most of Eastern Europe, which was thereby pulled largely beyond the influence of the Western powers. Moreover this was combined with a marked political radicalisation of the whole of war-torn Europe (not to mention East and Southeast Asia). Britain elected a Labour Government with a massive majority. In France, Greece, Italy, Yugoslavia and Albania, all countries where the Red Army had never set foot, Communist Parties emerged from the war with considerable strength and influence, whilst the future politics of Germany were very much of an unknown quantity. It seemed possible that the whole of Europe could embark on a steady leftward drift unless something was done to stop it.

This was the background to the launching of the Cold War and the Truman strategy of 'containment of Communism'. The essential purpose of this was to regain the political initiative for the right by branding Communists and their political allies as subversive agents of an anti-democratic external power, the USSR, whilst at the same time justifying to domestic public opinion and providing a cloak of legitimacy for US interventions all over the globe. This approach to the post-war world had been encouraged and indeed foreshadowed by Britain, not only in Churchill's famous 'Iron Curtain' speech but also in armed action against a native resistance movement in Greece even before the war was over. Politically, the strategy was a great success in Western Europe: Communist Parties were pushed out of government and the United States was able to orchestrate an all-encompassing political and military alliance. In the East it failed, only provoking a political homogenisation along Soviet lines.

Both this political strategy itself and its outcome, the creation of a major socialist geo-political zone designated as an overwhelming potential threat, had significant and very largely beneficial economic consequences for the capitalist world. It cemented an alliance based on the belief that major squabbles amongst the big capitalist powers would weaken them all in the face of the socialist challenge: therefore such squabbles had to be strictly controlled. Although still the richest and most powerful nations on earth, the advanced capitalist countries felt themselves to be in a position of historic weakness and on the defensive, with their wings sharply clipped as compared with 1939. In this situation the United States, not crippled by war and now unquestionably the dominant power, undertook from 1947 to finance the recovery of Western Europe and Japan. Later, it supported the creation of the European Economic Community even though such a bloc threatened in the long run to be a formidable commercial rival. Such generosity required the quelling of traditional US attitudes to Europe based on past commercial hostility; although originally inspired by the vivid contrast between the prosperity of the United States and the devastation of Europe, the Marshall Plan would in all probability never have been accepted by Congress had it not been seen as necessary to the struggle against Communism.

The impact of this was most marked in the former Axis powers now under occupation: Germany, Austria and Japan. Punitive attitudes were steadily abandoned as the United States came to perceive the strategic significance of these countries in its new conception of world politics. During the war the Allies had approved the idea of reducing Germany to a pastoral economy incapable of making war in the future, by dismantling industrial capacity, breaking up large firms and imposing limits on future output. But in the three Western Zones increasing hostility to the USSR led slowly to the total reversal of this policy, and in September 1949 the three Zones were united to become the Federal Republic of Germany. The aim by then was to build up the FRG as a politically stable bulwark against Communism, and for this a healthy economic revival seemed an indispensable requirement. Dismantling and deconcentration measures were halted, and the weeding out of former Nazis in high places quietly dropped. The FRG was incorporated into the Organisation for European Economic Co-operation (OEEC) as a full participant in the Marshall Aid programme. This turn of events has led one commentator to write: 'if there is a single factor that has been more decisive for Germany's recovery than any other, it is the East-West split' (Wallich, 1955, p. 323).

An essentially similar pattern was followed in Japan. The US authorities regarded the aggressive expansionism of pre-war Japan as the product of its highly stratified and feudal political and economic structure, and set out on a course of 'Punishment and Reform'. The punishment element consisted of reparations and a lack of concern for economic recovery. The reform element included the breaking up of the large industrial combines (*Zaibatsu*), land reform and political democratisation. By the end of 1947 this attitude was changing. The anti-*Zaibatsu* policy was moderated; trade union militancy, previously regarded sympathetically as a force for democratisation, was increasingly discouraged; reparations were halted. Full sovereignty was restored to Japan in 1952, and throughout the early 1950s US military expenditures played a highly significant role in alleviating balance of payments constraints on recovery.

It is difficult to exaggerate the significance of these events, especially when one considers that Japan and West Germany have since acquired an exceptional aura of economic success. The occupying forces could easily have allowed their economies to stagnate for years. For Western Europe as a whole, however, of much greater significance was the Marshall Plan. This derived from an offer made in a speech by US Secretary of State Marshall on 5 June 1947 in which he said that 'Europe's requirements for the next three or four years of foreign food and other essential products – principally from America – are so much greater than her present ability to pay that she must have substantial additional help or face economic, social and political deterioration of a very grave character'. The offer was made to all European nations, but was never really intended to include the USSR, which in any case refused to enter into a co-operative recovery programme with the Western countries (one of the conditions of the aid) and the rest of Eastern Europe followed suit.

The background to this was that Western Europe had emerged from the Second World War with severe balance of payments problems of a structural nature, which expressed themselves as a 'dollar shortage' – i.e. Western Europe wished to purchase imports from the dollar area to a far greater value than she was earning in exports. While it lasted this dollar shortage served as a graphic reminder of the new subordination of its erstwhile rivals to the United States. Its causes have been well summarised by the United Nations Economic Commission for Europe (1953). They consisted of

(1) A movement of the terms of trade against the industrial countries (in the 1930s food and raw materials prices had been exceptionally depressed);
(2) A reduction in the supplies of raw materials from non-dollar sources (Eastern Europe and the colonies);
(3) Greatly reduced income from foreign assets as a result of wartime sales and confiscations;
(4) Greatly reduced earnings from shipping due to wartime losses of merchant ships.

To overcome this structural problem would require a massive readjustment of Western European economies (a wartime estimate for Britain was that exports would have to increase by 50 per cent). Without a US loan the shortage of raw materials was becoming a bottleneck in the whole recovery process.

The reaction to Marshall's speech was swift. A committee of sixteen West European countries was set up in July 1947 to draw up a draft recovery programme; this committee was the embryo of the OEEC, which was to be the co-ordinator and debating chamber for the distribution of the programme's later stages. The aid received by these countries was substantial, being sufficient to pay for two-thirds of their imports of goods from the dollar area, or a quarter of their total import bill, over the period 1947–50 (OEEC, 1958, p. 33). It enabled them to overcome serious shortages of food, coal and steel. The point about the Marshall Plan was not that it was a piece of international Keynesianism, creating recovery by injecting demand. If it had been, the United States might just as well have spent the money at home. The point was that it eliminated a temporary maldistribution of foreign exchange, thus creating a breathing space in which Western Europe was able to overcome the structural difficulties with its balance of payments. In fact output and exports grew fast enough to eliminate the deficit on current balance with the dollar area by 1953.

Thus US policy and generosity supported the recovery and

development of the entire advanced capitalist world during the first decade of the post-war period. The political solidarity has survived much longer, and has sustained the relatively smooth pattern of international economic relations within the West ever since. The strong moves towards trade liberalisation did reflect, in part, a wish to avoid the disruptions of the 1930s, but the objections of particular interest groups would have got a much wider hearing if the relations between nations had not been dominated by strong feelings of shared interests. The adjustment system established under the Bretton Woods Agreement of 1944 did not work totally smoothly, since exchange rate changes were often bitterly resisted, but it certainly did not seriously hamper the growth of international trade, which steadily outpaced the growth of output. It enshrined the dominance of the dollar, but this was quite acceptable to most other countries until they began to feel that the United States was abusing its position (President de Gaulle's actions, however, demonstrate the difficulties that might have arisen in different political circumstances).

Trade liberalisation was of limited significance to the US economy, but of great importance elsewhere. European economies were much smaller – some very small – and needed secure trade arrangements in order to take advantage of opportunities for specialisation and economies of scale. The creation of the EEC and EFTA and the general trend towards tariff reduction created the confidence required for companies to invest on the assumption that such arrangements would continue. This is precisely what had not been possible before the war. The role of international monetary arrangements was to make sure that temporary maladjustments did not lead to the cumulative imposition of restrictions which would break that confidence. The availability of significant but limited and conditional short-term finance for balance of payments deficits from the International Monetary Fund largely prevented resort to irregular measures, even though countries tended to be reluctant to change their parities in either direction.

Thus after centuries in which international politics were dominated by the commercial rivalries between major capitalist nations, the period since 1945 has seen an alliance between them of unprecedented breadth and solidity, which has had profound and beneficial effects on economic development. This process, which was embryonic in the inter-war period, has occurred in response to the decline of empires and the expansion of socialism. The most sustained effects have been the commitment to freedom of trade and an orderly system of international economic relations. In addition, the US commitment to the recovery of Western Europe and Japan got these economies off to a flying start which they could never otherwise have achieved. This stimulated an investment boom, and fairly quickly created a belief that high growth rates could be sustained.

Nevertheless, it takes more than a favourable international environment to stimulate exceptional rates of investment and economic growth. In a large number of countries, investment ratios and growth rates exceeded those experienced over any period of any length in the past by some way.

Almost all commentators have cited a backlog of technological innovations built up over the recent past but not yet widely applied, as a major force behind the investment boom. In 1953 a normal pattern of investment had been possible in Europe for only about one decade in the last four. Of the previous forty years, roughly twenty had been taken up with war and its aftermath, and ten with a massive depression which greatly discouraged investment. If it can be argued in relation to the 1920s, as it has been (Svennilson, 1954), that investment was stimulated by the backlog of innovative possibilities built up since 1913, how much greater must the opportunities have been by 1945?

The same reasoning does not apply to North America, for in both World Wars the United States ultimately became a belligerent but derived many of the advantages of a non-belligerent: it was neither damaged by enemy bombs nor, because of its size, was it crippled by the war effort, whilst its economy received the stimulus of high government expenditures and a booming market. Its productivity lead of perhaps a quarter in 1913 was extended to the point where, by 1950, US productivity was about double that of Western Europe, an advantage far greater than could be explained by economies of scale, favourable natural resource endowments or a larger capital stock per employee. Thus Western Europe and Japan had tremendous scope for growth simply by importing US technology already in operation. The process was eased by a flood of overseas invest-ment by US firms after 1955.

Thus for Western Europe and Japan we can build up a highly plausible story of the availability of profitable technical innovations in the 1950s and 1960s. This does, however, leave open two related questions: why did the United States itself, the technological leader, experience a sustained investment boom? And why did the European and Japanese investment euphoria not peter out as the easy pickings disappeared? The answer would appear to be that the relatively high profitability and good demand conditions of the period, together with the allocation of substantial funds from the federal government, sustained a high and rapidly growing investment of resources in research and development (R & D), which was rewarded by continued outward movement of the technological frontier at rates which at least matched that of earlier historical periods. In the United States GDP per hour of work increased on average by 2.5 per cent per annum over the period 1950–70, a rate similar to that achieved in 1913–50, and greater than the 2.1 per cent p.a. averaged from 1870 to 1913 (Maddison, 1979, Table 1). If we make the over-simple assumption that this purely reflects the rate of outward movement of the technological frontier (thus ignoring the impact of structural changes, trends in capital intensity and the position of the US economy in relation to the frontier), then the proper measure of Western Europe's movement towards the frontier would be the excess of the growth of its GDP per hour of work over the US average of 2.5 per cent per annum. Since over this period Western Europe averaged an annual growth of GDP per hour of work of around 5 per cent, only about half of this growth represented a catching-up process, the rest reflecting the improvement required merely to maintain its relative position. The ability of US firms to exploit new scientific developments through R & D expenditure, in circumstances where they felt financially strong enough and confident enough to sustain a large volume of such expenditure, thus had a dual effect on growth. It stimulated a high rate of investment in the United States and throughout the advanced capitalist world, and it prolonged the catching-up process of Western Europe and Japan, so that these countries could go on growing fast by adapting imported technology rather than having to share in the costs of basic technical innovation. The result was that the investment boom in Western Europe did not peter out. Indeed business confidence reached such a pitch under the influence of surging demand that if anything the ratio of investment to GDP tended to increase over time.

We have already seen that US military expenditures made a significant contribution to the disappearance of 1930s unemployment rates. A question which requires answering is whether such expenditures also made an important *indirect* contribution to employment, through 'technological spin-off'. The argument would be that military requirements stimulated a considerable allocation of federal funds for research, the benefits of which could be reaped for civilian as well as military projects, so that industry got new inventions 'on the cheap' and undertook more investment than it would otherwise have done. The statistics show that the United States did spend a higher proportion of national product on R & D than other countries, and that the difference was indeed largely accounted for by the greater weight of military and space-related expenditures (United Nations, 1964). But the direct evidence for technological spin-off is weak. The fundamental obstacle was that the requirements of the military for limited quantities of specialised equipment of superlative quality regardless of cost were very different from those of the mass market for consumer goods, and there are very few instances of successful direct adaptation of military technology for civilian purposes (Clayton, 1970, pp. 100–3). Almost certainly of much greater importance was the rapid increase in US industry's own R & D expenditures, which reached 1 per cent of GNP by 1959, having increased threefold since 1950.

A further factor of major significance to the long post-war expansion was the quiescence of the work-force. The fears expressed by many economists around 1945, that the combination of full employment and democracy could give workers too much bargaining power and create serious inflationary pressures as the traditional constraints on industrial militancy disappeared, proved largely unfounded. Certainly workers in all countries obtained steady rises in real wages, shorter working hours and improvements in working conditions. But, in striking contrast to the 1970s, the pressure of their demands was never such as to threaten general business profitability. It has been common to attribute this success to money illusion – the failure of workers to take account of inflation in their wage bargaining –

but though this was an element in the situation, as a total explanation it is far too superficial.

The true answer probably lies in a combination of ideological and market factors. On the ideological side the two main forces at work were the Cold War atmosphere and the relatively demoralised state of the work-force of most of Continental Europe after two decades of depression and war. One striking symptom of the prevailing mood was the flowering in the years around 1960 of such notions as the withering away of class conflict and the embourgeoisement of the working class. In the later 1960s these ideas lost their intellectual appeal amidst widespread opposition to the Vietnam War and new evidence of industrial militancy in France (the May events of 1968), Italy (the hot autumn of 1969) and many other countries. But in the years from 1950 until around 1967 there was considerable evidence of integration of the working class into the social order. Politically the decade of the 1950s was stable and belonged to the right. In the inter-war era, by contrast, most of the major countries had experienced periods of intense class conflict and were politically much more volatile.

One reason was undoubtedly the psychological atmosphere created by the Cold War. The Cold War prolonged, in an attenuated form, the sense of patriotic solidarity and intolerance of dissent characteristic of wartime, with the added dimension that, with Communism designated as the enemy, militant or left-wing activities only avoided the tag of external subversion with extreme difficulty. Characteristic of this period were the division of the trade union movement along ideological and confessional lines effectively preventing any degree of unity in action (France, Italy, Belgium); the dominance of right-wing leaders (Britain, Germany); and the acceptance of either an incomes policy as part of long-term economic planning (Holland) or nationally negotiated but moderate wage increases as necessary to sustained economic growth (Sweden, Austria). This pattern was established in the late 1940s and only began to break down after 1960 (and even then only slowly). The trend towards *détente* undoubtedly helped the breakdown process.

But an equally and perhaps more important factor was the relatively low aspirations of working people in the late 1940s. This was a generation which had experienced two decades of deprivation: first depression and then war. Only in North America was the experience markedly different. Here the depression was bitter and prolonged, but war brought unprecedented prosperity. However in the United States there was a powerful factor working for moderation, namely the consciousness of being a member of the richest and most powerful nation on earth and markedly better off than one's European counterparts.

This history of depression and war meant that the post-war experience of political stability, a buoyant labour market and rising living standards represented a great improvement. Indeed the sense of security of employment combined with the prospect of a steady improvement in real wages over the years, at whatever rate, was something of a novelty for twentieth-century Europe. In fact, because productivity growth was so fast in most of Western Europe, real wages rose at rates which had not been matched in any sustained period of previous history. Such rates of real wage increase came as a bonus. As a result the one serious international inflationary boom (associated with the Korean War) and the occasional bouts of overheating experienced in many countries did not take the advanced capitalist world into an era of prolonged inflation and conflicting claims over resources such as has become familiar since 1973.

One might regard the industrial capitalist countries during this period as deriving the benefits of being caught in an unusually virtuous circle. Because of the exceptional opportunities for technical innovation, high rates of investment brought forth high productivity growth rates, whilst strong demand conditions held profits up. At the same time the depressed aspirations of the work-force implied that buoyant demand for labour could be consistent with a growth rate of real wages which was satisfactory to workers and yet did not exceed the rate of increase of productivity, so the share of profits was maintained. Firms therefore had both the confidence and the financial strength to continue with high rates of investment. In the short run this was wonderful. In a longer perspective, however, it could be seen to have shaky foundations, which would be eroded as popular aspirations adjusted to the new circumstances. The period before 1950 receded into the back of people's minds; a new generation who had never experienced it began to join the work-force. The very solidity and stability of the post-war environment encouraged people to take its achievements for granted, and this accelerated the process of rising aspirations. Popular perceptions of social wealth and their private expectations began to catch up with what the economic system could easily offer them. The goal of full employment increasingly came into conflict with the stability of prices and the maintenance of a social consensus: these problems were to emerge sharply from 1970 onwards.

It might seem strange to talk about market forces acting to moderate wage demands in a period when unemployment was lower than ever before. Yet, as we have seen, several countries (Italy, West Germany, Belgium) had significant unemployment in the 1950s. In Italy, it is probable that this did significantly weaken the trade unions, whose activities had noticeably more impact in the 1960s; indeed for a long time in the 1950s money wages increased more slowly than labour productivity. In West Germany the role of labour market competition is not quite so clear, despite the similarity to Italy in the time pattern of unemployment, because the urban housing crisis for a long time prevented refugees lodged in rural areas from competing effectively for jobs.

In other countries there was a massive structural change during the 1950s and 1960s, with very large reductions in agriculture's share of the total labour force, which has sometimes been asserted to reflect a degree of underemployment in the countryside similar to that found in underdeveloped countries (Kindleberger, 1967). Was this reserve army of labour of vital importance to the post-war boom? Although it was sucked into employment in other sectors by strong demand conditions and rising real wages, I doubt if it had much influence on wage bargaining in an immediate sense. Kindleberger's argument is that the existence of such an elastic supply of labour prevented the boom from being cut short by labour shortages and hence over-fast wage increases eating into profitability. But there were other sources of expanding labour supply: population growth, increasing participation of women in paid employment and immigration, whose relative importance of course varied from country to country. If one accepts that economic development necessarily involves structural change and a reallocation of labour between sectors, then the issue really comes down to whether it is in some sense easier or cheaper for expanding industries to draw labour out of agriculture than out of declining industrial sectors, and this I think remains to be proved.

Thus I consider there to have been three major factors which were exceptionally favourable to the accumulation of capital during this period: the new and long-lasting political solidarity between the advanced capitalist nations, a backlog of technical innovations to be exploited, and the depressed aspirations of the mass of the population. All of these were in large measure the product of the upheavals of the previous two decades. Of various other factors that could be mentioned (other than government policy which I shall discuss shortly) probably the most important was the steadiness of food and raw materials prices in the face of substantial increases in demand. Between 1953 and 1970 prices of these commodities did not increase at all relative to industrial prices and in some important cases (e.g. oil) actually declined.

Fiscal Policy

What I have attempted to do above is to show that there were various circumstances unrelated to doctrines of macroeconomic policy which were unusually favourable to high rates of growth and investment after 1945. But poor macroeconomic policy could still have managed to offset most of these advantages. The case for Keynesian economics is that it prevented this. But how much did governments really accept Keynesianism in this period? There are two sources of information here: one is their public statements, the other their behaviour in practice. Both are of interest.

There were certain governments which officially embraced Keynesian doctrine immediately after the war. The ones most commonly cited are Britain, the Netherlands and Sweden (as we have seen in Chapter 2, Sweden was already moving strongly in this direction in the 1930s). By 'Keynesian doctrine' I mean an acceptance that budgetary measures are to be judged by their impact on aggregate demand rather than on the financial balance of the government itself (i.e. the rejection of the balanced budget as a policy objective), and a willingness to use such measures in order to attain the desired level of effective demand. There is little doubt that Britain, the Netherlands and Sweden pass this test, although, as we shall see below, performance in practice was another matter. But what about other countries?

In the United States concern with the balance of the budget lasted longer than in most other countries, and was reflected in the public presentation of government policy. Nevertheless it did not lead to any serious policy mistakes as in the 1930s. On the occasion of the first downturn after the post-war boom, the Truman Administration felt obliged to argue vigorously against Congressional moves towards reducing the budget deficit, stating that the objectives of balancing the budget and reducing the national debt 'cannot be achieved without regard to the general state of the Nation's economy' (*Economic Report of the President,* July 1949, p. 7). Soon after this the task of economic management came to be dominated by the effects of the Korean War. The return of a Republican Administration under President Eisenhower in the 1952 election did not, however, induce any obvious retreat towards a balanced budget philosophy. In his first *Economic Report* the new President said:

> fiscal policy is a less flexible instrument than either monetary or debt management policy for keeping the economy on the narrow path that separates inflation from recession. But federal operations are now so large a factor in our economy that their variations, whether on the revenue or expenditure side, are bound to have a significant impact on our economy. The deliberate use of fiscal policy, in the interest of maintaining a sound economy, reflects this concern (*Economic Report of the President,* January 1954, p. 52).

The 1957 *Economic Report* expressed similar sentiments in the following sentence: 'the principle of flexibility in fiscal policy calls for relating the budget as far as feasible to economic conditions, helping to counteract inflationary or deflationary tendencies as the situation requires' (pp. 47–8).

Nevertheless Eisenhower placed much weight on the elimination on inflationary tendencies, and this caused his fiscal policy to become over-cautious in the latter part of his Administration. In 1958, as the economy turned downwards, the Administration took measures to bring forward various government purchases but resisted pressure from Congress for more vigorous action. The recovery began before the end of the year, but in its anxiety about inflation the Administration overestimated its strength and tightened fiscal policy too quickly. The expansion petered out in 1960 with unemployment still well above what it had been in the previous boom of 1956–7.

The Kennedy Administration came in with a political commitment to reaching full employment through fiscal expansion, in a situation where the high employment budget surplus was considerably larger than in 1959 or indeed any recent year (Teeters, 1965). Its advisers were committed Keynesians who had little doubt that discretionary fiscal policy was the path to be pursued. Fuelled by increasing federal expenditures (and later tax cuts) the economy moved into a long boom which lasted until 1968.

This was the era of the 'New Economics'. It did become part of the mythology of the time that Eisenhower's fiscal policy was still in many respects intellectually backward. He certainly had had a preference for a small and balanced budget, but it is doubtful whether this exerted any significant influence on his fiscal policy. His only real error lay in a serious misjudgment in 1959–60, and this was because his concern to stabilise prices made him very anxious not to overheat the economy. His errors were always more likely to be in a deflationary direction, but not because he rejected the principles of a Keynesian fiscal policy.

I have said that some European countries had fully absorbed the idea of budgetary policy as a tool of demand management early in the post-war period. But in the three major Continental countries there was no real commitment to an active fiscal policy until the 1960s (Hansen, 1969). When the Federal Republic of Germany was set up in 1949, it elected to power a Christian Democrat Government strongly inclined towards fiscal conservatism. The Government pursued a tight monetary and fiscal policy both to prevent inflation and to force domestic producers out into the world market in order to overcome a serious balance of payments deficit. Its ideology of *Sozialmarktwirtschaft* – a free enterprise economy backed by a broad, if not necessarily generous, system of social security – included a strong belief in the incentive effects of low taxes and an inegalitarian tax structure, which tended to inhibit the pragmatic adjustment of tax rates for stabilisation purposes. In the spectacular boom period of the 1950s, when the FRG still had considerable structural unemployment, the government felt happy to rely on monetary policy and automatic market adjustments, and its budget decisions took no account of the state of demand. Although government expenditures did play an expansionary role during the recession of 1958, this was largely the fortuitous result of the timing of rearmament, for which financial provision had been made for some years previously (the famous 'Julius Tower').

But as the economy approached full employment the tasks of demand management increased in difficulty, and a period of overheating followed by a deflationary package in 1964–6 led to a reappraisal. 'The lessons of this period seem to have brought about a basic change in the attitude of governments toward active demand management policy, although public opinion to some extent still lags behind, remaining strongly opposed, in particular, to large budget deficits' (Hansen, 1969, p. 47). The Stabilisation Law of 1967, reminiscent of the 1944 White Paper and the 1946 Employment Act elsewhere, directed the government to present an annual economic report and to frame its budget proposals in the context of the current economic situation; it also gave it significant powers to adjust expenditure and tax rates at short notice with a much abbreviated Parliamentary procedure.

But were German governments before this still attached to the balanced budget doctrine? The difficulty in answering this question lies in the fact that, because of the sustained boom, they were never really put to the test. In 1949, when unemployment had started to rise alarmingly, the government ranged itself against those who argued for an expansionary programme of public expenditure and measures to stimulate private investment. And yet, as unemployment continued to rise into 1950 and the government felt some action to be a political necessity, fiscal policy played a major part in the package of measures that was formulated (Wallich, 1955, pp. 79–87). A housing and work-creation programme was drawn up, and a new round of tax cuts prepared. Although war in Korea and delays in implementation ultimately caused these measures to be badly timed, the episode demonstrated that even a conservative German government could be persuaded of the need for the right sort of discretionary fiscal action if the situation appeared sufficiently serious.

In France the history of budgetary policy in this period reflects not so much the influence of any strongly defined ideology as the pressure of events. It is probably true to say that the implications of Keynes's *General Theory* were broadly accepted and not a major source of contention, but budgetary policy was not much used for demand management; the major fluctuations in the economy can be related directly to the Korean War and the Algerian involvement. Unemployment was low throughout the period, and up to 1965 three deflationary packages were introduced, which were all brought in to combat inflationary booms: the first, in 1951, to counteract the effects of the Korean War; the second, in 1957, after a considerable expansion in military expenditure in connection with Algeria which the government, for political reasons, was unwilling to counteract by raising taxes; and the third, in 1963, to combat an unexpected boom associated with high spending on housing and consumer durables by expatriates returning from Algeria. Reliance on monetary policy was probably encouraged by the fact that the main task of stabilisation policy in this period was to counteract bouts of overheating (direct controls of various kinds also retained a greater role in France than elsewhere). But since 1964–5 there has been a greater belief in and willingness to use fiscal policy for demand management purposes.

Italy was up until the early 1960s in a situation similar to that of West Germany, with substantial structural unemployment being gradually eaten away by a prolonged export-led boom. There was no great pressure on the government to pursue a particularly active fiscal policy, and there was little attempt to relate the budget to macroeconomic conditions, although once the balance of payments deficit had been eliminated public expenditure expanded quite strongly and the demand impact of fiscal policy in the later 1950s was generally positive. But in Italy the fiscal system was organised very poorly from the point of view of demand management. The tax system was so complex that, in addition to allowing great scope for evasion, the forecasting of revenue or the revenue implications of a change in tax rates was horrendously difficult. And on the expenditure side the budget presented to Parliament tended to be both incomplete and to represent a request for an 'authority to spend' rather than a plan of expenditures over the coming year. These features obviously made fine-tuning extremely hard – but there is no reason why they should have prevented extraordinary measures of expenditure or tax changes in the event of a serious recession. Indeed counter-cyclical measures *were* taken in the 1958 recession, and after some obvious overheating in 1963 there were moves towards the more consistent use of fiscal policy. 'Governments have several times declared themselves in favour of counter-cyclical budget policies; since the middle of the sixties no important ideological obstacles to demand management through fiscal policy seem to have been experienced' (Hansen, 1969, p. 51).

Thus it is striking that in both Germany and Italy a much more Keynesian approach to fiscal policy was instituted within a year or two of the limitations of the earlier more lax attitude being revealed. Moreover it is likely that in all these three countries Keynesian ideas had gained sufficient influence to stimulate an expansionary reaction to the threat of a *serious* recession. In fact no such threat materialised, but the actions taken in Germany in 1950 and in Italy in 1958 reinforce this impression.

In Japan the rate of investment was so high that the government never really faced a problem of having to give a stimulus to demand; stabilisation policy was however periodically confronted with some degree of overheating, when private investment accelerated too far and caused a deterioration in the balance of payments. Because monetary measures were extremely effective in countering this problem, by causing a sharp run-down in stocks and therefore in imports and also having some restraining effect on fixed investment, the government had no real need to consider the possibility of an active fiscal policy. Thus, although government expenditure grew fast along with the rest of the economy, it is hard to judge whether such a policy would have come up against serious ideological obstacles had it been required (it is perhaps worth noting however that large and increasing budget deficits did not prevent four years of strong fiscal expansion in 1975–8).

In Canada, the effective use of fiscal policy was hampered by the federal structure of the country, which meant that the federal government controlled only about 40 per cent of public expenditure, but there was also a noticeable political reluctance to incur sizeable budget deficits. In the absence of a vigorous macroeconomic policy, fluctuations in the Canadian economy naturally reflected those of its much larger neighbour. Like the United

States, Canada's economy was running at significantly less than its full potential in the decade between 1955 and 1965. In part this was a result of lower investment in the natural resource industries in the later 1950s, when they were suffering from previous over-expansion. But it is striking that, although there was a certain degree of flexibility in fiscal policy, the Canadian government never formulated a strong policy of expanding demand, along Kennedy lines, to meet the situation.

The above brief review of approaches to fiscal policy in some major countries suggests the following conclusions.

(1) There was a noticeable trend towards the improved use of fiscal policy over time (United States, West Germany, France, Italy).
(2) Although in many countries there remained scepticism about regular counter-cyclical fiscal action, there was no case of a serious policy mistake obviously resulting from adherence to the balanced budget doctrine, in marked contrast to the experience of 1929–33. Even the less 'Keynesian' governments were largely content to let the automatic stabilisers do their work – and the universal growth of the government sector meant that these automatic stabilisers were markedly more effective than before the war.
(3) There is an impression of a widespread recognition that *expansionary* fiscal action should be taken in the event of a serious collapse in demand, irrespective of the impact on the government budget.

The Record of Economic Stabilisation

The other aspect of the question is whether, whatever their stated attitudes, governments did in practice follow a budgetary policy designed to offset or reduce the natural fluctuations of the private sector. Anyone familiar with the literature on this subject will know that this question is not as easy to answer as might at first sight appear. It is comparatively simple to observe whether the budget surplus (or deficit) has varied in a pro-cyclical fashion. But the automatic effects of boom and recession on tax revenue and certain government transfer expenditures (such as unemployment benefits) mean that this could occur as much with a government unsuccessfully trying to balance the budget in each year as with a government committed to a full counter-cyclical fiscal policy. We would like to know (a) how strong these automatic effects are and (b) what measures the government has taken to enhance or reduce them. The direction of these latter, *discretionary*, measures is critical. A balanced budget policy would imply pro-cyclical discretionary measures; a Keynesian fiscal policy would require such measures to be counter-cyclical.

Since a discretionary fiscal action includes any change in the budget balance not defined as the automatic effect of a change in the economy itself, the question of how the automatic effects are defined becomes critical. A common method, which became part of the practice of the US Council of Economic Advisers in the 1960s, is to estimate what the budget balance would have been at some constant percentage rate of unemployment. A change in this adjusted budget balance from one year to the next would then be interpreted as discretionary action, the difference between the adjusted and the unadjusted balances for a given year reflecting the workings of the automatic stabilisers. A summary of the procedure, as applied to the fiscal stance of the US federal government, is given by Teeters (1965). The unemployment rate chose in this case was 4 per cent, which was thought to represent a close approximation to full employment. 'Full employment expenditures' were taken as actual expenditures minus appropriate reductions for unemployment benefits. 'Full employment revenue' was derived from applying federal tax rates to full employment GNP, estimated by interpolation between cyclical peaks (alternative procedures for estimating the trend of potential output are possible). The problem of cyclical variations in income shares affecting tax revenue because different tax rates apply to different forms of income was avoided by imposing constant income shares at full employment.

This is certainly not the only possible method of arriving at a constant employment budget balance. The OECD, for example, currently uses an econometric model which assumes that the economy is brought to the constant employment level through an exogenous change in stock-building. But whatever the method of estimation, the principle is the same: to measure discretionary action by changes in the budget balance after the elimination of cyclical effects. However, such a measure is certainly not without its problems.

(1) It makes no allowance for different impacts on demand of, for example, a rise in public employment and a fall in company tax rates. The implicit balanced budget multiplier is zero. This difficulty may however be removed by applying weights to the various budget items to reflect their estimated demand impact (for an example see Okun and Teeters, 1970). In the event of a marked change in the level and structure of tax rates movements in this weighted balance could be significantly different from movements in the unweighted balance.

(2) In an economy whose potential output is expanding (either because of a growing labour force or rising productivity), constant employment tax revenue at given tax rates will also grow from year to year (a phenomenon which has come to be known as 'fiscal drag'). The constant employment budget surplus (CEBS) will therefore increase unless government expenditure increases to offset this. Or to put it another way, the CEBS may have increased even though the government has deliberately increased its own spending since the previous year without changing tax rates. The CEBS measure of budgetary stance therefore does not treat expansionary measures required to offset fiscal drag as discretionary action.

(3) The example just cited refers to 'real' fiscal drag. But there also exists 'monetary' fiscal drag, which results from changes in the tax burden as prices and incomes alter in proportion to one another. Inflation can change real tax revenue at a given real GNP and given tax rates, particularly if direct taxation is progressive or indirect taxes are specified in terms of absolute amounts per item. Therefore it is necessary to decide whether discretionary action consists of a change in tax rates and thresholds in money terms, or in a change *relative to what they would have been had the thresholds been indexed against inflation*.

(4) The government may spend more either because it is purchasing a larger volume of goods and services or because their price has risen (ignoring transfer payments). The CEBS calculation does not ask why government expenditure has

changed; it merely records the fact. This implies that a change
in the relative price of goods consumed by the government is
a discretionary act. But if the relative price change reflects,
for example, the lagged adjustment of public sector wage
and salary movements to movements in private sector wages
and salaries, is it really discretionary?

These are all difficult technical issues, and I mention them
only because the choices made in the course of the analysis will
clearly affect the picture of discretionary fiscal action which
emerges at the end. In his important international study Hansen
(1969) finds good reasons for diverging from the CEBS approach
on points (1), (2) and (4); as regards point (3), it has now become
common to take indexation as the point of reference, which was
never done before 1970. Moreover all these measures refer only to
first-round effects; they take no account of the effect of changing
marginal tax rates on the size of the multiplier. Nevertheless if
one compares Hansen's estimates of discretionary fiscal action by
the US government with those of Teeters, the general picture is
very similar for the years 1960–4; for 1956–9, however, there is
some divergence.

Hansen's study is significant because it analyses budgetary
policy in seven OECD countries, comprising about two-thirds of
the total GNP of the OECD area, and applies identical
procedures to all of them. Moreover his main intention was to
investigate whether fiscal policy stabilised the economy, in the
sense of reducing the amplitude of the natural fluctuations of the
private sector. This remains a useful exercise despite the obvious
point that, in some countries and at some times, macroeconomic
policy may have been dominated by other considerations.

Of his seven countries, Hansen concludes that over the period
1955–65, the UK was unique in actually managing to destabilise
its economy through the budget, both through discretionary
measures and automatic effects. In two other countries, France
and Italy, discretionary measures were destabilising but not
sufficiently strongly so to offset the stabilising influence of the
automatic effects. In the other four countries (Belgium, Sweden,
the United States and the FRG) both discretionary and
automatic effects helped to stabilise the economy.

The mildly destabilising nature of the discretionary com-

ponent of UK fiscal policy accords with the conclusion of Dow
(1964) for the 1950s. That the automatic effects should also have
been slightly destabilising is something of a surprise. It resulted
from time-lags in the payments of company and personal income
taxes, the predominance of specific duties in indirect taxation,
and strongly pro-cyclical movements of government wages and
salaries in the later 1950s. In Italy discretionary policies were
destabilising because of the tendency to spend the proceeds of
fiscal drag with little reference to the overall economic situation,
although counter-cyclical measures were taken during the 1958
recession and as part of the 1963 stabilisation programme. In
France discretionary policies were pro-cyclical because of the
policy errors mentioned above and the need to make the 1957–8
devaluations work. In both France and Italy the strength of the
automatic stabilisers derived from the relative importance of
social security contributions and proportional indirect taxes in
government revenue. On the other hand Hansen judges that the
stabilising character of discretionary measures in Belgium and
West Germany was largely fortuitous, and in the latter case
might be reversed if a slightly longer historical period had been
taken (for Germany Hansen's estimates cover the period 1958–
65; he indicates that discretionary fiscal policy was probably
destabilising in both 1955–7 and 1966–7).

Conclusions

What does all this suggest by way of conclusions about the role of
fiscal policy in sustaining the prolonged boom which lasted from
the end of the Second World War to the early 1970s? I have
already shown, in the first part of the chapter, that *ex post* the
reason for the lower levels of unemployment as compared with
inter-war lies with private sector investment rather than the
government budget. The only (partial) exception to this is the
United States, and this does not help to explain the high levels of
demand in Europe. Then I proceeded to demonstrate that there
were a number of factors operating in the post-war period that
were highly favourable to economic development whatever
macroeconomic policy was pursued. But policy mistakes had
played a large part in the Great Depression, and they could easily

have undermined the 'investment euphoria', as Maddison has described it, of the 1950s and 1960s.

My survey of official attitudes and the record of budgetary policy in this period suggests that, although the conduct of policy could not be described as brilliant from a Keynesian standpoint in any country, it was never led into serious deflationary errors by the persistence of the balanced budget doctrine. Even in West Germany and Italy, two countries where official ideas seemed more traditional than most, one gets the impression that Keynesian ideas were sufficiently influential to induce counter-cyclical action if a recession began to look serious. Indeed such action was undertaken in the recessions of 1950 (Germany) and 1958 (Italy). Moreover, governments were able to rely on the enhanced effects of automatic stabilisers compared with the inter-war period, the result of the increased weight of their own operations in the economy. For the most part they managed to allow these to do their work in the downswing of the cycle.

There is legitimate room for speculation as to whether this improved conduct of macroeconomic policy had significant effects on business confidence and the propensity to invest. The argument that it did relies on a rational expectations type of story: although cyclical instabilities were much smaller than in the inter-war period, this was in part because business believed that macroeconomic policy would be effective in preventing them, and so the private sector did not cut back its investment plans markedly in a recession. In other words, the changed behaviour of governments induced the private sector to believe that the experience of 1929–33 would not be repeated; therefore investment was much less sensitive to cyclical fluctuations in demand and the private sector revealed a great deal more stability in its behaviour. This stability mitigated the need for discretionary fiscal action, but was itself dependent on expectations of such action. Although government discretionary action was not always stabilising *ex post*, this was a reflection of the difficulty of timing fiscal measures correctly in a world of much smaller fluctuations and not of a lack of willingness to undertake such action.

There is nothing wrong with this argument *a priori*; but like all propositions about expectations it is hard to demonstrate. It could be strengthened by widening the focus of attention beyond stabilisation policy alone. Such thoughtful observers of the post-war scene as Lundberg (1968), Maddison (1964) and Postan (1967) all emphasise the new role of government policy in promoting growth. Indeed the acceptance of economic growth as a policy objective was considerably more widespread than the methods used in pursuit of it. In France the state played a considerable part in organising private sector investment through the planning process; in West Germany the emphasis was on private initiative, the reduction of taxation and price stability. But the general acceptance of economic growth as a policy goal meant (or should have meant) that obstacles to growth were systematically identified and action formulated to deal with them; to the extent that such obstacles were removed, private investment should have increased. Moreover, recessions took on a new aspect in the light of this new commitment. They were no longer just unfortunate phases of the cycle; they were also periods of negative growth. This should have encouraged governments to find ways of getting out of them more quickly.

A further dimension to the growth commitment was the encouragement which it gave to the increase in governments' own spending. In the absence of growth, this would have had to have been justified as necessary reform, and would have been questioned as a possibly unwarranted expansion of the public sector. With a broad commitment to economic growth, these hindrances to planned expansion of government expenditure disappeared. This encouraged governments deliberately to offset fiscal drag, and indeed in all countries they did even more than this (Maddison, 1980, Table 2). This was important: with the policy attitudes of pre-1929, they would have been more inclined to pocket the extra tax revenue and build up ever larger surpluses, especially in countries with a large public debt.

Thus it is plausible to argue that in several ways the political focus on economic growth encouraged actions which also helped to support employment. And this is before taking into consideration the various forms of subsidy and tax privileges to private investment which became increasingly common as the years went by. My own view is that the commitment to growth did significantly strengthen the impact of post-war stabilisation policy in the sense relevant here: that business came to assume that governments would act to support effective demand where necessary, and prevent a serious recession from developing.

Since we are essentially inhabiting the realm of speculation, the conclusion that Keynesian ideas did underpin the post-war boom in important ways is certainly open to challenge. But when we consider that

(1) the investment patterns of the period suggest a strong belief in the continuation of high demand, despite early fears of a post-war recession;

(2) governments gave out fairly strong hints of their willingness to take discretionary action to support demand if urgently required;

(3) built-in stabilisers helped quite substantially to reduce cyclical fluctuations and were not generally offset by perverse discretionary action; and

(4) despite fast-rising tax revenue the expansion of public expenditure fully offset the demand impact of this fiscal drag;

it seems unlikely that the official adoption of Keynesian ideas failed to make any significant contribution to the generally confident state of business in this period.

Note to Chapter 4

1. Though this omission is probably less significant than in the case of Britain or the USA because of the smaller degree of slack in France in 1938 than in either of those countries.

5
The Theoretical Reaction Against Keynesianism

The 1960s and 1970s have witnessed a powerful theoretical reaction against Keynesianism. In most countries (and especially the United States) there has been a noticeable swing back towards pre-Keynesian analytical ideas. Has this counter-revolution succeeded in demolishing Keynes's arguments about the instability of a capitalist economy, or has it merely resurrected the old pre-Keynesian assumptions in a more sophisticated form? This is the question to which this chapter is devoted.

The great strengths of Keynesian economics were its ability to explain the economic problems of the 1930s and to provide a convenient framework for guiding post-war government policy in pursuit of the objective of full employment, a capacity which it had already demonstrated in tackling the problems of war finance. It was the natural economic orthodoxy of the post-war period. But it had one significant weakness: it did not offer any framework within which to analyse the apparent rise in class conflict and the worsening problem of inflation, which first became of major concern around 1965. Keynes had given good reasons why wages and prices might be resistant to downward pressures, but having freed them from a rigid relationship with the money supply as expressed in the quantity theory of money, he was left with no fundamental theory of why they were what they were. The wage rate seemed to have become a sociological variable, from the investigation of which economists were cordoned off by long-standing academic barriers. Economic forecasters therefore had recourse to apparently reliable empirical relationships such as the famous Phillips curve, whose theoretical foundation was never entirely clear.

The less tractable the problem of inflation became, the less satisfactory this situation appeared to be (particularly when the Phillips curve started to break down). The apparent chink in the Keynesian armour widened and gradually opened the way for a revolt against the new orthodoxy. The revolt took the form of a rebirth of the quantity theory of money, and acquired the name 'Monetarism'. It was associated to a quite exceptional degree (much more than the Keynesian revolution) with the thinking of one man, Milton Friedman. Monetarism clearly evolved as it went along, but at each stage the new ideas can be traced back to Friedman's research and writings. This is true, at any rate, for Monetarism proper. The 1970s offshoot which has now taken over the running, and has been dubbed the 'New Classical Macroeconomics', is the work of a younger generation of theorists. In this chapter we shall look first at the evolution of Monetarism, and then at the much more dramatic assertions of the New Classical Macroeconomics.

Monetarism

What is Monetarism? It would be hard to find a question to which modern economics has given a more diverse and self-contradictory set of answers. Certainly the participants in the debate have not always been able to define the issues clearly: there are few more confusing and depressing experiences than to read the proceedings of one of the staged confrontations between Friedman and his critics which took place in the early 1970s (Gordon, 1974; Stein, 1976).

By no means the worst possible definition of Monetarism would be to avoid technical issues altogether and to describe it as 'a revolt against the real and imagined consequences of the Keynesian revolution'. This would capture the more important motivations underlying it, including its fondness for the free market and its antipathy to all forms of state intervention. But it does not help us to understand the issues involved in the long debates about economic theory and policy. A recent, fairly comprehensive summary of the positions taken up by Monetarism has been made by Laidler (1981). He describes the key characteristics of Monetarism as:

(1) a quantity theory of money approach to macroeconomic analysis both in the sense of a theory of the demand for money and in the sense that changes in the money stock are the most important cause of changes in money income;
(2) the expectations-augmented Phillips curve;
(3) the monetary approach to the balance of payments;
(4) antipathy to activist stabilisation policy and support for long-run money supply rules or targets.

The central idea that emerges from this is the notion that money matters, and indeed that it matters more than anything else in macroeconomics. The second important component is the rejection of the orthodoxy of the immediate post-war period, in particular the twin ideas that governments should intervene actively to manipulate the level of effective demand in the economy, and that a certain amount of inflation is an acceptable price to pay for a high level of employment. According to the expectations-augmented Phillips curve, if the inflation rate remains above what had been generally anticipated for a prolonged period, then expectations will be adjusted upwards and the inflation is liable to accelerate. These policy issues have been the meat and drink of the Monetarist argument; they have been less concerned to attack Keynesian ideas at a purely theoretical level.

For a long time, the overriding concern of Monetarism was to reinstate the supply of money as a central determinant of effective demand. It was reacting against a view which had been prevalent in the 1940s and 1950s, that monetary policy was an almost totally useless instrument of demand management (this view was based on the experience of the 1930s and on empirical studies which seemed to show that interest rates had little effect on investment decisions). The first salvo was the publication, in 1956, of *Studies in the Quantity Theory of Money*, edited by Friedman. This book contained a number of empirical studies of the relationship between money and prices, the most striking of which was Cagan's study of 'hyper-inflations'; in all of Cagan's historical episodes of astronomical rates of inflation there was almost equally astronomical expansion of the money supply. As an introduction to these studies, Friedman presented a theoretical restatement of the quantity theory of money. He defined it as a theory of the demand for money rather than a mechanical relationship between money and income. For utility-maximising individuals, he argued, the marginal utility of holding wealth as money should equal the marginal utility of holding it in any other form, such as a larger stock of consumer durables or non-monetary financial assets. If then the money supply was significantly increased, people would attempt to exchange it for other assets. For the community as a whole this is not possible, and the prices of other assets would rise until the population was happy to hold the enlarged stock of money. This idea of money as one amongst a number of possible forms of wealth-holding is in the tradition initiated by Keynes's theory of speculative demand. The emphasis in Friedman's theory, however, was very much on the expansion of demand for goods rather than financial assets in response to an excess supply of money.

At the same time, Friedman was working on a theory of consumption which suggested a much smaller value for the Keynesian multiplier than was commonly supposed. In *The Theory of the Consumption Function* (1957) he introduced the idea that consumers had quite long planning horizons in matching their expenditures to their income. Short-run changes in income would therefore only affect consumer spending to the extent that they affected long-run expectations. Thus spells of unemployment which were confidently expected to be temporary, for example, would only result in small reductions in consumption. Whilst the new quantity theory emphasised the power of monetary policy, Friedman's new ideas on consumption simultaneously threw into question the effectiveness of fiscal policy.

Friedman then began, together with some associates, an intensive historical study of money and business cycles in the United States, and in 1959 he published an article which argued that turning points in the money supply series led turning points in economic activity by a reasonably regular period. The point was that if the former preceded the latter, this suggested that the fluctuations in the stock of money were causing the fluctuations in activity, whereas if vice versa, the obvious conclusion would be that the authorities were merely accommodating the change in the demand for money that had resulted from changes in money income. Comparing timings of peaks and troughs of the *rate of growth of the money supply* with peaks and troughs in the *level of money income* he found an average lag of sixteen months for peaks and twelve months for troughs. From this Friedman concluded that fluctuations in the money stock had been a major causative factor in US business cycles. The obvious objection to make to this procedure, and the one which was widely made, was that like was not being compared with like: rates of growth should be compared with rates of growth and levels with levels, but not rates of growth with levels. It was subsequently shown that for an appropriate comparison, the two series moved very closely together (Brown *et al.*, 1962). Friedman therefore stood accused of choosing his method to suit his results.

The culmination of this intensive examination of historical statistics on money was the publication by Milton Friedman and Anna Schwartz of an article on 'Money and Business Cycles' summarising the results, together with a weighty book on the *Monetary History of the United States 1867–1960*. The article (Friedman and Schwartz 1963b) once again compared the timing of movements in the rate of growth of the money stock with movements in the level of money income, and argued that the former series leads the latter. It also provided evidence to show that the periods when the rate of growth of the money stock was changing fastest were quite well correlated with those when the rate of growth of net national product was changing fastest. But perhaps more persuasive than such comparisons of statistical series was the argument that if one examined the monetary history of those six episodes which Friedman and Schwartz classified as deep rather than mild depressions, then the monetary contraction on each occasion could be shown to have been caused by factors independent of the decline in money income, and could not plausibly be described as purely the result of the demand for money following income downwards. Therefore the causation must have run from money to income and not vice versa.

The *Monetary History* was a verbal account intended to complement the statistical studies of the trade cycle. It laid great emphasis on the money supply as a causal influence in economic fluctuations. The most striking and controversial single point was the assertion that the Great Depression only became great because of a fall of one-third in the money stock as a result of bank failures – before the failures started in late 1930, the authors claimed, the recession was sharp but not essentially out of the ordinary. They then proceeded to argue that the Federal Reserve System might have prevented the banking collapse if it had pursued its role as lender of last resort with much greater vigour. If this had happened, the money supply would not have collapsed and therefore, according to this line of reasoning, neither money income nor real output would have done so. The underlying assumption was that the money stock was the major determinant of money income, and that if money income had not collapsed, there would not have been the catastrophic rise in unemployment. This essentially monetary explanation of such a major historical episode (and one which had seemed to many to be the living proof of the inherent instability of a capitalist economy) provoked a considerable stir, but has only recently elicited a significant response (Temin, 1976; Brunner, 1981). It implied that timely action by the monetary authorities was sufficient to prevent abnormal economic fluctuations, a position which was to become an increasingly prominent feature of Monetarist doctrine.

Up until this stage the Monetarists had attempted to prove their point by using relatively crude statistical techniques, but in 1963 Friedman and Meiselman published a piece of work in which they applied econometric methods in a direct confrontation of Keynesian and Monetarist models as an explanation of United States consumption expenditure from 1897 to 1958. The aim was to estimate how much of the variation in consumption could be explained by changes in the supply of money and how much by changes in autonomous expenditure (i.e. the effects of the Keynesian multiplier). They compared two equations:

$$C = a + bA + u \qquad (5.1)$$

$$C = c + dM + v \qquad (5.2)$$

where C denotes consumption expenditure, A autonomous expenditure (whose precise definition I discuss below), M the money supply, u and v are random errors and a, b, c and d the parameters to be estimated. Friedman and Meiselman claimed that apart from a short period around the late 1920s the second equation gave much the better explanation. This experiment was reproduced for the UK by Barrett and Walters (1966). They found the money supply to be very important before 1914, but the inter-war period was strongly Keynesian, with neither equation performing very well over the period 1948–63.

However the Friedman and Meiselman paper attracted a good deal of criticism. First the measure of autonomous expenditure employed – the sum of investment, the budget deficit and the balance of payments surplus on current account – was argued to bias the results of the first equation downwards, since there would be a negative influence of C on A through induced changes in imports and tax revenue in addition to a positive stimulus to C from A. With a narrower specification of A designed to eliminate this feedback some other investigators got better results from equation (5.1) (e.g. Ando and Modigliani, 1965). Secondly there was a great difference in the relative performance of the two equations in different time periods, and the monetary equation had had no clear superiority in the recent period. And the third point which was consistently made was that crude single-equation estimates of this sort were a poor substitute for simulations on a full-scale econometric model.

Everything which Friedman had written on these matters up until the mid-1960s could be interpreted as an argument that the quantity of money is an important influence on effective demand, and one that is frequently of greater importance than fiscal policy. Friedman has since claimed that whatever the weaknesses of his joint work with Meiselman, the controversy generated by it conclusively put paid to the view that 'money does not matter' (Friedman, 1973, p. 10). But it was not clear that there was anything particularly anti-Keynesian about Friedman's positions. Keynes himself had argued that changes in the money supply could influence aggregate demand via interest rates and investment. Moreover Friedman's claim to be giving written expression to a non-Keynesian oral tradition of quantity theorists at the University of Chicago has been seriously questioned (Patinkin, 1969).

The majority view in the economics profession at this time was that Friedman's ideas could be perfectly well fitted into the conventional interpretation of Keynesian economics, as presented in the IS–LM diagram due to Hicks (1937) (Figure 5.1).

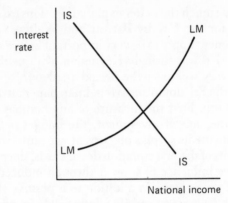

Figure 5.1   *The IS–LM diagram*

In this diagram (an explanation of which may be found in any macroeconomics textbook) a Keynesian equilibrium is given by the intersection of the IS and LM curves. An increase in the money supply will shift the LM curve to the right, and a fiscal stimulus (such as an increase in government expenditure) will shift the IS curve to the right. In either case, the size of the impact on output and employment will depend on the relative slopes of the two curves. Changes in the money supply will have only small effects on real output if either the IS curve is close to being vertical or the LM curve is close to being horizontal. The former will be true if investment is insensitive to changes in the rate of interest, while the latter will occur if the demand for money is highly sensitive to changes in the rate of interest. Conversely fiscal policy will have only small effects on output if LM is near-vertical, because then the multiplier effects will be 'crowded out' by the impact on private investment of the large changes in interest rates required to alter the speculative demand for money in tune with the changing transactions demand as income changes. Thus it was generally believed that the Monetarist position rested on beliefs about the size of the interest-elasticities of investment spending and the demand for money, and this seemed to be confirmed by Friedman's repeated assertions that the issues were essentially empirical.

On the other hand, Friedman's verbal statements often seemed to imply quite extreme positions. In the *Monetary History*, as one reviewer pointed out, the flavour of the narrative is much closer to the view that 'money is all that matters' than Friedman and Schwartz's own statistical studies would warrant (Tobin, 1965). But Friedman has always refused to be nailed down to any extreme theoretical position, such as a vertical LM curve (Friedman, 1966, 1970). It was this which made the debates of the early 1970s so unproductive. The anti-Monetarists were reconstructing Friedman's theoretical model out of his historical and statistical studies, and did not believe it to be the same as his stated theory; while Friedman himself was quite happy to lay claim to a theoretical framework broadly acceptable to everyone, and to argue that the issues were purely empirical.

The only theoretical difference that could be agreed on was whether, as Friedman believed, undesired money balances were likely to be exchanged directly for goods or whether, as Keynesians thought, the effects of a money supply increase operated mainly or exclusively via changes in the interest rate. But even this was not a major issue, since Keynesians could accept that the money supply could influence consumption as well as investment spending by raising the value of financial assets and hence consumers' wealth.

Meanwhile, however, Friedman himself had injected a whole new set of issues into the debate with his Presidential Address to the American Economic Association, 'The Role of Monetary Policy' (1968). The main thrust of the lecture was to back up the case for pursuing a simple, known target rate of growth of the stock of money as the leading principle of monetary policy, irrespective of the current state of the economy, a policy which Friedman had been advocating for nearly a decade. Previously he had argued that stabilisation policy had often been counter-productive because the authorities had underestimated the time-lags required for their measures to take effect; now he added to that a much more powerful and more obviously anti-Keynesian proposition: that the economy contained strong self-stabilising tendencies of its own.

The central idea was that aggregate demand management would have only temporary effects – an expansionary monetary policy could cause unemployment to fall below its 'natural rate' at which the labour market was cleared, but in the medium term it would return to this level, which Friedman described as that 'which would be ground out by a Walrasian system of general equilibrium equations'. The mechanism was as follows. The monetary stimulus would increase prices of goods, but wages, often being set by contract in advance, would react more slowly. Money wages would therefore rise but real wages would fall; employers, in response to the fall in real wages, demand more labour and increase output. Workers are presumed not to have recognised that prices have risen more than they had anticipated, so they believe that real wages have *risen*, so they are consequently willing to supply more labour. Gradually, however, workers recognise the truth and force employers to increase wages, at which employment falls back to its 'natural' level, and the extra effective demand is absorbed entirely in price increases.

Thus the story depends on an asymmetry between employers and employees. Employers are fully aware of what wages and prices are doing, whereas employees can be fooled by the actions of the monetary authorities. Indeed this is the only reason why output deviates from its full employment level. Keynesian ideas of effective demand have disappeared out of the window; it is never suggested that lack of demand could constrain output. We are back in a completely neoclassical world, where it is assumed that if the real wage is such as to equalise the demand and supply of labour, full employment follows automatically. But none of this is argued out; *it is simply assumed.*

Friedman's version entailed a complete reversal of the causality of the Phillips curve. Phillips and almost everyone else had assumed that the observed statistical relationship between money wage changes and unemployment reflected the strengthened bargaining position of workers in times of low unemployment. But according to Friedman it is the rise in money wages which *causes* unemployment to fall, by fooling workers into believing that their real wages have increased. The Phillips curve is simply tracing out the supply curve of labour.

The policy implications of the Monetarist position could be summarised as follows:

(1) The stance of monetary policy should be judged by the behaviour of the money supply rather than of interest rates (this follows from the assertion that there could be direct substitution between money and goods).

(2) Monetary policy is a noticeably more powerful instrument of stabilisation policy than fiscal policy.

(3) The time lags in the effect of policy measures are fairly long and variable, so that it is difficult for the authorities to exert any consistent stabilising influence on the natural fluctuations of the private sector: in practice they would do better to give up the attempt and to prevent monetary policy itself from becoming a source of disturbance by adopting a fixed target rate of growth of the money stock independently of the state of effective demand.

Besides generating a heated academic debate this Monetarist assault made a major political impact. Friedman himself was a gifted propagandist who was never frightened to argue the vices of state intervention and the virtues of the free market. Meanwhile the political right latched on to Monetarist ideas as a way of attacking state expenditure and intervention for stoking inflation. Money supply control seemed to promise a new era of financial stringency in the public sector and an altogether more discriminating attitude towards its activities. Whereas the experience of depression and war, together with the intellectual backwash of the Keynesian revolution, had long sustained a pronounced growth of state spending and intervention and the development of an extensive welfare state, by the end of the 1960s the rising burden of taxation was beginning to eat a hole in people's pockets and a reaction set in against the cost and the dubious justifiability of various state expenditures. For the political right, Monetarism was to become the way to link popular dissatisfaction about taxation, public generosity and the suspicion that it was being abused by 'scroungers' with the other great source of anxiety, inflation. Thus despite the technical and involved nature of the academic debate, in the wider world Monetarism became a key component of the right-wing critique of the Keynesian/social-democratic consensus of the post-war period, a consensus which had been characterised by great optimism about how the state could be used to improve the lives of the community.

The New Classical Macroeconomics

Friedman's 1968 lecture really marked the end of developments in Monetarism proper. During the early 1970s the ideas came to be disseminated more widely and were increasingly heeded by governments. In addition the monetary approach to the balance of payments began to be developed; but this was really a sideshow. However it was precisely at this time that the first steps were taken in the construction of what has since become known as the New Classical Macroeconomics. It is fair to say that this new school of thought could not even have begun without the groundwork which had been done by Friedman, particularly in his 1968 lecture, but it has succeeded in giving a whole new lease of life to what was fast becoming a very stale debate.

The essential novelty in the New Classical Macroeconomics was its treatment of expectations. Although macroeconomics had recognised the critical importance of expectations of the future to the behaviour of the economic system for a long time, the practice had tended to be to assume such expectations about the future values of variables to be constant, or more recently, where precise assumptions about how they might adapt were required for empirical purposes, to construct some mechanical formula of how they responded to past experience. Thus in general one could say that the approach was to treat expectations of a variable x at time t, which we shall denote by x_t^e, as a weighted function of its past observed values:

$$x_t^e = b_1 x_{t-1} + b_2 x_{t-2} + b_3 x_{t-3} + \ldots \qquad (5.3)$$

The advocates of the New Classical Macroeconomics argued that this hypothesis about expectations formation was open to two fundamental objections: first, it did not allow people to adjust their expectations of x_t in the light of other variables whose value at time $t-1$ is known, and which they might believe would influence x_t. There was an implicit assumption that people had no knowledge of the economic system and did not perceive any interrelationships between variables. Therefore they could take the past values of x alone and not the past values of any other variables as a guide to future values of x. The second objection was that it was perfectly possible to imagine situations in which expectations formed in this way would be systematically wrong over any sustained period of time. For example, in any system where the sum of b_1, b_2, b_3, . . . is one, a continuous upward trend in x will mean that x_t^e is always less than x_t, and a continuous downward trend will mean that x_t^e is always greater than x_t. But since the selection of any particular values for the b's is essentially arbitrary, then one would expect economic agents to be willing to change them if they were proved systematically wrong. Thus any model of expectations formation of this kind could be expected to be true only for limited periods, after which it would be modified in the light of experience.

This critique is based on the insight that if people find they are making systematic expectational errors (which may be very costly to themselves), then one would expect them to consider it worthwhile to invest a little bit of effort in seeking out ways to improve their forecasting. An obvious step would be to purchase the services of a professional economic forecasting organisation (e.g. in the UK, by subscribing to the National Institute Economic Review) and to base decisions on the information thus obtained. This sort of reaction to expectational error could be described as 'rational' in a double sense. First, expectations of economic agents will now be formed, or at least influenced, by a process of theoretical reasoning based on analysis of past economic data and incorporating the insights of economic theory. And secondly, so long as the expected gain exceeds the costs of acquiring the information, it is the sort of behaviour which would be predicted of a rationally self-interested human being, the *homo oeconomicus* with which economic theory has for so long been at home.

However the assumptions about expectations formation preferred by the New Classical Macroeconomics actually go much further than what has just been said, and have become known as the hypothesis of Rational Expectations, in capital letters. As developed in economics over the last ten years (though originally dating back to Muth, 1961), Rational Expectations assumes that economic agents are completely aware of the true structure of the economy (i.e. the form of each equation and the size of the coefficients in the econometric model which mirrors it) and make full use of this knowledge in forming their expectations. Ignoring the role of government policy for a moment, this would imply (assuming the model was not liable to unforeseen changes in its structure) that expectations about economic variables can only be wrong because of random shocks, represented by disturbance terms in the equations and caused by events which could not be foreseen at the time that the expectations were formed. Since expectational errors must therefore be random, there is no incentive for any economic agent to switch to any other form of forecasting. What happens is that any new piece of information, such as the national income statistics for the latest quarter, is plugged into the econometric model in people's heads, so that they fully anticipate its consequences. Since they are assumed to know the true model, they cannot be wrong about these consequences, apart from the effects of unforeseen disturbances to the system which are assumed in the Rational Expectations hypothesis to be random events.

What about government policy measures designed to manipulate the level of aggregate demand? First of all, under Rational Expectations, the government is no better informed than the private sector about the true structure of the economy. Moreover, if the government has been following a systematic policy in the past (e.g. trying to iron out economic fluctuations), then the private sector can be expected to have perceived this and built it into its expectations of the future. For example, suppose real government expenditure (G) has followed a pattern such as:

$$G_t = aG_{t-1} + bU_{t-1} \tag{5.4}$$

where U_{t-1} is the unemployment rate at time $t-1$; then the private sector, observing G_{t-1} and U_{t-1}, will expect the level of G_t that this equation would predict. The argument then is that, *ex post*, no effects from the policy described by equation (5.4) will be observable, since no one will change their consumption and investment decisions at time t when the government actually does spend the anticipated amount. If, however, real government expenditure is greater or less than this, then there will be reactions from the private sector, because its anticipation of government policy will have been proved wrong. In other words government policy has effects not because it has changed since the previous period ($G_t \neq G_{t-1}$) but only if it is different from what was expected ($G_t \neq G_t^e$). Amongst other things this implies that macroeconomic policy can have effects even if the government changes none of its policy instruments, simply because the private sector had predicted from the government's previous behaviour that it would do something.

The idea is perhaps best illustrated by reference to the stock market. On the day when a company's results are reported, one often hears in radio financial reports that 'the profits of company X were much as expected, and left the share price unchanged'. In other words the market had formed expectations of what the announced profit would be, and these had already been 'discounted in advance', so there was no change after the announcement, even though the profit figures may have been much better (or worse) than last year's. Only if expectations had been wrong would there have been a price change.

It may be seen that Rational Expectations is equivalent to an assumption of costless information. If everyone was a rational self-seeker, they would only invest in information search while the marginal benefit exceeded the marginal cost. Since in Rational Expectations there is no information available which people do not have, implicitly acquiring it is costless to them in both time and money. This is a strong assumption which one can expect to be dangerously false over large areas of economic life. The markets which would seem to come closest to it are those for financial assets and commodities, since these are the ones where transactions are simple and relatively cheap, but the scope for making (or losing) money through speculative purchases and sales is enormous. To take an example: suppose that I had observed that the demand for copper had in the past been related to OECD industrial output but no one else had observed this. Then I could expect to make a fortune by buying copper when I saw a recovery in the world economy starting and selling it when I saw a boom ending. But this only works so long as other people have not observed the same pattern. For me to buy, someone else has to sell. But if everyone had the same information as me no one would be willing to sell, and any sign of an upturn in the world economy would immediately be reflected not in a surge of buying (because there are no sellers), but in a large jump in the price of copper sufficient to wipe out my anticipated profit. Under Rational Expectations (or any other system in which the expectations of all agents are identical and sensitive to new information) there would be many price movements in these markets with relatively few transactions.

This illustrates the point that *informational advantage* can be translated in these markets into speculative profits but not information which is common to everyone. One obvious source of information is past movements in price. If only one person was searching for systematic relationships in past data then that person could exploit them to his/her own advantage; if everyone is, these observed relationships will simply disappear as soon as they become observable. The same principle applies to systematic government policy under Rational Expectations. Just like the relationship between the price of copper and OECD industrial output, the observable impact of stabilisation policy on private sector decisions disappears as soon as economic agents have been able to gather sufficient information to deduce what policy reaction will be triggered by what state of the economy.

Whilst the Rational Expectations hypothesis is the great technical novelty introduced by the New Classical Macroeconomics (and it is certainly the shiniest new toy in the playground of academic macroeconomics) it is only one of three central postulates. The other two provide the link with Monetarism proper, because they hark back to the ideas of Friedman's 1968 lecture. The first additional postulate is that prices are sufficiently flexible to clear all markets in each time period. Whatever is produced is sold, though of course maybe not at a price which satisfies the producers. As in Friedman's interpretation of the Phillips curve, a rise in aggregate demand pulls up prices, and vice versa. As pointed out above, this runs very much counter to the Keynesian tradition of assuming relatively sluggish price adjustments.

The third postulate is an aggregate supply curve which is a rising function of the difference between actual and anticipated prices (Figure 5.2). If price expectations for period t turn out to be correct then it is assumed that output and employment will be at their normal full employment equilibrium level (or 'natural rate' in Friedman's terminology). But if prices are higher (or lower) than anticipated then output will exceed (or fall short of) its natural rate. This aggregate supply equation may be written:

$$y = y_N + c(p - p^e) \qquad c > 0 \qquad\qquad (5.5)$$

where y denotes the logarithm of real output, y_N the logarithm of the natural rate of real output (i.e. the output produced when all

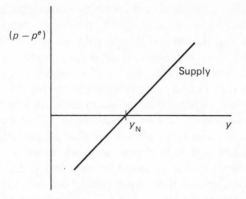

Figure 5.2 *Aggregate supply in the New Classical Macroeconomics*

those willing to work at the going –and correctly anticipated – real wage are employed), p the logarithm of the price level and p^e the logarithm of the price level expected in advance (the logarithmic transformation is not necessary but is usually mathematically convenient). It may be perceived that this was the sort of aggregate supply curve that Friedman was describing in his 1968 lecture. Since a supply curve of this nature is of critical importance to the New Classical Economics, it is worth examining the justification for it.

In Friedman's exposition, this supply curve results from the fact that workers are assumed to be less perceptive about current price movements than their employers. Such a justification would seem to suffer from two weaknesses. The first is that it fits uneasily into the hypothesis of Rational Expectations, which attributes great sophistication to workers along with everybody else. The second is that if the supply curve of labour is 'backward-bending' (i.e. if workers work fewer hours when their real incomes are higher because they can afford to give up overtime and secondary jobs) then c will be negative, which reverses the whole aggregate supply curve and also, incidentally, undermines the whole Friedman interpretation of the Phillips curve. Yet such a backward-bending supply curve is theoretically perfectly plausible and may well be quite frequent in practice.

Luckily, the New Classical Macroeconomics has been able to

rely on an alternative and even more ingenious justification of its favourite aggregate supply curve produced by Lucas and Rapping (1969). Lucas and Rapping do not assume that anyone misperceives their current real or money wage, but they do assume that workers have an idea of a normal wage and price level which they expect to be resumed in the future. Thus, even though the *real* wage may not be abnormally high in the current period, if *money wages and prices* have been pulled up by strong demand, Lucas and Rapping assume that people believe this to be exceptional and will choose to work more today, simultaneously planning to work less in the next period. In other words people bring forward their work plans because today's money wage is exceptionally high when taken in relation to the wages and prices anticipated for tomorrow. Another way of expressing it would be to say that they believe that the return on savings between this period and the next (the expected real interest rate) is exceptionally high, so their response is to earn today in order to spend tomorrow.

The difficulty with this idea is the notion of a normal wage and price level to which current prices are expected to return. In current inflationary conditions this sounds distinctly out of date, although the theory could be reformulated, perhaps somewhat less convincingly, in terms of normal trends rather than levels. But even in this form it means that if inflation was moving along at 5 per cent p.a., and this year it suddenly moves up to 6 per cent, people will *reduce* their expectations of next year's inflation to 4 per cent. This stretches the imagination somewhat, and yet the assumption is critical to Lucas and Rapping's entire argument. A justification of an aggregate supply curve which stands or falls by this assumption must be judged a little tenuous.[1]

With these three ingredients well mixed – Rational Expectations, price flexibility and the above aggregate supply curve – the New Classical Macroeconomics has no trouble in producing its most startling concoction: the proposition that no predictable government policy, whether a simple money supply rule or a very sophisticated attempt at fine-tuning, will have any influence on real output (strictly speaking, this proposition is usually proved only for monetary policy; fiscal policy is more complex since it can have supply-side effects). This is the effect of applying Rational Expectations to a model with a very strong natural tendency towards stability. First of all, the aggregate supply equation means that $y = y_N$ unless people's price expectations are falsified. But how can price expectations be falsified? If for the sake of example we assume that a very simple quantity theory holds:

$$MV = PY \tag{5.6}$$

where M is the money supply (assumed determined by the government), V its velocity of circulation (which we assume constant), P the price level and Y real output, then the government can alter the price level by altering the money supply. But under the hypothesis of Rational Expectations equation (5.6) also tells us how the expectations of the private sector are formed. Taking logarithms (denoted by lower case letters), then rearranging and taking mathematical expectations, we have:

$$E(p) = E(m) + v - E(y) \tag{5.7}$$

This tells us that anything which is likely to influence $E(m)$ will influence price expectations; since m is assumed to be determined by the government, this must consist of an assessment of the government's likely policy reaction to the present. Equation (5.7) also contains a term in $E(y)$; but this complication is easily removed by returning to the aggregate supply equation (5.5). The strict definition of Rational Expectations is that the expectation of the future value of any variable is equal to its mathematical expectation, given the information currently available. Thus under Rational Expectations $p^e = E(p)$, so we can deduce from equation (5.5) that $E(y) = y_N$ (assumed constant). Thus equation (5.7) becomes:

$$E(p) = E(m) + v - y_N \tag{5.8}$$

With V and Y_N assumed constant, this tells us that a 1 per cent increase in the expected money supply will be immediately translated into a 1 per cent higher expected price level. Any systematic monetary policy, predictable from past behaviour, will be anticipated (i.e. will enter into $E(m)$), and will therefore affect price expectations. It is only by surprising the private sector that the government can falsify its price expectations and cause Y to deviate from Y_N. But in this case it cannot be said to be helping to stabilise output, since it is simply imitating any other sort of unanticipatable random disturbance.

Under some other rule of expectations formation in which the private sector does not learn to anticipate the government's behaviour, the government would have no difficulty in falsifying the private sector's price expectations. Moreover this could be stabilising because, now that private sector price expectations can be systematically wrong (because of an unperceived trend in , for example), the government could set its monetary policy so as to correct these errors. Thus the policy ineffectiveness result depends crucially on Rational Expectations. But even with Rational Expectations, the two other assumptions, originating from Friedman, are critical, because they imply that even if the government did not exist the economy would have a very strong tendency to stability around the natural level of output. It is only because of these other assumptions that $E(y) = y_N$. Suppose that in period t there is a negative demand shock which causes prices to be lower than expected. With the price flexibility assumption, producers still sell all their output, although they have to accept a lower than anticipated price and therefore they produce less than Y_N. But the form of the aggregate supply curve means that this does not bother them when considering plans for period $t + 1$. At the worst this negative shock in period t could cause economic agents to expect lower prices in period $t + 1$, but their supply decisions do not depend in any way on the *level* of expected prices, only on how correct these expectations turn out to be. Thus they do not plan to supply any less than Y_N in period $t + 1$.

If, on the other hand, we drop the price flexibility assumption, then a negative demand shock will be reflected in unemployment and an accumulation of unsold stocks. And with a different aggregate supply function, producers can no longer rely on the thought that provided their price expectations prove correct, then they can sell all the output which it is profitable to produce; so they must form expectations of next period's level of effective demand as well as price. They can no longer assume, as they can under New Classical Macroeconomics assumptions, that real effective demand will be sufficient to buy full employment output. In general expectations of next period's real effective demand are likely to reflect the state of excess supply in the current period. If this is so, then they will also reflect expectations of how the government will respond. In these circumstances, systematic government macroeconomic policy *can* affect the path of real output because its reactions influence expectations of future real effective demand and not simply prices.

The New Classical Macroeconomics has therefore highlighted the issue of the natural stability, or otherwise, of capitalist economies. By adding the hypothesis of Rational Expectations to the assumptions of Friedman's 1968 lecture, it has been able to show that any systematic government policy is ineffective in stabilising real output, whilst an unsystematic one is not particularly beneficial. This proposition has, however, not had the same political impact as Monetarism proper. This is partly because the arguments are more complex and difficult and therefore less easy to popularise. But the proposition is also hard to sell because it is counter-intuitive – and this reflects the fact that it is only true under the heroic assumptions which the advocates of the New Classical Macroeconomics have been willing to make but many others have not.

All of the three assumptions are open to serious question. Rational Expectations assumes that everyone knows the true economic model and can solve it (or pay someone to solve it for them), whereas in reality one of the few things that the population as a whole is sure about is that even the economists themselves do not know the true economic model. Many empirical studies of price-setting go against the notion of price flexibility, whilst the theoretical foundations of the aggregate supply function are rather less than totally convincing. Nevertheless, in theoretical terms the New Classical Macroeconomics has definitely taken over the running from old-style Monetarism. This is because Monetarists have been quite willing to accept the assumptions, whilst the Rational Expectations postulate is such a powerful one that it is difficult to resist. In practical terms, the New Classical Macroeconomics seems to imply that Friedman's money supply rule is no less stabilising than any other 'stabilisation policy', and at least has the advantage of being non-inflationary. So the New Classical Macroeconomics certainly does no harm to the Monetarists' case, and throws serious doubts on that of their opponents.

Rational Expectations is appealing because it is the simplest case of expectations being based on a process of reasoning, and some of the points which have been made about macroeconomic policy by advocates of the New Classical Macroeconomics are important precisely because they hold wherever people are capable of learning about changes in policy and anticipating its effects. For example, Lucas (1976) has made a famous critique of conventional policy debates in which he points out that an econometric relationship observed by the government when it is pursuing macroeconomic policy X will not necessarily hold if it then tries to exploit that relationship and switches to macroeconomic policy Y, because the private sector, once having observed the switch in policy, will form its expectations differently and the econometric relationship which the government is seeking to exploit will either be modified or disappear altogether. This point is valid whenever expectations are sensitive to perceptions of government policy, and does not depend on the extreme assumption of Rational Expectations, but it obviously has far-reaching consequences which were not previously noted.

The New Classical Macroeconomics throws a question mark over active stabilisation policy, which had previously been regarded as one of the lasting achievements of the Keynesian revolution. Not surprisingly, it has met a vigorous counter-attack. Besides the points which have already been made, it was pointed out that the policy-ineffectiveness proposition would break down if the government had more information than the private sector (or got the information earlier), or if the private sector entered into wage or price contracts for more than one period ahead which could not be renegotiated in the light of events. The first criticism is fairly trivial since, under New Classical Macroeconomics assumptions, the government could not do any better than to eliminate its informational advantage by immediately publishing any information which it gets. The second is more substantial, and arises out of the fact that the private sector is no longer free to take full advantage of new information: some prices are now effectively fixed. In this situation systematic government policy can help to stabilise real output.

A further criticism is that in a New Classical Macroeconomics world, the unemployment rate should fluctuate randomly around its natural rate, whereas in reality there is a high degree of correlation between unemployment rates in successive time periods (Hall, 1975). The New Classical Macroeconomics has reacted to this by modifying its aggregate supply equation to include a term in last period's output, but the justifications for this procedure leave something to be desired: it is essentially an *ad hoc* accommodation of an awkward fact. Finally, even if one accepts all the other assumptions, but allows for the fact that the structural relationships in the economy may change periodically, then it becomes very implausible to assume that economic agents always know the true model (Shiller, 1978; Friedman, 1979). At first they will not be able to distinguish the change in the structure from a random disturbance, but presumably after a few quarters they will deduce that there has been a structural change from the fact that their errors are no longer random. But this puts them in the position of not knowing the true model, and they will have to wait for twenty or so quarters' data to have accumulated before they can estimate the new model. Then they can start forming expectations on the basis of these estimates, but this will itself change the structure of the system in ways which it will take another five years to estimate. So the approach to a Rational Expectations equilibrium is an iterative process and the New Classical Macroeconomics, like other neoclassical constructs, can only properly be viewed as a description of a long-run equilibrium, deductions from which are unlikely to be relevant to short-run situations.

Conclusion

In this chapter we have seen that the theoretical reaction against Keynesianism has moved increasingly towards a questioning of the value of government attempts to stabilise the economy at all. In the early days of Monetarism, the emphasis was on the assertion of the power of monetary policy, and the theoretical rehabilitation of the quantity theory of money was really a means towards this end. But the failure of demand management to find a satisfactory solution to the more complex challenges of the 1960s and 1970s opened the door to a much more comprehensive critique. As we have seen the theoretical basis for this critique has been a return to neoclassical assumptions of complete information and price flexibility. This has stood out most clearly in the stark propositions of the New Classical Macroeconomics, and is in sharp contrast to theoretical developments elsewhere in economics, which have increasingly concentrated on situations where information is only limited. No attempt has been made by Monetarists or New Classicists to justify their summary rejection of Keynes's theoretical arguments; they simply choose to dismiss them by assumption. It is therefore not surprising that their conclusions are firmly anti-Keynesian.

Note to Chapter 5

1. A further difficulty is that in practice post-tax real interest rates have often been negative, which should be sufficient to deter the rational person with normal preferences from earning today in order to spend tomorrow. As Minford and Peel (1980) have pointed out, Lucas and Rapping's argument makes this period's output a function of the difference between this period's prices and *next* period's expected price level, not this period's. In other words, it implies a supply curve of the form

$$y_t = y_{Nt} + c(p_t - p_{t+1}^e).$$

But, as is made clear below, p_{t+1}^e will depend on government policy in period t, so how governments choose to react to the observed price level in period t will influence, via p_{t+1}^e, the level of output in period t. The 'policy ineffectiveness' result about to be described no longer holds. The alternative justification of equation (5.5) offered by Sargent and Wallace (1975), to the effect that suppliers of goods and labour come to know about price changes for their own commodities faster than for commodities in general and therefore assume them to be *relative* price movements, seems implausible given that inflation statistics are published every month. Moreover this justification is open to the same objection as Friedman's: that if people are putting massive effort into solving a sophisticated econometric model to generate expectations of the future values of all economic variables, it makes little sense to assume that they do not make the effort to find out what the current price level is.

6
The Current Recession

The breakdown of the post-war boom was symbolised, like the beginning of the Great Depression, by a dramatic event – the 'energy crisis', i.e. the restriction of supplies of oil followed by a massive increase in prices imposed by OPEC in late 1973. Since that date, the economic performance of the advanced capitalist countries has clearly deteriorated. Growth rates have fallen. The rate of unemployment has increased and stayed high. The threat to industries and jobs has revived protectionist pressures reminiscent of the 1930s, whilst the debts hanging over a number of sizeable nations have caused tension and strain in the international financial system. There is a pervasive atmosphere of depression and crisis. Many underdeveloped countries are suffering badly from the combination of high oil prices and depressed export markets, and even the socialist bloc, seemingly less dependent on events in the major capitalist countries than any other part of the world, has experienced these difficulties.

In figures, the shift of gear is illustrated by Table 6.1. Real output in the advanced capitalist countries is growing at half its former rate, and unemployment has moved sharply upwards. The average for the whole period obscures the fact that unemployment has tended to increase: it was much higher in the early 1980s than at the height of the previous recession (1975). The figures may not be as horrendous as in the 1930s but the prospect of a prolonged period of depressed demand for labour is similar. The inflation rate has doubled (Table 6.2). The dates chosen in the tables do introduce a certain bias against the recent period, which includes two recessions (1974–5 and 1979–82) and

Table 6.1   *Growth and unemployment in the OECD countries, 1962–81*

	1962–73	1974–81
Growth of real GDP at market prices (% p.a.)	5.0	2.4
Standardised unemployment rates (%)	3.0*	5.3

* 1966–73.

SOURCE   OECD, *Economic Outlook*, No. 32 (December, 1982), Tables R1, R12.

only the one intervening recovery; but the contrast between the two periods is reinforced by the observations that *in no single recent year* has the growth rate reached the *average* of the period up to 1973 (the highest being 4.8 per cent in 1976), and in all years since 1975 the unemployment rate has exceeded the *maximum* recorded in the earlier period.

Is this something which Keynesian economics could and should have prevented? Has Keynesianism been exposed in the last decade as a hollow doctrine, of no relevance to the economic problems of the 1980s? These are the questions with which this chapter is concerned. We shall look first at the record of macroeconomic policy. Most people are aware that in the last decade previously unthinkable levels of unemployment have become reality and indeed are often regarded in official circles as tolerable. Phrases such as 'the fight against inflation must have priority over the reduction of unemployment', 'the need to accept slower growth of living standards' or 'public expenditure cannot be allowed to expand at the same rate as before' testify to a marked change of attitude amongst policy-makers. Our investigation fleshes out these impressions with figures.

But why has such a deterioration in economic performance been tolerated? Twenty years ago it was generally believed that Keynes had proved such a prolonged waste of resources to be both unnecessary and relatively easy to prevent. Now it has happened, and not because ministers and government officials have in any immediate sense forgotten the lessons of history, but because they believe themselves to be following the best course of policy open to them. They believe that the remedies of the 1930s are in critical respects no longer adequate to the current slump.

Thus if the practical message of Keynesian theory is that fiscal policy can be used to stabilise capitalist economies and prevent unnecessary losses of output, then either it has failed, or the current loss of output is in some sense 'necessary'. But in what sense? To answer this at all convincingly requires an analysis of some of the deeper forces underlying the breakdown of the boom. Accordingly the bulk of this chapter is concerned with this. We need to evaluate all of the various factors which economists have cited as significant causes: fundamental changes in international economic relations; errors of macroeconomic policy; structural, legislative and other 'supply-side' constraints; inflationary expectations; distributional conflicts; the growth of the public sector; the oil price shocks and other commodity price increases. All of these have influenced or have been alleged to have influenced the pattern of economic development, and must therefore affect our judgments of recent macroeconomic policy. But to give some indication of my conclusions, I shall be arguing that the central role has been played by distributional conflicts, and that the impact of other influences has been determined in large part by their relationship to these conflicts. It is the intensity of these conflicts which marks the essential difference between the 1970s and 1980s on the one hand, and the 1930s and the 1950s on the other. Since Keynesian theory was never intended as an analysis or as a pointer to the resolution of such conflicts, its role in practice has been as an aid to the manipulation of them, and this is how the macroeconomic policy of the past decade should be interpreted.

Macroeconomic Policy Since 1973

Fiscal and monetary policies are adjusted relatively frequently, and by the use of a variety of instruments. Since we are concerned with broad changes in pattern between the periods before and after 1973, we require simple summary measures, and also, since we are interested in the world as a whole and not just one country, ones that can be meaningfully aggregated internationally. A useful approximation is to confine attention to the seven major OECD countries (United States, Japan, Federal Republic of Germany, France, United Kingdom, Italy and Canada), which together account for over 80 per cent of OECD output.

Of various possible monetary measures, the best is probably the growth rate of a broad measure of the real money supply (M2 deflated by a price index), for which figures are given in Table 6.2.[1] Taken by itself, the growth in the money supply shows no change in pattern: indeed the average over the two periods is almost exactly the same. But the rate of inflation was so much higher after 1973 that the growth of real M2 dropped from an average of 7.0 to 1.8 per cent. The figures for the individual years 1972 to 1975, also shown in the table, indicate a very sharp break in trend around 1973–4. In the years up to 1973, real M2 grew by less than 5 per cent in only one year (1969, when it was 2.0 per cent), whereas since 1973 real monetary growth has exceeded 3 per cent only in the years 1976–8 (5.0, 4.1 and 5.0 per cent respectively). In the absence of any perceived *change in trend* in the velocity of circulation of money, this must be interpreted as a marked and sustained shift of monetary stance in a restrictive direction.

Table 6.2 *Money supply growth and inflation in seven major OECD countries, 1965–82*

	Average percentage change from previous year					
	1965–73	*1974–82*	*1972*	*1973*	*1974*	*1975*
Money supply (M2)	11.5	11.3	15.5	15.2	10.7	11.0
Consumer prices	4.5	9.5	4.3	7.5	13.3	11.0
Real money supply	7.0	1.8	10.2	7.7	−2.6	0.0

SOURCES   OECD, *Monetary Targets and Inflation Control* (Paris, 1979), p. 10; OECD, *Economic Outlook*, No. 32 (December 1982), Table R10 and No. 33 (July 1983), Table R10 and p. 32.

A more detailed examination of the post-1973 picture reveals that *nominal* monetary growth has been very steady, exhibiting a gradual deceleration from about 13 per cent in 1976 to around 9 per cent in 1983. This steadiness presumably reflects the widespread adoption of monetary targets.[2] In consequence the pattern of *real* monetary growth has been strongly influenced by changes in the inflation rate, being strongest in the periods of lower inflation (1976–8 and 1982–3) and weakest (and for a time negative) in 1979–81, when the impact of the second oil price shock once again pushed consumer price increases into double figures.

Fiscal policy is less easy to summarise. The best indicator of the intentions of the budgetary authorities is a measure of their discretionary action, but this must clearly be related to macro-economic conditions, which brings in to some extent the action of automatic stabilisers as well. Moreover, discretionary actions identified *ex post* may not always have been fully intended and, as discussed in Chapter 4, may be highly sensitive to the method of estimation. This is particularly true of the internationally standardised measures calculated by the OECD which we shall be using, since these perforce cannot be adjusted to suit particular national circumstances.

Table 6.3 indicates that the demand impact of discretionary action was no stronger in the higher unemployment period of 1974–8 than it had been on average over the years 1965–73, and in several important cases it was weaker (though for the United States the comparison is influenced by the obvious fiscal overheating of the Vietnam War years 1966–8). Thus the general impression given is that no vigorous attempt was made to reduce unemployment through fiscal measures in the mid-1970s. Table 6.4 gives an alternative measure of fiscal stance over the years

Table 6.3 *Discretionary effects of fiscal policy in seven countries 1965–78. Percentage of previous year's GDP at constant prices*

	US	Japan	FRG	France	UK	Italy	Canada
1965	1.29	1.25	2.07	0.72	−0.06	1.16	1.26
1966	2.68	1.45	0.38	−0.46	0.34	0.97	1.51
1967	3.03	1.03	0.43	1.45	1.71	0.11	1.36
1968	1.25	1.41	0.88	1.61	−0.07	1.05	1.59
1969	−0.62	0.38	0.30	0.63	−1.48	0.77	0.36
1970	0.51	0.92	1.76	1.06	0.26	0.32	1.72
1971	0.67	1.65	1.09	0.94	1.28	1.07	1.76
1972	0.49	1.52	0.91	0.93	2.54	1.44	1.10
1973	0.49	0.73	0.48	0.96	1.68	1.18	1.29
1974	−0.02	0.74	1.44	2.59	1.13	0.66	1.51
1975	1.23	1.88	1.37	0.27	−0.38	1.22	1.91
1976	0.30	0.82	0.30	1.69	−1.00	−0.14	0.10
1977	0.52	0.99	−0.11	1.10	−1.28	0.60	0.76
1978	0.91	1.41	1.03	1.14	0.56	−0.28	1.04

SOURCES OECD, *Budget Indicators* (Paris, 1978), p. 12; OECD, *Economic Outlook*, No. 23 (July 1978), p. 18.

Table 6.4   *Discretionary and automatic changes in budget balances of the seven major OECD countries as a percentage of GNP, 1971–82*

	Change in actual budget balance	Discretionary change	Built-in stabilisers	Unemployment rate (%)
1971	−0.8	−0.6	−0.2	3.8
1972	+0.1	−0.3	+0.4	3.8
1973	+0.6	−0.2	+0.8	3.4
1974	−0.7	+0.4	−1.1	3.7
1975	−3.5	−1.8	−1.7	5.5
1976	+1.3	+0.7	+0.6	5.5
1977	+0.8	+0.4	+0.4	5.4
1978	−0.2	−0.7	+0.5	5.1
1979	+0.6	+0.5	+0.1	5.0
1980	−0.7	+0.2	−0.9	5.6
1981	−0.1	+0.7	−0.8	6.5
1982	−1.5	+0.1	−1.4	7.9

SOURCES   *Public Sector Deficits: Problems and Policy Implications* (OECD, *Economic Outlook Occasional Studies*, June 1983), Table 5; OECD, *Economic Outlook*, No. 33 (July 1983), Table R12.

1971–82.[3] According to this measure, strong action was taken to stem the slump in 1975, but fiscal policy then became restrictive for two years before imparting another expansionary stimulus in 1978. Since 1979 it has been consistently restrictive despite a substantial further rise in unemployment. Over the years 1979–82 fiscal policy was on average expansionary only in the United States and Italy of the major countries, and then only very mildly so (moreover the sizeable US fiscal stimulus of 1982 was largely the unintentional result of deadlock between President Reagan and Congress about how to reduce the budget deficit, which both sides believed to be too large).

Thus the general picture which emerges might be summarised as follows. In 1974–5 monetary policy was tight, but fiscal policy became strongly expansionary when it was realised that the recession was an unusually deep one. After the middle of 1975, once it had become clear that a recovery was beginning, anxiety switched quickly to the other tack. There was a general fear that if recovery was too swift it could rekindle inflationary pressures (see, for example, the Introduction to EO 19[4]). Thus in the period 1976–8, although monetary policy was less tight than before because of the fall in inflation rates, fiscal policy was very cautious, playing a negative role in the recovery during 1976 and 1977, and only switching to an expansionary stance in 1978 when it was realised that the recovery was virtually petering out (in the US, where the recovery had been markedly stronger than elsewhere and inflation had shown signs of a re-acceleration, fiscal policy remained restrictive). Although there were marked differences between countries, for the advanced capitalist world as a whole unemployment declined only a little and inflation decelerated very slowly, to about 7 per cent in early 1978. The second oil price shock of 1979–80 stimulated a concertedly restrictive response, with monetary policy not accommodating the new inflationary pressures at all, and fiscal policy aiming (unsuccessfully) at reducing budget deficits, which widened considerably as unemployment shot upwards. The effect was a longer and deeper recession than 1974–5, with unemployment noticeably higher. By late 1982, thanks in part to a drop in the oil price, inflation rates had come down quite substantially to around 6 per cent p.a., although once again the deceleration was much slower than the preceding acceleration.

Thus the general impression is that the advanced capitalist countries have been moving gradually away from any commitment to an active fiscal policy to reduce unemployment. One justification of this runs in terms of conflicts between economic objectives: governments have only slowly come to realise how hard the inflation problem is to solve, and macroeconomic policy since 1979 has been dominated by a determination not to allow the problem to get any worse. But the reality is somewhat more complicated. With the arrival of political Monetarism in power in countries such as the US and the UK, belief in the effectiveness and desirability of an expansionary fiscal policy has perceptibly declined in a more general sense. Not only have Keynesian remedies scarcely been applied to the current recession, but in many ways they look less and less likely to be applied as time goes on. Sometimes it seems almost as if the current recession is witnessing a replay of the theoretical developments of the 1930s – *in reverse*.

Before proceeding any further we should confront two issues which arise from the above discussion of monetary and fiscal policy. One is the argument that it is wrong to discuss these policy instruments as if they were entirely independent, because a budget deficit has to be financed either by the creation of money or in some other way which may have further repercussions, notably higher interest rates. Before 1973 this relationship was of no significance, because monetary policy was relaxed and budget deficits small. Now that budget deficits are much larger and the stance of monetary policy is judged by monetary growth rather than interest rates, the question arises whether, *for a given stance of monetary policy*, fiscal policy may prove a relatively ineffective instrument for stimulating demand. Given monetary targets, any increase in the budget deficit must be financed by increased sales of government securities, and the resulting rise in interest rates may 'crowd out' the fiscal stimulus.

Amongst the major countries there is evidence of this relationship influencing the conduct of macroeconomic policy at various times in the UK, West Germany and Italy (OECD, 1982, p. 107), and more recently the United States (indeed this is probably the most important case). What it means is that a commitment to a restrictive monetary policy will also tend to bias fiscal policy in a deflationary direction. But it also implies the converse: that a commitment to a reflationary fiscal policy would bias monetary policy in an expansionary direction. Thus this relationship does not in itself justify a restrictive policy stance; it merely implies that if you believe monetary targets to be an essential weapon of anti-inflation policy, you cannot fully offset their effects on real output through fiscal policy. Monetary and fiscal policy are to some extent tied to one another. However the restrictiveness of fiscal policy has not been confined to those countries concerned about this connection between fiscal and monetary policy, so we must conclude that though it may have had some influence at the margin in a few countries, it cannot explain the *general* picture of restriction and caution.

This caution might of course be justified if it could be shown that the apparent degree of slack in the advanced capitalist world today was just a statistical artefact. Arguments of this sort have been made, and they usually focus on one of two points: (a) the assertion that much measured unemployment is voluntary; or (b) the observation that capacity utilisation rates have not fallen to match the rise in unemployment (EO 31, Chart D). The second point implies that in all probability the production capacity does not at present exist to give employment to the whole of the labour force. But it does not imply that unemployment is thereby invalidated as an indicator of slackness in resource use, because the obvious explanation for the phenomenon in question is that the volume of production capacity has been adapted to cautious business expectations about future demand. Thus the phenomenon is itself a result of depressed demand conditions, and being influenced by demand, cannot be used as an independent yardstick of it.

Unless one is going to claim that there has been a massive shift in taste towards leisure as against income, of which I have seen no convincing evidence, the argument that voluntary unemployment has mushroomed depends on unemployment having become more financially attractive relative to employment. In a few countries (notably France) this has occurred, but in others (notably Britain) the trend has been very much in the opposite direction, and in most the changes have been small (UN, 1982, p. 31). Since the increase in unemployment has been universal, this evidence seems inconsistent with the voluntary unemployment thesis. Moreover all arguments of this kind must be set against the other misleading part of the unemployment statistics: those who are discouraged from considering entry into the labour market by the lack of jobs (e.g. married women, potential immigrants, those who retire early).

The Breakdown of the Boom

One might evaluate this policy restrictiveness by considering the justifications that have been offered for it, the most common of which has been 'the inflationary problem'. But this and other phrases uttered by governments can have a multitude of meanings, and a more rounded approach is to build up an integrated picture of the significant changes in the economic environment that have occurred since the 1960s. Accordingly in this section I shall consider some of the forces behind the breakdown of the post-war boom. It is perhaps useful to start by summarising schematically the alternative explanations which have been offered by earlier writers.[5] Different schools of thought have interpreted current problems as:

(1) The result of earlier policy errors. The purest example of this is what I shall call 'the simple Monetarist position'.
(2) The result of exogenous shocks (notably the rises in oil prices in 1973–4 and 1979–80).
(3) The consequence of developments internal to the advanced capitalist world.

The simple Monetarist position results from the application of the theory of the expectations-augmented Phillips curve (Friedman, 1968; 1975). It argues that governments, inspired by Keynesian economics, made two fundamental errors in the 1960s and early 1970s. First, they underestimated the officially measured unemployment rate which corresponded to an economic definition of full employment. This led them to adopt expansionary policies in pursuit of the full employment objective, when their economies were already at full employment, thus creating substantial excess demand. And secondly, they failed to recognise that creeping inflation did not represent a stable equilibrium, as the Phillips curve suggested, but depended on people largely ignoring price increases as far as their economic behaviour was concerned; when the inflation rate began to move up another notch or two people suddenly woke up to it and built it into their expectations, with the result that a constant demand pressure in the economy became associated not with a constant but with an accelerating rate of inflation. After 1973 policy-makers therefore had to adjust to a legacy of excess demand and quickly-adjusting inflationary expectations; these expectations could only be altered by a course of deflationary medicine which would mean a temporary period of 'stagflation' and unemployment before a world of constant prices could once again return.

According to this theory the current policy restrictiveness is a necessary cure for its earlier laxity. As we saw in the last chapter, it is assumed that the labour market is competitive, so that cost-push forces can be ignored, as can also exogenous price shocks (since if they are not accommodated by monetary expansion they should affect only the relative price of the commodities involved and not the general price level). This school tends to stress the increase in state intervention and regulation as a cause of the deterioration in growth rates (Feldstein, 1980, Introduction). Overall, this explanation is strongly neoclassical, and despite its intellectual coherence it is unrealistic and ignores factors which, I shall argue, have been of critical importance.

Explanations which run in terms of supply-side shocks emphasise the rise in oil prices (and secondarily that of other raw materials). This caused a significant acceleration of inflation and a sharp increase in the price of energy relative to other inputs to the production process. The worsening of inflation caused macroeconomic policy to be more cautious than it would otherwise have been and thus explains the rise in unemployment; the relative rise in energy prices caused a progressive substitution of labour and capital for energy over the subsequent years, which explains the slowdown in the growth of labour productivity, and also induced a once-for-all reduction in productive potential by making some capital equipment economically obsolete (Bruno, 1982).

In its most extreme form this explanation suggests that, in the absence of these external shocks, the post-war boom in the advanced capitalist countries could have been prolonged much further. For reasons discussed below, I regard it as seriously inadequate as a primary explanation. The true significance of these external shocks arose from their interaction with internal factors.

Emphasis on developments internal to the advanced capitalist world which would point to a deceleration of economic development has come particularly from Marxists (e.g. Mandel, 1975; Glyn, 1982), although by no means exclusively from them. Mandel and Glyn both attribute the change to a fall in the rate of profit, as a result of a rise in the capital–output ratio and/or a fall in the share of profits in output because of 'the increasing pressure of the class struggle'. Mandel emphasises the exhaustion of the reserve army of labour in the countryside and elsewhere as a factor increasing workers' bargaining power. My view is that these authors have focused on a fundamental aspect of the problem, although by itself each of their analyses is seriously inadequate.

These three types of explanation differ radically in their perspective on current problems. Although elements of all three can be integrated together (OECD, 1977; Maddison, 1980), it remains significant where the central emphasis lies (Maddison stresses internal developments rather more strongly than the

OECD Report). Having said this by way of introduction, I shall now turn to some of the factors at play in the transition from boom to recession.

The International Monetary System

In the 1960s the most pressing difficulty in world economic relations was the progressive crisis of the international monetary system. However the connection between the death throes of the Bretton Woods arrangements and the end of the post-war boom is far from obvious. In many respects the recurrent and very public crises were more of a symbol than a cause of economic difficulties, though it has been argued that the pattern of the breakdown contributed to inflationary pressures at a vital moment in the early 1970s (OECD, 1977; Maddison, 1980). There is no doubt that the 'adjustable peg' system was successful in providing a framework for fast expansion of international trade, the effect of which was to make the advanced capitalist economies increasingly 'open'. But after the establishment of general currency convertibility in December 1958 the difficulties in the Bretton Woods arrangements displayed a definite tendency to increase. From around the middle of the 1960s the worry that fast-growing international trade was being covered by a more or less constant level of world foreign exchange reserves became a matter of increasing official concern. The fear was that with generally inadequate reserves temporary balance of payments difficulties would be more frequently met by measures of deflation or trade restriction, with adverse consequences for output and investment, and this led in 1969 to the creation of IMF Special Drawing Rights. But the Bretton Woods system suffered from several much more deep-rooted problems than this, the combination of which eventually finished it off for good. These were:

(1) Increasing speculative pressures due to structural changes in the world economy associated, in part, with the success of the Bretton Woods system itself.
(2) Reluctance to adjust exchange rates.
(3) Acceleration of inflation and in particular the increasing divergence of inflation rates which accompanied it.

(4) Decline of the United States from its former position of absolute dominance in the world economy.

Speculative pressures increased with the growth of trade relative to GDP and the internationalisation of the operations of large companies and banks. Since in the adjustable peg system a currency was only ever likely to move in one direction, 'hot money' could gamble on large gains for the risk of only a small loss (interest differentials and transactions costs) by participating in a speculative run. Because speculation fed on itself (the larger a speculative movement became, the greater the incentive to join it in the expectation that governments would have to give in and adjust exchange rates) the explosion of hot money apparent in the 1960s greatly increased the frequency and seriousness of foreign exchange crises.

Reluctance to adjust exchange rates, even in the face of 'fundamental disequilibrium', arose from political pressures; governments felt that they were much more likely to be blamed for the consequences if they changed the exchange rate, which involved a positive decision on their part and was bound to antagonise significant bodies of opinion, than if they resisted pressure for a change. This created a serious asymmetry in the system, since governments could be forced to devalue by the imminent disappearance of their foreign exchange reserves, but there was no corresponding sanction in the opposite direction. Revaluations were consequently extremely rare, and there were only three out of a total of 250 exchange rate changes up to January 1970 (Machlup, 1972). This reluctance to alter exchange rates increased in significance as accelerating inflation caused actual and equilibrium exchange rates to diverge more quickly from each other. Such problems would of course have been magnified many times over had the Bretton Woods arrangements lived beyond the early 1970s.

The adjustable peg enshrined the economic dominance of the United States by expressing all the other countries' exchange rates in terms of the dollar. This automatically made the US dollar the principal reserve currency, so that the US was under much less pressure than any other country to remedy a persistent balance of payments deficit. More important, however, was the fact that the United States could not devalue its own currency. By

the mid-1960s, when a major US balance of payments problem
first developed, that country no longer had the kind of absolute
political and economic dominance of the West which, had the
problem occurred a decade earlier, would probably have enabled
it to force a general revaluation of other currencies. Since the
United States was not willing to solve the problem by domestic
deflation, it essentially ignored it, thereby challenging other
countries either just to accept the dollars or to make the necessary
adjustments themselves. Between 1969 and 1973 other countries
therefore experienced a massive increase in their official reserves,
stemming directly from the US deficit. This tactic did force a
realignment of currencies (the Smithsonian Agreement of 1971)
but speculative crises continued and by 1973 all the major
currencies were floating in relation to the dollar.

This system of floating rates between major countries, or at
least between major blocs of countries (the EEC having made
persistent attempts to maintain 'fixed rates internally) has
continued ever since. There is no obvious case for stating that the
disappearance of the Bretton Woods system has contributed to
the subsequent recession, despite the coincidence of timing. There
was no breakdown of international economic relations in the
1970s as there had been in the 1930s. Exchange rate uncertainties
did not seem to inhibit international trade to any significant
extent, and over the long run exchange rate changes seemed to
reflect the adjustments required to maintain trade competitiveness. In the short run movements have often been large and
sudden, with a tendency to 'overshooting'; this has resulted from
the crowd psychology of speculators combined with the absence
of any obvious criterion for judging when the exchange rate
adjustment has gone far enough (a consequence of the well-
known 'J-curve effect').[6]

Thus the workings of the floating rate system have certainly not
been as smooth as its most ardent advocates suggested.
Speculative movements have on several occasions caused major
headaches through their impact on the exchange rates of
important currencies. But overall, floating rates have enabled
these speculative pressures to be absorbed without adverse effects
on trade volumes. The creeping protectionism of recent years
owes far more to depressed demand conditions than to the
workings of the international monetary system.

It has been persuasively argued that, even if the breakdown of the Bretton Woods arrangements was inevitable and perhaps desirable, the *manner* in which it occurred did contribute to the end of the post-war boom because the expansion of the world money supply associated with the massive US payments deficit increased inflationary pressures at a vital moment in the early 1970s (OECD, 1977, pp. 52–6).[7] Since this is related to the issue of macroeconomic policy errors, I shall discuss it under that heading.

Errors of Macroeconomic Policy

As already suggested, the argument that macroeconomic policy errors brought an end to the boom has been most closely associated with the Monetarist school, which has argued that a period of deflation has been necessary to weed out inflationary expectations. The analysis was originally formulated in the wake of the evident overheating of the United States economy in 1966–8, but was widely applied to the monetary expansions of the early 1970s. Indeed it was commonly argued by Monetarists that the price explosion of 1974 was the direct result of the earlier monetary growth, the time-lags being consistent with what they had predicted.

A slightly different line of argument is that demand conditions in 1972–3 were responsible for the commodity price boom, which then fed through at a critical time into the prices of all other goods. This issue has been closely examined by the OECD. They argue that there was an unfortunate synchronisation of the trade cycle in the major countries over the period 1969–73, the consequences of which were exacerbated by the monetary ease associated with the breakdown of the Bretton Woods arrangements.

With the benefit of hindsight we judge that the shift of policies, particularly monetary policies, in 1971 to settings which were effectively 'all-systems-go' in many countries simultaneously was the most important mishap in recent economic policy history. It contributed to an extremely rapid and synchronised boom, which in conjunction with a number of important shocks led to an outburst of world-wide inflation almost unprecedented in peace-time, driven primarily not by wage increases but by price increases, in which primary products and speculative elements played a leading part (OECD, 1977, p. 51).

What was significant was not the height of the cyclical peak, which was unexceptional, but the speed of the upswing. This produced a spectacular rise in the price of raw materials, which immediately became the focus of anticipatory and speculative buying facilitated by easy credit conditions. Spot prices of industrial raw materials more or less doubled in 1972–3. These increases were passed on by manufacturers as higher prices of industrial products. Consumer price inflation in OECD countries moved up from an average of 5.2 per cent p.a. in the second half of 1972 to 7.8 per cent during the first half of 1973 and 10.3 per cent in the second half. This was a price acceleration on a global scale unknown since the Korean War.

Towards Full Employment and Price Stability, which was written before any clear picture of subsequent growth trends could be obtained, makes much of this episode in its analysis of the difficulties facing the advanced capitalist countries in the mid-1970s. Although the authors do not neglect other contributory factors (e.g. poor grain harvests in the USSR and elsewhere), the main thrust of the argument is that policy errors created excessive demand pressures, which resulted in a commodity price boom. Such a boom was by its nature temporary and bound to be reversed, but its effects were less transient because of the impact on inflationary expectations. The dynamics of popular expectations turned a once-for-all price rise into a shift in the trend.

There are two quite separate issues involved in this explanation of events. One is the degree of responsibility of macro-economic policy errors for the acceleration of inflation at this time; the other is the plausibility of expectational factors as an explanation of the subsequent persistence of inflation. This latter point is crucial, since without it one cannot regard the recession solely as retribution for the sin of earlier policy excesses. It is the cornerstone of the Monetarist interpretation of 'stagflation', and I shall criticise it in some detail below. But first, if we accept that the commodity price boom did significantly exacerbate the inflationary problem in the advanced capitalist countries, was it the result of earlier policy errors?

In part it must be ascribed to a cyclical pattern of sorts in commodity markets. The Korean War price bubble encouraged investment in raw materials so that, even though there was a sustained expansion of demand over the next two decades, supply kept pace with it and the trend in the terms of trade ran gently in favour of industrial goods. Once this new pattern of relative price stability had been recognised however, new investment tended to be discouraged. New sources of supply ceased to be opened up at the same rate. Thus by the early 1970s the situation was probably ripe for a new price bubble when demand began to accelerate unusually fast. Moreover the political situation in the under-developed countries had shifted considerably since the 1950s: sentiment had moved strongly in the direction of nationalism and a perception of injustice in past economic relationships. For most commodities, however, this point had little significance, since producer countries were unable to establish any real control over market forces. The one great exception to this, oil, was of such importance that I shall discuss it separately.

Nevertheless recognition of this pattern cannot eliminate the fact that there must have been something unusual about demand conditions in this period to produce such a price explosion. Here the conditions created by the crisis in the Bretton Woods system would seem to be the key to the matter. The United States had in the early 1970s a massive current account deficit, which it was deliberately ignoring as part of a plan to force other major countries to revalue their currencies. At the same time the situation stimulated large speculative movements out of the dollar, which the United States government could meet simply by printing more, since the US dollar was the major reserve currency. Thus the US had a major balance of payments problem but was refusing to meet it by domestic deflation. The counterpart to this was an unusually strong current account and reserve asset position for the rest of the world, which relaxed the international constraints on domestic expansion. Governments were therefore formulating policies to counter the 1971 recession at a time of exceptionally rosy balance of payments prospects and with hot money flows running against the currency whose government was least likely to be forced to introduce a major deflationary package to meet them. This was compounded by a general underestimation of the ease of monetary policy, because of the emphasis on interest rates rather than some measure of money supply as an indicator. The outflow of dollars, presented at central banks and exchanged for domestic currency, fuelled a massive monetary expansion outside the United States, but this failed to reduce interest rates very much because of the attractiveness of borrowing money to speculate in property and raw materials. This demand for money, essentially based on inflationary expectations, was largely accommodated by monetary authorities in the belief that to do otherwise would raise interest rates and make monetary policy unduly restrictive.

It is unlikely that the same combination of monetary laxity and absence of balance of payments constraints would have occurred but for the impasse reached by the Bretton Woods system. If countries other than the US had permitted a general realignment of currencies amounting to a US devaluation then the United States would not have been forced to resort to deliberate neglect of its external balance and the massive dollar outflow could have been avoided. Alternatively had a system of floating rates been resorted to, the dollar would automatically have fallen with similar results. If we regard what happened to the Bretton Woods system as an international policy failure, then weaknesses of government policy must bear a considerable responsibility for the commodity price boom.

Having said this, however, one must place it in perspective. The events of 1971–3 did see the most significant policy errors, on a global scale, since the Second World War, but their long-term significance is uncertain. An acceleration of inflation was already apparent in the later 1960s and in the recession of 1970–1 prices were moving upwards at a rate significantly above that of previous recessions. The loss in the terms of trade imposed by the commodity price boom on the industrial countries was to a large degree reversed (if we exclude oil) in the subsequent recession; and the much more enduring oil price explosion was stimulated rather less by the demand conditions of the time than by political factors (the Arab–Israeli war). For these reasons I regard the combination of 'unfortunate events and policy errors' of the early 1970s (other than the happenings in the oil market) as very much in the second line of explanatory factors. The events of this period are supposed to have been significant because they were inflationary, but the critical issue in relation to inflation is not the initial acceleration but why that acceleration has proved so difficult to reverse in the recession years.

Reduction in Growth Potential

As Table 6.1 indicates, the reduction in the growth rate of real output in the advanced capitalist countries since 1973 has been very marked. This has been accompanied by a downward shift in the trend of labour productivity growth, not just in the fast-growing countries but in the slow-growing ones as well, which has led to the flowering of ideas about increasing supply-side constraints on economic development, i.e. a reduction in growth potential. The significance of such constraints is potentially considerable because the greater they have been, the smaller the shortfall in output that can be attributed to depressed demand.

If the deceleration had been confined to the fast-growing areas, the natural explanation would have been the slowing down of the catching-up process. But, as Table 6.5 shows, the pattern is not really consistent with this. Productivity growth in North America has been cut back to virtually nothing. Moreover the change in trend is sharp, with the break occurring in 1973–4. Neither of these features is as expected if the explanation was the

Table 6.5 *Labour productivity growth in the advanced capitalist countries, 1960–80. Annual average percentage change in real GDP per person employed*

	1960–7	1967–73	1973–80
United States	2.7	1.6	0.2
Japan	8.6	8.3	3.0
Fed. Rep. of Germany	4.0	4.8	2.8
France	5.0	4.7	2.6
United Kingdom	2.4	3.4	1.1
Italy	6.3	5.2	1.7
Canada	2.5	2.9	0.0
Major 7 OECD	4.0	3.7	1.4
Total OECD	4.0	3.8	1.5

SOURCE OECD, *Economic Outlook Historical Statistics 1960–80* (Paris, 1982), Table 3.7.

natural exhaustion of the process of technological catching-up with North America by Western Europe and Japan. If, as suggested in Chapter 4, catching-up represented a significant cause of the exceptional dynamism of the post-war decades, the exhaustion of such possibilities should have been reflected in a gradual deceleration towards North American rates of productivity growth, as the other countries approached the technological frontier. But before 1973 there was no particular sign of this deceleration, whereas after 1973 it has been general.

This suggests strongly that the fundamental explanation must lie in a change of conditions that took place around 1973–4: either the oil price shock or the weakening of demand. Of these two, I would attach weight to the latter far above the former, for reasons which I discuss below. But it is still possible that behind the veil of depressed demand, quite significant changes have taken place in the growth potential of the advanced capitalist world. In this section I briefly review some of these arguments.

It is almost impossible to judge the contribution which might have been made by the gradual exhaustion of the catching-up process, except to make comments based on general considerations. It seems inconceivable that the Japanese economy could go on indefinitely achieving the productivity growth rates of the 1960s as it approached the technological frontier across an ever-widening field of activity, and similar comments could be made about the most advanced countries of Western Europe. But when and to what degree this process would have made itself felt, had other circumstances been propitious to growth, is largely a matter of conjecture. There was certainly little sign before 1973. It is interesting to note that the absolute difference in productivity growth rates between Western Europe and North America has remained almost unaltered through the recession, although the employment experience has been quite different (employment has continued to grow strongly in North America but stagnated in Europe). However the Japanese advance over West Germany and France has been almost eliminated.

Another possibility is that the rate of technical progress (i.e. the outward movement of the technical frontier rather than the approach of economies to that frontier) has slowed. Casual observation does not suggest strong evidence for this (witness the publicity surrounding the micro-chip and its potential effects on employment), but industrial research and development expenditure, which had grown fast up until 1967, has stagnated in real terms since then, exhibiting a trend away from 'basic' research and more risky projects to ones with a more certain return.[8] It is possible that this reflects a perception by companies that the returns to R & D expenditure have fallen off, but since these are hard to calculate, it is more likely that it is simply a response to increasing financial pressures on firms and governments. In any case it is hard to believe that this stagnation of expenditure has yet had adverse effects on the rate of innovation, because of the speed of growth up until 1967. The plateau of expenditure which has been reached is a high one by historical standards, and there is a significant time-lag before these additions to the stock of intellectual know-how find their full use in the production process (Griliches, 1980).

It has been suggested that the high productivity growth rates of the 1960s represented a once-for-all shift towards more capital-intensive techniques, as a consequence of a general state of business euphoria, fast-rising labour costs and increasingly generous tax treatment of investment (sometimes supplemented by government subsidies).[9] There is some evidence for a rise in the capital–output ratio during this period, so that a part of the increase in labour productivity could be ascribed to a movement along a production function rather than a movement of the function itself. But given that the relative cost trends have not since been sharply reversed, it is difficult to use this idea to explain the subsequent productivity slowdown, and I do not see it as more than a rather small factor in the overall pattern.

A further argument which has been made is that more stringent environmental protection regulations have deterred firms from investing in new equipment. Since the gainers cannot be charged for the cleanness of the atmosphere and the rivers, the extra capital costs must be borne by the firm and will depress the rate of return on the project. This point has been emphasised particularly in the United States, where its effects have been compounded by new regulations on health and safety at work. In their 1979 *Annual Report* the Council of Economic Advisers put the possible effect of compliance with the regulations as high as a 0.4 per cent fall in the productivity growth rate, with pollution abatement accounting for as much as 5 per cent of business fixed investment in 1977. A figure of 4 per cent for the same year has been cited for West Germany (Giersch and Wolter, 1983). However for the OECD as a whole in the 1970s, a more realistic estimate of the effects on productivity growth would be not more than 0.2 per cent p.a. (Lindbeck, 1983).

Possibly of slightly greater importance has been the impact of structural changes in the economy. The service sector, characterised by relatively slow productivity growth, has grown in importance in all countries, whilst the flow of labour out of agriculture into higher-productivity occupations is now much reduced. Lindbeck calculates the effect of the greater weight of the service sector as a reduction of productivity growth rates of about 0.3 per cent p.a. as compared with the 1960s, and the effects of reduced outflow from agriculture at roughly 0.2 per cent (but this must reflect in part the depressed demand for labour in other sectors rather than the shrinkage of rural labour reserves).

A final supply-side factor is the energy price shock. The impact of OPEC actions on distributional conflicts, macroeconomic policy and expectations in the advanced capitalist countries I shall discuss below. Here I merely consider the question of whether the tremendous increase in the relative price of energy could have some direct bearing on the productivity slowdown. The argument is that firms were induced to carry out a substitution of other inputs into the production process for energy, including labour. This adaptation could not all be carried out immediately, and so it expressed itself in a depressed rate of productivity growth over some years rather than a sudden fall. Though superficially appealing, this argument suffers from three major weaknesses.

(1) The rise in energy prices to final users was much less than that of the world crude oil price, because of the element of transport costs and taxation in the consuming countries; taxation policy in particular has been directed towards cushioning the effect on the consumer (though this has been markedly less true of the second oil price shock than the first).

(2) Energy is not a sufficiently large input into the economy, and the fall in its consumption per unit of national income

insufficiently great, to explain more than a tiny proportion of the productivity slowdown.

(3) Casual observation suggests that energy conservation has principally taken the form of influencing the design of new capital equipment rather than direct substitution in the immediate production process (this is most obvious in the energy-intensive transport sector, where the number of drivers per motor vehicle is still one, but considerable and successful efforts have been made by vehicle manufacturers to improve fuel consumption on new models).

Thus direct substitution effects of the oil price increase can be disregarded as far as productivity trends are concerned. This is even more true of other raw materials whose prices boomed in 1972–4. Producers of these were unable to form an effective cartel to stabilise prices in the face of depressed demand, and with some cyclical fluctuations their terms of trade gains have been steadily wiped out. By 1982 non-oil commodity prices had fallen to their lowest level relative to the prices of manufactured exports since the Second World War (EO 32, p. 40).

Altogether, I find it difficult to attribute to supply-side factors more than about one percentage point of the deceleration of labour productivity growth in the advanced capitalist countries since 1973.[10] This is substantial, but as Table 6.5 shows it accounts for less than half of the deceleration which has occurred. The remainder has to be explained by the depressed demand conditions and their impact on the rate of investment (investment decisions are so clearly sensitive to macroeconomic conditions that reduced capital inputs cannot seriously be regarded as an exogenous supply-side factor). Investment I discuss in more detail below; suffice it to say at this point that since it has held up quite well it cannot explain very much of the productivity deceleration (Matthews, 1982). This leaves us with the direct relationship between demand and productivity growth.

There is a well-known *short-run* relationship between demand and labour productivity, according to which productivity rises above trend in booms and falls below it in slumps: this pattern is normally attributed to the costs of hiring and firing labour, in terms of both money and goodwill. Such an explanation will not do for a prolonged deceleration, since it would pay firms to have a big shake-out of superfluous labour. But it is not easy to find alternative ideas in the literature, which tends to arrive at a conclusion about the effects of altered demand conditions as a residual after making estimates of other factors, and leave it at that.

My own instinct is to believe that this longer-term sensitivity of productivity growth to demand conditions reflects a combination of inertia and the conflicting interests of the parties in the production process. When both the level and the growth rate of demand are high, as was the case before 1973, pressures and attitudes are favourable to productivity growth. For management, there is a continuous pressure to increase output to meet the growth of demand, despite frequent delays in recruiting additional labour and replacing workers who leave. This pressure of orders automatically takes up any areas of slack in resource use and is transmitted down the hierarchy of the firm to production workers, who may be offered financial incentives to finish projects more quickly or agree to productivity-enhancing reorganisations of the work process. On the workers' side, there is little reason to oppose such improvements, since they know that demand for the firm's output is growing and jobs elsewhere are not hard to come by. This may not be true of declining industries or skilled crafts threatened with extinction by technical change, but as a generalisation it is true that workers feel secure about their employment prospects in such conditions.

When the level and growth rate of demand are low, as has been the case in the last decade, all this goes into reverse. Workers perceive that the job market is extremely bleak, and that with output stagnant, productivity improvements are liable to lead to redundancies. They feel insecure, and as far as possible they hide any elements of spare capacity in their own job; such elements will in any case tend to persist much longer when demand is weak. And whilst workers try to reduce the intensity of work to preserve employment, the pressure on and from management to increase output is also weakened. Short order books encourage vigorous marketing but not the speeding up of production. The inertia of the system now operates to preserve slack rather than to eliminate it.

This seems to me a plausible explanation of the ways in which weak demand conditions can operate to reduce productivity growth in the medium term, and I see no reason why its effects could not amount to 1–1½ per cent p.a., which is the order of the deceleration to be explained (consider, for example, the role often ascribed to the human element in the growth performance of Japan or the UK). Structural changes, environmental protection measures and the approach of other economies to US standards of living may all have contributed something to the slowdown, but by no means everything. If my estimates of the demand effect are correct, then the cumulative shortfall in productivity had reached 10–15 per cent by 1983 (compared with the level that could have been expected under stronger demand conditions), so that if we allow 5 per cent for reduced employment, the cost in lost output would amount to 15–20 per cent of GNP. This is a very large cost, and macroeconomic policy must be judged against this background.

The Inflationary Process

Inflation figures in all explanations of the breakdown of the post-war boom, but its causes remain a matter of dispute. There are certainly many historical circumstances in which inflation has emerged as a consequence of excessive effective demand, and Monetarists view current inflationary problems in similar light. Most non-Monetarists, however, regard this approach as too simple, and stress various elements of 'cost-push' in modern inflation which differentiates it from earlier historical episodes. I do not wish to retrace the well-trodden paths of this controversy, but the Monetarist stress on price expectations deserves a more critical analysis than it often receives.

The principal reason for examining this issue is that, as mentioned in the section on policy errors, the blame for the current recession can only be attached to past over-expansion of demand if it can be plausibly maintained that the inflationary process has been sustained during the recession by sticky expectations. The appeal of this hypothesis has been weakened by the lack of symmetry between the acceleration and the much slower deceleration, but it still commands a fair degree of support.

The theoretical argument for including price expectations in the theory of wage- and price-setting was one of the novelties introduced by Friedman, and it has been accepted with remarkably little fundamental criticism by other economists. To Friedman the justification was the neoclassical argument that competition in the labour market would determine the *real* wage, combined with the empirical fact that wage contracts were typically negotiated in money terms but covered significant periods of time, so that the real wage to which they would correspond was uncertain and would depend on the prices that would prevail on average during the period of the contract. Friedman postulated that if everyone anticipated price rises of 5 per cent, the money wage negotiated would be 5 per cent higher than if stability of prices was expected.

But can this superficially appealing idea be justified in microeconomic terms? Not on the basis of perfect competition, because then the wage-rate would be reset every day and price expectations would not enter into it. There would be no incentive for any employer to offer wage stability over any greater time period, since on any particular day either he would be paying over the market rate, or he would find no takers because he was offering less than his competitors. Thus perfect competition offers no solution; it cannot explain lengthy wage contracts. An alternative is to assume that the labour market is basically a competitive one, but information on the state of the labour market is hard to come by, thus making use of some form of search theory as in Phelps (1968). But besides the fact that there are important ways in which the predictions of search theory contradict observed reality (Tobin, 1972), these theories are not based on expected *prices* but on the expected *wage offers* of other firms. There is no intrinsic reason why workers should believe these to be moving in line with prices, or more closely in line with prices than the wages paid by their existing employer – and without this assumption, prices do not enter into the theory. But in a general competitive model with lengthy wage contracts, a positive inflation rate implies a higher real wage at the beginning of the contract than at the end, so a wage increase below the expected inflation rate is still attractive initially. Expected prices will only induce workers to reject such a wage offer if one imposes the assumption that they cannot quit and find a higher-paying job half-way through the contract, when the real wage falls to the level at which they would prefer to be unemployed. Without this assumption, it is hard to see why an employer (who presumably already has sufficient labour at the old wage, or wages would have been increased previously) should face a withdrawal of labour on the basis that the offered increase does not match the workers' price expectations, since it still represents a short-run increase in the real wage.[11]

Thus the picture offered by Monetarists, of price expectations influencing wage determination in a competitive market through the decisions of individual economic agents in isolation from one another, lacks any ready microeconomic justification. Let us turn now to the Monetarist explanation of recent historical experience. The acceleration of inflation is attributed to bouts of excess demand, whilst its reluctance to decelerate in the face of obvious excess supply can only be explained by the 'stickiness' of expectations, i.e. that inflationary expectations are dominated by recent experience. This has been heavily criticised by exponents of the New Classical Macroeconomics, who have used the idea of rational expectations to show that it would be sufficient (under Monetarist assumptions) for the government to announce that money supply growth was going to be halted, for inflation to stop – provided the government is believed. Governments have made many attempts to persuade people that their policies would bring about radical reductions in the inflation rate, and in the Monetarist model it would only have been necessary for one of these attempts to have been successful for the inflation rate to fall. Thus Monetarists are really forced to argue that people are so certain of their own inflation forecasts (which are simply based on past experience and not on any economic theory) that they ignore the statements of governments completely.

But why should this happen? If the government is trying hard to persuade people that the inflation rate next year will be lower than this, there is an obvious incentive for employers to offer wage contracts on this basis. But by the same reasoning as before, there is no obvious reason for workers to reject them, because the real wage is highest at the beginning of the contract. To break into an inflationary spiral founded on sticky expectations alone should not be difficult.

I would suggest that what governments have found hard to influence is not price expectations but real wage aspirations. In an imperfect labour market, wages are not determined purely by market forces but by a bargaining process, and it is more or less impossible to distinguish the element of *price expectations* in wage claims from the element of compensation for *past inflation*. To accept wage increases based on an assumed deceleration of inflation implies that there will not be full compensation for the erosion of real wages during the previous wage contract. This is the real problem. Where workers have accepted lower wage increases in return for the promise of lower inflation, they have often later sought to make up for the adverse impact on their real wages by demanding higher wage increases, which then erase all of the gains on the inflation front (a classic example of this is the UK experience of 1975–9). This phenomenon is not explicable by the 'sticky expectations' thesis. In sum, I would suggest (and I shall elaborate on this in the next section) that price expectations are not the essence of the modern inflationary process; distributional conflicts are.

Distributional Conflicts

In Chapter 4 I suggested some reasons why distributional conflicts were muted in the advanced countries in the immediate post-war period: popular aspirations were depressed by recent historical experience; growth rates were high and employment unusually secure; the atmosphere of the Cold War bred a sense of external danger which discouraged internal dissent and split the labour movement in many countries. The slogan with which Macmillan won the 1959 election in Britain – 'you've never had it so good' – expressed a genuine feeling of contentment with post-war experience. Ten years later the same slogan would have been even more true in an economic sense – but it had ceased to represent the popular mood in any country.

Over the last quarter of a century we have witnessed a sharp increase in the intensity of distributional conflicts. The resulting upward pressure on production costs has been met by raising prices – a process which governments have generally permitted in order to protect company profitability. The conflicts have involved several dimensions: producers of raw materials, state expenditure and the burden of taxation, and enhanced popular aspirations.

Popular aspirations have risen with the apparent stability of the new regime of full employment, prosperity and growth and the fading from memory of the earlier era of insecurity. People have come to expect that work will be readily available for those who are seriously looking for it, and that economic development will make their lives steadily easier and materially better. In the 1960s expectations adapted to the historical realities of the post-war period. The rate of growth of real wages set up in the 1950s, and then historically unprecedented in most countries, came to be built into people's aspirations. The breathing space gained by capital in the 1950s came to an end. At the same time the lessening of international tensions created a more favourable atmosphere for the expression of internal discontent.

This is a highly schematic view, but one which is broadly reflected in the politics of the period. The 1950s were undoubtedly a period of the dominance of the right in the major countries, although in France a stable regime of this kind was not established until 1958. During the 1960s the right either lost power for a prolonged period (United States, Britain, West Germany, Canada) or came under increasing challenge from the left (France, Italy). There were increasingly overt signs of discontent amongst various social groups (racial minorities, students) and, towards the end of the decade, a marked rise of industrial militancy (Crouch and Pizzorno, 1978). All these events reflected, I would argue, the erosion of fundamental satisfaction with the evolution of the post-war world which had existed earlier. Ambitions for improvements in the quality of life began to dominate gratefulness for a new security, and this was expressed in demands for higher wage increases, longer holidays and challenges to management control over production. The 1950s had appeared to many to signal the integration of the working class into a newly stabilised and democratic capitalism; the later 1960s in particular saw the shattering of this illusion.

The theme underlying this analysis is that the aspirations of the populace reflect with a certain time-lag the growth rates which the economic system generates. It is not sufficient for capitalism just to provide a high *level* of consumption for the mass of the population; any level, once it becomes a matter of habit, is built into the worker's idea of fair compensation for work. Discontent could be stifled by growth: the continual provision of higher levels of real wages to which the population has not yet adapted psychologically. But growth is far from being a secret. New products, technological breakthroughs in consumer goods and fundamental improvements in the production process receive a great deal of publicity. Particularly after 1960, growth rates received an enormous amount of attention, especially in the form of international comparisons. The growth process is built into the social imagination' through science fiction and futurology. Thus people have come to demand, in the post-war period, a living standard which exceeds their previous experience and reflects the growth of labour productivity. In itself, this need not be inflationary or eat into company profitability. But it does mean that the room for manoeuvre provided by the gap between productivity growth rates and workers' aspirations in the 1950s has been eroded, and the equilibrium acquired a new delicacy which could easily be disturbed by any adverse circumstances.

Such adverse trends became significant in the 1960s because of the growth of state expenditure and the movements of commodity prices, which first of all ceased to be favourable (relative to industrial products) and then in the early 1970s became seriously unfavourable (OECD, 1977, Chart 9). The OECD countries as a group are essentially importers of food and raw materials and exporters of manufactures. Any unfavourable trend in the terms of trade between industrial and primary products therefore implies that the real income of these countries will grow more slowly than their output. Events such as the commodity price boom of 1972–3 can thereby add an important extra twist to distributional conflicts in the industrial countries. If workers try to compensate for the erosion of their real wages by demanding higher money wage increases, then the whole inflationary process is shifted up several notches. This is what happened in 1972–3. It is what did *not* happen in the Korean War price boom: the working population could be more easily induced to accept the extra cost burden, because their aspirations were not so elevated, and the inflationary bubble was quickly deflated.

Public expenditure is less straightforward because it confers benefits as well as imposing costs in the form of taxation. Thus, even if state expenditure and taxation grow in line with national income, so that post-tax and pre-tax incomes rise at the same rate, we cannot be sure that the perceived benefits of state expenditure are rising in line with their cost. Nevertheless, it is not unreasonable to suppose that, if the tax burden does no more than keep pace with income as income rises, the population would regard that as acceptable. This is broadly what was happening in the advanced capitalist countries from the end of the Korean War to around 1960, and it was accompanied by a marked shift in the composition of public spending away from military to other purposes, associated with the decline in international tension.

Since 1960, however, the picture has been rather different. Declines in military expenditure as a share of GDP have been much smaller, and insufficient to compensate for continued growth in the share of other areas of public expenditure. In the average OECD country public expenditure grew 21 per cent faster than GDP between 1960 and 1976, with the share of GDP at current prices represented by public expenditure rising from 28.5 per cent in 1955–7 to 34.5 per cent in 1967–9 and 41.4 per cent in 1974–6 (OECD, 1978b). This is a substantial increase. One element of it has been the expansion of current expenditure on goods and services (this was negligible in France and Japan, but amounted to about five percentage points of GDP for the average country). This was almost entirely due to the so-called 'relative price effect': in volume terms public consumption did not increase its share of GDP as conventionally measured, but its relative cost increased because of slow productivity growth. But the more important element has been the increase in government transfers to households, which grew from an average of 7.5 per cent of GDP in 1960 to 13.9 per cent in 1976. The bulk of this has come from an extension of the coverage of income maintenance and public health schemes and, to a lesser extent, educational expenditures; demographic changes and improvements in benefits have also played a minor part.

This expansion in welfare expenditures obviously reflects a strong social preference for the development of adequate insurance against poverty, ill health or misfortune as real income rises. In this period the existence of such schemes was commonly regarded as the test of a caring, civilised society. Yet a striking feature of such programmes is that they essentially involve a transfer from the economically active to the economically inactive – the aged, unemployed, disabled, students. Those who pay the additional taxes do not by and large receive the benefits, at least in the present; their acceptance of the burden depends on their sense of belonging to a caring community and the thought that in the future they may well themselves be beneficiaries of the system. Moreover, although as electors they support the extension of welfare benefits, they may not appreciate the full cost to themselves in additional taxation; the individual does not make a co-ordinated decision to pay additional taxes for such-and-such a purpose, and may well believe that the revenue should be raised from some other source. Thus the existence of obvious benefits from welfare expenditure does not necessarily signal that the additional tax burden is willingly accepted. This is even more true of the expansion of the share of public consumption caused by the relative price effect, which simply reflects the slower productivity growth of the public sector.

There is quite strong evidence that in this period there *was* considerable reluctance to accept the additional tax burden (which mainly took the form of an increasing share of social security contributions and direct taxes on households), in the sense that workers tried to compensate for it by demanding higher money wages (OECD, 1978b, Appendix B and references there cited). If it is true that by the early 1960s workers' aspirations for real wage increases were close to the rate of growth of labour productivity, the effect of the increasing tax burden on *post-tax* real wages growth was sufficient to create substantial discontent, and probably had much to do with the growth of industrial conflict in Western Europe in the later 1960s. The pressure for higher money wages was largely accommodated, because oligopolistic market structures permitted companies to defend their profits by raising prices. In this, however, they were not entirely successful: although the share of profits was broadly maintained up until 1969, there are signs of a decline after that date in a number of countries (US, Japan, West Germany, UK, Italy; Hill, 1979). The failure to insulate profits completely is usually attributed to an intensification of competition associated with the fast growth of international trade (Lindbeck, 1983).

Thus by the late 1960s distributional pressures were leading to a significant intensification of the inflationary process, as a result of the growth of popular aspirations combined with a rising burden of taxation. The problem was then seriously exacerbated, first by the commodity price boom of 1972–3, and then by the four-fold increase in oil prices imposed by OPEC in late 1973. Since the working population was not in a mood to accept the burden of this worsening of the terms of trade, the immediate effect was a sudden and sustained rise in inflation rates to double-digit levels.[12]

The reaction of governments, as we have seen, was to switch over to a much more restrictive policy stance, which they justified by reference to the inflation problem. It is worth asking, however, why they should have reacted in this way. It is far from obvious that inflation discourages investment. Because business profitability could be protected by price rises, the impact of cost pressures on profits in conditions of high demand was mild overall, although noticeable in some countries, and firms benefited from low real interest rates. The purely *economic* disadvantages of inflation for capitalist development do not seem great. The political effects are, however, potentially very damaging. Inflation creates an enormous degree of insecurity. In between pay settlements, wage and salary earners experience a continuous fall in their living standards with no guarantee that their next pay increase will be sufficient to compensate. Everyone feels that they have to run very fast in order to stand still; if they stop they will suddenly find their living standards cut by 10 or 20 per cent. Inflation is therefore experienced as very threatening, and liable to create quite arbitrary and sudden changes in income distribution. These effects can of course be reduced by indexation, but this practice was not widely adopted, in part because it automatically insulates wages against adverse movements in the terms of trade, and more generally, leads to wage bargaining in real rather than in money terms, which was felt, in the circumstances of the time, to be a dangerous idea. Thus inflation at double digit levels was unacceptable not because of its direct economic effects but because it threatened quickly to erode the political and social stability of the advanced capitalist countries.

The Oil Price Shocks

The first rise in oil prices, which was followed by a second massive increase over the years 1978–80, was important chiefly for two reasons: the distributional effects, and the impact on expec-

188 The Rise and Fall of Keynesian Economics

tations.[13] For the average OECD country, the terms of trade loss
of each of these two increases amounted to about 2 per cent of
GNP, that is to say less than a year's growth of per capita output
at pre-1973 rates. But despite the atmosphere of crisis surrounding the first oil shock workers were reluctant to accept any
downward shift in the trend of real wages. This pushed the costs of
the increase on to companies, the result being a marked fall in the
share of profits and a rise in the labour share of value added in
manufacturing (EO 32, Chart J). Real wage resistance also
meant that the deceleration of inflation was very slow: from a
peak of 13 per cent in 1974, the rate of increase of consumer prices
fell to 11 per cent in 1975, 8 per cent in 1976 and 7 per cent in 1978
(weighted average of seven major OECD countries).

The caution of macroeconomic policy during this period was a
direct response to the acuteness of conflicting claims over
resources. Although action was taken to support demand in late
1974 and 1975, as soon as the recession seemed to be over the main
concern was that the recovery should not be of such a speed as to
rekindle inflationary pressures.[14] Likely sources of such pressures
were (a) acceleration of wage increases with falling unemployment, (b) further rises in the relative price of oil if demand for it
continued to grow strongly, and (c) sharp increases in the prices of
other commodities, such as had occurred in 1976 when speculators bought in anticipation of a repeat of the 1972-3 price
explosion. Cautious demand management was a way of keeping
the lid on these pressures.

The result of these policies was that the recovery was a very
weak affair. For the OECD as a whole unemployment in 1978
was only a little below its 1975 peak. Despite slow progress on
conservation and substitution, the real price of oil even declined a
little, and other commodity prices fell back again. But depressed
demand squeezed profits, both through low capacity utilisation
and weak productivity growth, so that even though real wages
grew markedly more slowly than they had before 1973, the profits
share did not recover. The sizeable deficits in government
budgets opened up by the 1975 recession were not much reduced.

Clearly the 1973-4 oil price increase would have caused
difficulties in the advanced capitalist countries in any circumstances, because of the dependence on oil built up over the
previous two decades of declining relative price. But these

difficulties were immeasurably compounded by the distributional conflicts analysed above. If workers had been willing to forgo a year's growth in their real income, then the oil price increase could have fed through into consumer prices without further inflationary effects. The rate of inflation would have risen sharply in 1974, but fallen back equally sharply in 1975 (as happened in Japan), because money wages were not responding to the increase. It was the aspirations and frustrations built up over the previous years that fuelled real wage resistance and made workers unresponsive to official calls for sacrifice and restraint, despite the general atmosphere of crisis.

The second oil price shock, stimulated by the effects of the interruption of Iranian supplies on the spot market, provoked a much more concertedly restrictive response in the advanced capitalist countries than the first. The main reason for this was that the problems posed by the first increase had not yet been resolved: the inflationary bubble had proved so difficult to burst that it seemed vital to prevent the whole experience being repeated at a yet higher rate of inflation. This restrictive stance has been broadly maintained ever since. As a result unemployment has again increased markedly: on internationally standardised definitions it reached 8 per cent in 1982, compared with 5 per cent in 1979 and $5\frac{1}{2}$ per cent in 1975 (weighted average of seven major countries). This time money wages did not compensate to the same degree for the rise in energy prices, and the upward trend in real wages decelerated even further (EO 32, Table 20). With the help of further falls in commodity prices and a cut in the oil price in the face of the cumulative effects of conservation measures taken since 1974 and the rise in non-OPEC sources of supply, inflation in the major OECD countries managed to dip below 5 per cent in the first half of 1983. Despite a widespread commitment to cut the share of public expenditure in GDP, such a cut has not occurred, and restrictive fiscal action has taken the form of raising effective tax rates (OECD, 1983).

The past decade of economic history in the advanced capitalist countries could thus broadly be summarised as follows. The oil price shocks accentuated the inflationary problem because they came on top of distributional conflicts which were already acute; otherwise they would have merely resulted in a once-for-all jump in the price level. From 1975 onwards profits have been severely depressed by the combination of distributional pressures and weak demand; governments have deliberately allowed demand to remain weak to prevent these pressures from getting out of hand. In its immediate effect this policy has had a fair degree of success. Real wages growth decelerated significantly in 1974–8 and again after 1979; commodity prices have remained low; oil prices have started to fall back. But inflation remains at unacceptable levels and profit margins have not been rebuilt, because productivity growth has slowed down so much.

The deceleration of real wages represents an adjustment of aspirations in the face of a deteriorating economic environment, but it is a critical point whether this is just a temporary result of high unemployment or whether it would be maintained in the event of a strong recovery. If workers were now content with real wages growing much more slowly than in the 1960s, there could be little objection to a policy of vigorous expansion. There is no reason to be inhibited by the current size of the budget deficits, since with the exception of a few cases (notably Japan) they reflect cyclical influences and the recent high cost of debt finance rather than 'structural' factors (OECD, 1983). Productivity growth would accelerate and this would raise the share of profits and prevent rises in commodity prices from rekindling inflation. A virtuous circle of rising productivity, profits and investment might be established. But if workers react to any signs of an end to the recession by trying to make up for their recent sacrifices, money wage increases will accelerate and inflation will re-emerge. It is the fear of this – that the adjustment of aspirations is not yet complete and the basis of a non-inflationary expansion has not yet been laid – that sustains the generally cautious policy stance.

The aspirations problem offers an interesting perspective on political Monetarism of the Thatcher–Reagan variety. Behind a veil of archaic and dubious economic arguments this school clearly recognises the *ideological* component to the current problems of the advanced capitalist countries, in the sense that the expectations and assumptions built up in the post-war period are now inhibiting development. The emphasis on individualism and self-reliance and the extensive critique of the welfare state, state intervention and the collectivist mentality could be interpreted as a direct confrontation of the aspirations problem, attempting to reorganise the individual's expectations of society on to a much lower plane (for a more detailed exploration of these ideas see Bleaney, 1983). The risk that is being run, however, is that to change beliefs Monetarism has also had to change governmental practice, and the abandonment of Keynesian reflexes increases the danger of a serious collapse in demand, not only because of the way governments might react in a crisis but also because of the effect on business expectations.

Expectations and Investment

In the early 1930s investment collapsed, because of an unusual fallback in demand combined with a series of shocks to confidence. The 1973 oil price increase represented the nearest that we have since come to a repetition of these events. First of all the negative demand shock (because OPEC could not initially spend more than a fraction of its increased revenues) was added to policy measures that were already moving in a restrictive direction to produce a recession significantly deeper than any other in the post-war period, and which affected all the major countries simultaneously. In the second quarter of 1975 industrial production in the advanced capitalist world was more than 15 per cent below its previous peak (seasonally adjusted weighted average of seven major countries; EO 18, Table 16), and over the two years 1974 and 1975 growth in real GDP was virtually zero, compared with 7 per cent over the worst two-year period between 1960 and 1973. In conjunction with the obvious shift of macroeconomic policy in the direction of caution, this must have caused a sudden and major downward revision of demand forecasts in every industry.

Secondly, there was the traumatic realisation that the life-style of the West had become dependent on a resource which was (a) finite in quantity and (b) under the control of people who could no longer be persuaded or forced to supply what was demanded at prices little above short-run marginal cost. Between 1950 and 1970 the price of oil had not risen at all, so that there had been a steady substitution of it for other energy sources, which could not be immediately reversed. At the same time political developments in the oil-producing countries, as in the rest of the developing world, had caused their governments to abandon the consistently pro-Western positions of the 1950s and take a much more nationalistic, anti-imperialist line. The ability of OPEC to raise oil prices massively and make the increase stick underlined both the political changes and the absence of alternative sources of supply – a reflection of the paucity of known reserves at existing prices and rates of extraction. It thus emphasised both how much the boom had been dependent on plentiful and cheap sources of energy and how unlikely such an era was ever to return. Indeed a much more immediate.question was whether producers of other raw materials would be able to establish a cartel of similar effectiveness.

Thus the OPEC action was widely perceived as marking the end of an era in which conditions for economic growth in the advanced capitalist countries had been exceptionally favourable; the general expectation was that macroeconomic policy would now face more difficult problems and would be considerably more cautious than before. The period 1973–5 thereby re-enacted two of the conditions that had precipitated the Great Slump of 1929–33: a sharp recession, combined with a severe expectational jolt. On that occasion business confidence was damaged first by the Wall Street crash and then by bank failures, and investment spending collapsed. What prevented a similar collapse of investment in the mid-1970s?

Although other factors are involved, I would suggest that the strong action taken by governments to support demand in 1975 through fiscal measures was very important. Budget deficits were allowed to rise from an average of only 1 per cent of GNP in 1974 to over 4 per cent in 1975. As Table 6.3 indicates, not only were the automatic stabilisers permitted to do their work fully, but the strongest positive discretionary measures of the decade were taken in that year, involving six out of the seven major countries (the exception was the UK). A policy reflex of this kind was the product of a Keynesian era and its importance in putting a stop to the decline should not be underestimated. After 1929 the world economy found itself trapped in a vicious circle of decline in which bankruptcies caused financial crises leading to a fall back in investment which cut demand, causing more bankruptcies and inducing governments to bring in measures to reduce budget deficits, thus cutting demand and investment even further. The fiscal measures of 1975 were a firm brake on that downward spiral. Precisely what would have happened otherwise we can never know, but one point in particular should be remembered: if Keynesian theory had not existed to say that a fast-rising budget deficit in such a situation was acceptable, then in all probability good reason would have been found for regarding it as unacceptable, and the recession would have been compounded by government deflationary action as in 1929–33.[15]

After 1975, macroeconomic policy was first of all cautious and then, from 1979 onwards, actively restrictive. Yet private investment expenditure has been surprisingly buoyant: as Table 6.6 shows, it has grown much more slowly in the 1970s than before, but it still managed to be higher in 1980 than in 1973. Moreover this is clearly not because companies are expecting demand to grow at the same rate as before 1973. The evidence of rising capacity utilisation rates relative to unemployment rates (EO 31, Chart D) suggests that the investment which has taken place since 1973 has been predominantly defensive and rationalising: cutting costs by introducing new techniques but not markedly increasing potential output. Factors which may have helped to maintain investment include the following:

Table 6.6 *Growth rates of private non-residential fixed investment, 1967–80*

	Average % p.a.	
	1967–73	1973–80
United States	4.3	2.0
EEC	8.2	1.3
Japan	13.5	2.4

SOURCE   OECD, *Economic Survey of Japan* (July 1981), p. 37.

(1) The major relative price change (for energy) was upwards rather than downwards, as had been the case after 1929 (agriculture and raw materials). This stimulated new investment in oil exploration and energy conservation, whereas the effect of the collapse of primary product prices in the early 1930s was precisely the opposite. In addition the knock-on

effect on the absolute price level in the mid-1970s helped to keep real interest rates low or even negative, whereas the falling prices of 1930–2 pushed real interest rates very high.

(2) The absence of a major financial crisis, which in the 1930s had devastating effects on confidence. This is related to the first point, since bank failures in the United States had been closely linked to the inability of farmers to repay loans or even maintain interest payments on their debts. Improved policy reactions were also of some importance here, central banks having acted swiftly to support the banking system during the secondary banking crisis of 1974.

(3) The existence of considerable fiscal incentives to investment, in the form of subsidies and tax reliefs, which had become available in almost all major countries during the post-war period, and were if anything strengthened in the 1974–5 recession (additional incentives introduced in this period are summarised in EO 19, pp. 29–31).

(4) The greater resilience of the international monetary system to the strains which were imposed on it. In the 1920s tariff barriers were already higher than they had been in 1913, and this tendency was greatly accentuated by the slump. Moreover the impact on confidence of the collapse of the gold standard system was severe. In the 1970s the flexible exchange rate system, which had been forced on the major countries by events, did permit the strains to be accommodated more easily. But the most important factor was the greater commitment of the advanced capitalist countries to a collective solution to the crisis. This did not generate anything very positive, but it did mean that governments were reluctant to give way to the rising political pressures for protectionism. As I suggested in Chapter 4, this owed more to changes in world politics than to intellectual conversion.

(5) Continued competitive pressure on companies to introduce new techniques and more advanced products. Despite the continued trend towards industrial concentration within countries, the reductions in tariff barriers and transport costs have reduced national markets to sections of a world market, in which product innovation and technological sophistication have been the main competitive weapon (consider, for example, the car industry). This has imposed on each

individual company high levels of research and development expenditure and periodic retooling, under threat of being left behind by its competitors.

The buoyancy of investment in the 1970s and 1980s has clearly been important in restricting the extent of the slump. It may be, however, that with governments moving away from Keynesianism, any further major shocks to confidence could lead to sizeable cutbacks in investment expenditure, of an order which we have not yet seen.

Conclusions

In this chapter I have offered an interpretation of the current position of the advanced capitalist countries which sees restrictive demand management as an attempt to restore stability to an economic system threatened by severe distributional conflicts. Inflation is the safety valve which releases the pressure in the short run, by allowing wages and prices to leapfrog over one another, but it creates such tremendous insecurity in the population as to threaten the existing political order if ignored for any length of time. Since direct state regulation of wages has not been regarded as politically acceptable, and milder forms of incomes policy have had limited success, the restriction of demand has been the chief weapon for relieving the pressure on profit margins, although its effects on productivity growth have meant that the share of profits has remained low.

These distributional conflicts were not significant in the 1930s, but the slump was certainly exacerbated by misguided policy actions. The experience of 1974–5 shows that those policy lessons had been well learnt. Monetary authorities were keenly aware of the dangers of a banking collapse, and sizeable discretionary fiscal measures were taken to support demand. Without this, a repetition of 1929–33 was certainly a possibility, although by no means inevitable. Since then fiscal policy attitudes have shifted significantly back towards pre-Keynesian notions, and though this has been partly offset by political commitments to high military expenditures, the combination of this with the strains on the banking system from major debtor nations does raise the possibility of a further collapse. Since the price in sacrificed output that has been paid for these policies is already enormous, such a prospect is horrific to contemplate.

This retreat from Keynesianism can be seen as a reflection of the fact that the recession has so far only done half its job in recreating the conditions for a renewed phase of expansion in the capitalist world. A temporary move down the Phillips curve (expectations-augmented or not) has proved not to be enough; the pressures on profitability could not be dissipated as easily as that. Popular aspirations have been depressed by adverse circumstances, and the pretensions of commodity producers have been similarly checked; but profitability has also suffered badly from these same policies, and the pressures threaten to re-emerge as soon as the recession seems to be over. The ideological atmosphere of the 1950s has not yet been recreated; the atmosphere of the 1960s still persists quite strongly under the veil of sharply changed macroeconomic conditions. Given the opportunity workers would want to start again where they left off in the early 1970s, and any vigorous pump-priming experiment on a world scale would at the moment in all probability lead to a re-eruption of inflationary pressures.

The recognition that the problems are deep-seated has encouraged the more structural approach characteristic of Monetarism, which confronts the ideological issues more directly than any government committed to the consensus of the post-war period has done, but in the process has been forced to challenge a whole range of established beliefs. Keynesian notions have not escaped the assault, because of their association with a commitment to full and secure employment of the workforce no matter how 'unproductive' and inefficient such work might be. It is possible to understand the logical steps by which we have reached the present situation; what is much less comprehensible is the deeper logic of accepting such immense sacrifices of output for the preservation of a social system dominated by private economic interests.

Notes to Chapter 6

1. Interest rates would seem to be a poor measure of monetary stance in this period for the well-known reason that their movements will reflect, in part,

changes in the expected rate of inflation, whilst a narrower measure of the money supply than M2 is more likely to be influenced by the feedback effect of economic activity on money demand. In a time of important changes in import prices even a very broad measure of changes in the price of domestic value added, such as the GDP deflator, will not reflect the direct impact of import price movements, so that the narrower (and politically more sensitive) consumer price index seems preferable.

2. For the dates at which the major countries first adopted published monetary targets, see OECD, *Monetary Targets and Inflation Control* (Paris, 1979), Table 1.

3. The measure used in this table, which is that currently favoured by the OECD, differs from that used to derive Table 6.3 chiefly in abandoning any form of weighting of different items in the budget. It is also of opposite sign, and gives a slightly different picture of discretionary action for the years for which the two calculations overlap. Comments in the narrative are based on the source for Table 6.4, since it is the later publication and uses simpler estimating procedures.

4. Since I shall be making a number of references to *OECD Economic Outlook* in the course of this chapter, I use the convention of referring to it as EO followed by the number of the relevant issue.

5. A somewhat similar categorisation appears in OECD (1977).

6. There is also the point that 'overshooting' is in part self-justifying through its impact on the domestic inflation rate.

7. M2 grew at an annual rate of more than 15 per cent over the three-year period 1971–3 in the seven major OECD countries.

8. For a detailed discussion of R & D trends in an international context see OECD, *Technical change and economic policy: science and technology in the new social context* (Paris, 1980), especially Chapter 3.

9. See the chapters by Sargent and Glyn in Matthews (1982).

10. This 1 per cent would consist of 0.2 for environmental protection, 0.4 for structural changes and 0.4 for the slowdown of catch-up (consisting of zero for North America and an average of 0.7 for the rest of the OECD area).

11. The above argument considers only the situation of a worker who receives a wage offer implicitly based on an expected inflation rate lower than his own. However, Friedman assumes that the whole population has the same expectations, so that one could argue that employers would always willingly offer wage increases consistent with workers' price expectations. But my analysis suggests that there is little incentive for them to do so, since workers would accept a lower offer. Employers would do better to offer smaller increases, combined either with a shorter contract period or some form of indexation.

12. My explanation emphasises ideological factors rather than the erosion of labour surpluses and the tightness of labour markets in the sixties as compared with the fifties, a point which is stressed by Mandel (1975) and many other Marxists. My scepticism with regard to this argument derives from a number of considerations: the failure of the reappearance of significant labour market slack after 1974 to produce a rapid resolution of inflationary pressures; the similarity of patterns of money wage movements

between countries with and without significant reserves of labour at the beginning of the period; and the lack of strong evidence that labour reserves were a major factor containing industrial militancy in the 1950s, other than in Italy.

13. The imbalances created in the international balance of payments by the fact that the OPEC nations could not immediately spend their vastly increased foreign exchange earnings created difficulties initially, but by 1975 the advanced industrial countries had succeeded in passing the counterpart deficit onto the developing world. In subsequent years the deficit shifted between these two groups of countries, but it never operated as a major constraint on macroeconomic policy in the advanced countries (the OPEC surplus disappeared in 1982 under the impact of falling oil prices). The deflationary impact of OPEC saving did, however, add to the depth of the 1975 recession.

14. For a semi-official statement see EO 19. The 'narrow path of recovery' recommended by the international group of experts who wrote *Towards Full Employment and Price Stability* reflects a similar line of thinking.

15. It is worth mentioning that this 'public sector automatic stabiliser' was augmented by a 'private sector automatic stabiliser' which had developed since the 1930s, namely the reduced sensitivity of employment to short-run fluctuations in output. This has helped to maintain workers' consumption during recessions, though at the expense of greater fluctuations in productivity (relative to trend) and in company profits.

7
Conclusion

From the mid-1960s Keynesianism clearly began to fall out of fashion in the academic world, and though this process may now be beginning to reverse itself, the influence of Keynesian ideas on policy-makers is as low as it has ever been since 1945. Nowadays there is a general fatalism about macroeconomic questions and a widespread belief that a policy of fiscal expansion cannot achieve very much to reduce unemployment. The experience of the Socialist Government in France, which attempted to expand in isolation and fairly quickly had to backtrack and introduce an austerity package, has reinforced such beliefs, although in today's highly integrated world the chances of success for an *individual* country which bucks the general trend towards deflation are far lower than for an *international* policy shift, because of the tendency to suck in imports and the interactions between monetary policy, expectations, exchange rates and inflation.

Is such disillusionment with Keynesianism justified? On the theoretical plane, I have argued quite categorically that it is not. The fundamental Keynesian arguments have not been demolished by Monetarism and its offshoots; they have simply been ignored. The *General Theory* was essentially an elaborate discussion of the point that the price mechanism could not be relied on to cure the short-run instabilities of a capitalist economy, as the neoclassical tradition had implicitly assumed. Through the multiplier mechanism, disturbances would be amplified, and falls in money wages and prices would not necessarily stop the rot because of their potentially damaging effects on confidence. The Great Depression represented a state where business confidence, or 'the state of long-term expectation', was so depressed that there was no obvious cure without vigorous governmental action to expand effective demand. Neoclassical economics had assumed that price adjustments would act as a powerful stabilising force, as indicated in their simple models of individual markets, but it had always neglected the point that the demand and supply curves in one market would be shifted by disturbances in other markets. It was Keynes who exposed the seriousness of this omission.

The Modigliani–Patinkin response that Keynes's unemployment equilibrium was unlikely to be a long-run equilibrium engaged more with the title of the book than the meat of the argument. It appeared to restore to neoclassical theory the claim to generality, but only by basing long-run propositions on the short-run model. In Keynes's formal exposition he took expectations as exogenous, but his verbal comments indicate that it is precisely the endogeneity of these expectations which carries the danger of converting a short-run disturbance into a deep depression. No amount of playing with the formal model will ever come to grips with this point.

It is the enduring merit of the Clower–Leijonhufvud interpretation of Keynes to have placed his ideas within the context of the neoclassical general equilibrium model, and to have demonstrated their applicability to the issue of the stability of that equilibrium, a matter which the neoclassical tradition had systematically ignored. This brings the emphasis back to the short-run dynamics of the system, where Keynes himself placed it. By emphasising the loyalty of Keynes to traditional neoclassical assumptions, this interpretation has also brought out what the Keynesian revolution was *not* – it was not a radically new vision of socio-economic life as a whole. The demonstration of the short-run instabilities of a capitalist economy had powerful implications and revolutionised macroeconomic theory, but it emerged from an essentially neoclassical structure.

The Monetarists have not entered into these debates at all. In Friedman's 1968 lecture and in the writings of the New Classical Macroeconomics, policy conclusions are drawn from models in which the price mechanism does for the macroeconomy exactly what it did for Alfred Marshall in his fish market: if there is excess supply prices fall and if there is excess demand they rise to the point where the market is cleared. When we come to the issue of expectations, anxieties about possible demand constraints on sales are removed altogether by assumption. All producers are allowed to assume that they can sell anything which they think they can profitably produce. With these two hypotheses we are back in the world of Say's Law. Yet no reason has been offered by these writers for rejecting the arguments of the *General Theory*.

As far as practice is concerned, I have argued, in the preceding chapters, that Keynesian fiscal policies made a substantial contribution both to the recovery of some countries in the 1930s and to the long post-war boom. After the war the commitment to active fiscal measures when required sustained business confidence and helped to create a remarkably stable environment for investment and technical innovation. When this began to change in the early 1970s, Keynesian reactions prevented a repetition of the 1930s collapse.

But this period of spectacular growth, high employment and massive structural change also bore within it the seeds of some fundamentally new developments. In particular some trends which had been observable since the breakdown of feudalism reached their logical conclusion. For the first time democratic political institutions became firmly established throughout the advanced capitalist world. Traditional peasant agriculture, which had formed such a large segment of the economic activity of many countries up until 1945, contracted at a hectic rate, and brought the vast majority of the population into contact with urban and industrial conditions. The global challenge of socialism reached a new dimension.

With these developments came important changes in social thought. Traditional ideologies of hierarchy were displaced by various forms of egalitarianism. The commitment to economic growth reflected competition between rival social systems and a desire that affluence should become the privilege of all. The insecurity which had been a characteristic of working-class experience in earlier phases of capitalism largely disappeared; few lamented it, and belief in the capacity and desirability of the state to assuage the harsh outcomes of market forces steadily grew. Outside North America the speed of change contrasted vividly with the rather sluggish pace of pre-war life, and in the new solidly democratic atmosphere this stimulated great ambitions for the future. The combined effect of all these developments was to generate strong expectations of continuous and noticeable rises in living standards. In the 1960s these expectations, based on the spectacular growth of the 1950s, began to come into conflict with what the economic system could deliver without significant distributional shifts. In the 1970s such shifts began to occur and over time might have seriously reduced the share of profits and the incentive to invest; however the pressures on production costs and profitability were suddenly and dramatically increased by rising commodity prices. This created an inflationary crisis which marked the end of the immediate post-war era.

Cautious demand management was an attempt to manage these problems. Initially there was optimism that this need only be temporary, but in the wake of the reluctance of inflation to decelerate in 1975–8, the second oil price shock led to considerable policy restrictiveness, and a large degree of slack has now emerged in the economies of the advanced capitalist world. Keynesian theory has not been forgotten; it is simply that depressed demand is required to relieve the pressures on profitability of which inflation is the expression. So far the successes of this policy have largely been cancelled out by its negative effects on productivity growth, and expansionary policies which might raise productivity growth are still ruled out by the fear that they would also relieve the downward pressure on real wages and commodity prices. The rise of Monetarism reflects a general appreciation of how deep-seated the problems of the advanced capitalist countries have now become, since it involves a clear shift of emphasis away from modes of thought characteristic of short-run demand management to a medium-term structural perspective. But the Monetarist project has encountered bitter resistance and its practical achievements fall far short of the rhetoric. This is another aspect of the aspirations problem: people are no more willing to accept a demolition of established public services and benefits than to see their real disposable incomes slashed.

Thus my thesis is that expansionary fiscal policies are currently rejected because they are inconsistent with the requirements of restabilising the socio-economic systems of the advanced capitalist world. This is different from the common accusation that they are no longer effective, in the sense that they no longer produce the increases in employment that were formerly expected of them.

This accusation rests on one or more of the following three points: (a) the openness of the advanced capitalist economies; (b) inflation; and (c) 'crowding out'.

The openness of the average industrial capitalist economy clearly limits the ability of one country to reduce its own unemployment, since a fair proportion of any demand stimulus will be exported, resulting in balance of payments deficits and a falling exchange rate, which will tend to push up inflation rates. Since the adjustment of trade flows to exchange rate changes is nowadays fairly slow, the disadvantages of such a change will tend to be evident earlier than the advantages, and will also tend to erode them. But these arguments apply only to the individual country pursuing a policy markedly more expansionary than its neighbours'; they do not apply to a co-ordinated or generalised policy of fiscal expansion. Accordingly their implication is that such a policy should if possible be co-ordinated internationally, rather than abandoned altogether.

The argument that expansionary policies lead to inflation can be based on a general relationship between demand and prices, particularly through wages and raw materials prices or (for the individual country) the exchange rate. It is also sometimes based on the thesis that most of the officially measured unemployment is voluntary and so prices might be pulled up by excess demand. The mechanical way in which such arguments are usually expressed is, however, quite unconvincing. It is true that stronger demand would tend to raise commodity prices; but it would also tend to raise productivity. The critical question is therefore its impact on money wages. This returns us to the problem of real wage aspirations which, as I have tried to indicate, cannot be reduced either to demand and supply relationships or to price expectations; it has a large *ideological* component. If aspirations are low in relation to productivity growth, as in the 1950s, the assertion that expansionary policies would lead to inflation is invalid; if they are high, the expansion will hit an inflation barrier based on industrial militancy as economic prospects improve. Thus I regard this argument as, essentially, a primitive expression of the analysis which I have tried to develop above.

The argument based on 'crowding out' is interesting. It rests on the assumption that monetary policy must remain relatively restrictive. If this is so, then the effectiveness of fiscal measures can certainly be impaired, perhaps seriously, by the impact of higher interest rates. But in the 1930s this problem was avoided simply by pursuing an accommodating monetary policy to keep interest rates low. Why not do the same today? This brings us back to the aspirations issue. The general adoption of monetary targets in the mid-1970s represented a well-publicised signal from governments that employment would not be insulated against the effects of excessive wage increases. The targets were meant to indicate to workers that if wage increases were too high, monetary policy would automatically become more restrictive. But having taken on this role of an informal incomes policy, monetary targets cannot be released from it until the threat of a wage explosion has been completely removed. Since they are playing an important role in regulating wage behaviour, they cannot be used to accommodate a fiscal expansion. If they could, it would signal that the aspirations problem had been solved, the danger of recovery being associated with a re-eruption of inflation having passed. Thus I do not regard 'crowding out' as a separate objection to fiscal action from the danger of inflation; they are alternative expressions of the fact that, though the growth of real wages has been significantly reduced by the recession, aspirations have not been reduced to the same extent, and improvements in the labour market and in medium-term economic prospects would result in strong pressure on money wages to make up the difference, including some of the shortfall built up during the recession. Whilst macroeconomic policy is designed to resolve *this* difficulty, it cannot be switched back to the conventional objective of controlling the level of output.

References

Addison, P. (1977) *The Road to 1945* (London: Quartet).

Ando, A. and Modigliani, F. (1965) 'The Relative Stability of Monetary Velocity and the Investment Multiplier', *American Economic Review*, LV, 693–728.

Arndt, H. W. (1944) *The Economic Lessons of the Nineteen Thirties* (London: Oxford UP).

Bailey, S. K. (1950) *Congress makes a Law: the Story behind the Employment Act of 1946* (New York: Columbia UP).

Barkai, A. (1977) *Das Wirtschaftssystem des Nationalsozialismus: der Historische und Ideologische Hintergrund 1933–36* (Cologne: Bibliothek Wissenschaft und Politik).

Barrett, C. R. and Walters, A. A. (1966) 'The Stability of Keynesian and Monetary Multipliers in the United Kingdom', *Review of Economics and Statistics*, XLVIII, 395–405.

Beveridge, W. H. (1944) *Full Employment in a Free Society* (London: Allen & Unwin).

Bleaney, M. F. (1976) *Underconsumption Theories: a History and Critical Analysis* (London: Lawrence & Wishart).

Bleaney, M. F. (1983) 'Conservative Economic Strategy', in S. Hall and M. Jacques (eds), *The Politics of Thatcherism* (London: Lawrence & Wishart).

Brown, E. C. (1956) 'Fiscal Policy in the Thirties: a Reappraisal', *American Economic Review*, XLVI, 857–79.

Brown, E. C., Solow, R. M., Ando A. and Kareken, J. (1962) *Lags in Fiscal and Monetary Policy* (Washington: US Commission on Money and Credit).

Brunner, K. (ed.) (1981) *The Great Depression Revisited* (Boston: Nijhoff).

Bruno, M. (1982) 'World Shocks, Macroeconomic Response, and the Productivity Puzzle', in R. C. O. Matthews (ed.) *Slower Growth in the Western World* (London: Heinemann).

Carré, J.-J., Dubois, P. and Malinvaud, E. (1972) *La Croissance Française* (Paris: Editions du Seuil).

Clayton, J. L. (ed.) (1970) *The Economic Impact of the Cold War* (New York: Harcourt Brace & World Inc.).

Clower, R. W. (1965) 'The Keynesian Counter-revolution: a Theoretical Reappraisal', in F. Hahn and F. Brechling (eds), *The Theory of Interest Rates* (London: Macmillan).

Crouch, C. and Pizzorno, A. (1978) *The Resurgence of Class Conflict in Western Europe since 1968*, 2 vols (London: Macmillan).

Davis, J. R. (1971) *The New Economics and the Old Economists* (Ames: Iowa UP).

Dow, J. C. R. (1964) *The Management of the British Economy 1945–60* (Cambridge: Cambridge UP).

Feinstein, C. H. (1972) *National Income, Expenditure and Output of the United Kingdom, 1855–1965* (Cambridge: Cambridge UP).

Feldstein, M. (1980) *The American Economy in Transition* (Chicago: Chicago UP).

Friedman, B. M. (1979) 'Optimal Expectation and the Extreme Information Assumptions of "Rational Expectations" Macromodels', *Journal of Monetary Economics*, V, 23–42.

Friedman, M. (ed.) (1956) *Studies in the Quantity Theory of Money* (Chicago: Chicago UP).

Friedman, M. (1957) *The Theory of the Consumption Function* (Princeton: Priceton UP).

Friedman, M. (1959) 'The Demand for Money: some Theoretical and Empirical Results', *Journal of Political Economy*, LXVII, 327–51.

Friedman, M. (1966) 'Interest Rates and the Demand for Money', *Journal of Law and Economics*, IX, 71–85.

Friedman, M. (1968) 'The Role of Monetary Policy', *American Economic Review*, LVIII, 1–17.

Friedman, M. (1970) 'A Theoretical Framework for Monetary Analysis', *Journal of Political Economy*, LXXVIII, 193–238.

Friedman, M. (1973) *Money and Economic Development: the Horowitz Lectures of 1972* (New York: Praeger).

Friedman, M. (1975) *Unemployment versus Inflation? An Evaluation of the Phillips Curve* (London: Institute of Economic Affairs).

Friedman, M. and Meiselman, D. (1963) *The Relative Stability of Monetary Velocity and the Investment Multiplier in the United States 1897–1958* (Englewood Cliffs: Prentice-Hall).

Friedman, M. and Schwartz, A. J. (1963a) *A Monetary History of the United States 1867–1960* (Princeton: Princeton UP).

Friedman, M. and Schwartz, A. J. (1963b) 'Money and Business Cycles', *Review of Economics and Statistics*, XLV, Supplement, 32–78.

Garvy, G. (1975) 'Keynes and the Economic Activists of Pre-Hitler Germany', *Journal of Political Economy*, LXXXIII, 391–404.

Giersch, H. and Wolter, F. (1983) 'Towards an Explanation of the Productivity Slowdown: an Acceleration–Deceleration Hypothesis', *Economic Journal*, XCIII, 35–55.

Glyn, A. (1982) 'The Productivity Slowdown: a Marxist View', in R. C. O. Matthews (ed.) *Slower Growth in the Western World* (London: Heinemann).

Gordon, R. J. (ed.) (1974) *Milton Friedman's Monetary Framework* (Chicago: Chicago UP).

Griliches, Z. (1980) 'Research and Development and the Productivity

Slowdown', *Papers and Proceedings of the American Economic Association*, LXX, 343–8.

Guillebaud, C. W. (1939) *The Economic Recovery of Germany 1933–38* (London: Macmillan).

Hall, R. E. (1975) 'The Rigidity of Wages and the persistence of Unemployment', *Brookings Papers on Economic Activity* 2 (1975) 301–35.

Halperin, S. W. (1965) *Germany tried Democracy: a Political History of the Reich from 1918 to 1932* (New York: Norton).

Hansen, A. (1963) 'Was Fiscal Policy in the 1930s a Failure?', *Review of Economics and Statistics*, XLV, 320–3.

Hansen, B. (1969) *Fiscal Policy in Seven Countries 1955–65* (Paris: OECD).

Harrod, R. F. (1939) 'An Essay in Dynamic Theory', *Economic Journal*, XLIX, 14–33.

Harrod, R. F. (1952) *The Life of John Maynard Keynes* (London: Macmillan).

Hickman, B. G. and Coen, R. M. (1976) *An Annual Growth Model of the U.S. Economy* (New York: American Elsevier).

Hicks, J. R. (1937) 'Mr Keynes and the "Classics": a Suggested Interpretation', *Econometrica*, V, 147–59.

Hill, T. P. (1979) *Profits and Rates of Return* (Paris: OECD).

Johannson, O. (1967) *The Gross Domestic Product of Sweden and its Composition 1861–1955* (Stockholm: Almqvist & Wiksell).

Jonung, L. (1979) 'Knut Wicksell's norm of price stabilisation and Swedish monetary policy in the 1930s', *Journal of Monetary Economics*, V, 459–96.

Kahn, R. F. (1931) 'The Relation of Home Investment to Unemployment', *Economic Journal*, XLI, 173–98.

Kalecki, M. (1938) 'The Lesson of the Blum Experiment', *Economic Journal*, XLVIII, 26–41.

Keynes, J. M. (1930) *A Treatise on Money*, 2 vols (London: Macmillan).

Keynes, J. M. (1936) *The General Theory of Employment Interest and Money* (London: Macmillan).

Keynes, J. M. (1937) 'Alternative Theories of the Rate of Interest', *Economic Journal*, XLVII, 241–52.

Keynes, J. M. (1940) *How to Pay for the War* (London: Macmillan).

Kindleberger, C. P. (1967) *Europe's Post-war Growth: the Role of Labour Supply* (Cambridge: Harvard UP).

Laidler, D. (1981) 'Monetarism', *Economic Journal*, XCI, 1–28.

Leijonhufvud, A. (1968) *On Keynesian Economics and the Economics of Keynes* (Oxford: Oxford UP).

Leijonhufvud, A. (1981) *Information and Co-ordination: Essays in Macroeconomic Theory* (Oxford: Oxford UP).

Lewis, W. A. (1949) *Economic Survey 1919–39* (London: Allen & Unwin).

Lindbeck, A. (1983) 'The Recent Slowdown of Productivity Growth', *Economic Journal*, XCIII, 13–34.

Lucas, R. E. (1976) 'Econometric Policy Evaluation: a Critique', in K. Brunner and A. H. Meltzer (eds), *The Phillips Curve and Labour Markets* (New York: North-Holland).

Lucas, R. E. and Rapping, L. A. (1969) 'Real Wages, Employment and the Price Level', *Journal of Political Economy*, LXXVII, 721–54.

Lundberg, E. (1968) *Instability and Economic Growth* (New Haven: Yale UP).

Machlup, F. (1972) *The Alignment of Foreign Exchange Rates* (New York: Praeger).

Maddison, A. (1964) *Economic Growth in the West* (London: Allen & Unwin).

Maddison, A. (1977) 'Phases of Capitalist Development', *Bana nazionale del Lavoro Quarterly Review*, XXX, 103–39.

Maddison, A. (1979) 'Long Run Dynamics of Productivity Growth', *Banca Nazionale del Lavoro Quarterly Review*, XXXII, 3–44.

Maddison, A. (1980) 'Western Economic Performance in the 1970s: a Perspective and Assessment', *Banca Nazionale del Lavoro Quarterly Review*, XXXIII, 247–90.

Mandel, E. (1975) *Late Capitalism* (London: New Left Books).

Marjolin, R. (1938) 'Reflections on the Blum Experiment', *Economica* (N.S.), V, 177–91.

Marx, K. (1954) *Capital*, vol. I (Moscow: Progress).

Matthews, R. C. O. (1959) *The Trade Cycle* (Cambridge: Cambridge UP).

Matthews, R. C. O. (1968) 'Why has Britain had Full Employment since the War?', *Economic Journal*, LXXVIII, 555–69.

Matthews, R. C. O. (ed.) (1982) *Slower Growth in the Western World* (London: Heinemann).

Minford, P. and Peel, D. (1980) 'The Natural Rate Hypothesis and Rational Expectations – a Critique of some Recent Developments', *Oxford Economic Papers* N.S., XXXII, 71–81.

Modigliani, F. (1944) 'Liquidity Preference and the Theory of Money', *Econometrica*, XII, 45–88.

Muth, J. F. (1961) 'Rational Expectations and the Theory of Price Movements', *Econometrica*, XXIX, 315–35.

Okun, A. M. and Teeters, N. H. (1970) 'The Full Employment Surplus Revisited', *Brookings Papers on Economic Activity*, 1, (1970), 77–110.

OECD (Organisation for Economic Co-operation and Development) (1977) *Towards Full Employment and Price Stability* (Paris: OECD).

OECD (1978a) *Budget Indicators* (Paris: OECD Economic Outlook Occasional Studies).

OECD (1978b) *Public Expenditure Trends* (Paris: OECD).

OECD (1982) *Budget Financing and Monetary Control* (Paris: OECD).

OECD (1983) *Public Sector Deficits: Problems and Policy Implications* (Paris: OECD Economic Outlook Occasional Studies).

Organisation for European Economic Co-operation (OEEC) (1958) *Ninth Report of the OEEC – A Decade of Co-operation: Achievements and Perspectives* (Paris: OEEC).

Overy, R. J. (1982) *The Nazi Economic Recovery 1932–1938* (London: Macmillan).

Patinkin, D. (1956) *Money Interest and Prices* (New York: Harper & Row).

Patinkin, D. (1969) 'The Chicago Tradition, the Quantity Theory and Friedman', *Journal of Money Credit and Banking*, I, 46–70.

Patinkin, D. (1976) *Keynes's Monetary Thought: A Study of its Development* (Durham, NC: Duke UP).

Peppers, L. C. (1973) 'Full Employment Surplus Analysis and Structural

Change: the 1930s', *Explorations in Economic History*, X, 197–210.

Phelps, E. S. (1968) 'Money-wage Dynamics and Labour-market Equilibrium', *Journal of Political Economy*, LXXVI, 678–711.

Pigou, A. C. (1943) 'The Classical Stationary State', *Economic Journal*, LIII, 343–51.

Pigou, A. C. (1950) *Keynes's 'General Theory': A Retrospective View* (London: Macmillan).

Postan, M. M. (1967) *An Economic History of Western Europe 1945–64* (London: Methuen).

Roose, K. D. (1954) *The Economics of Recession and Revival: an Interpretation of 1937–38* (New Haven: Yale UP).

Samuelson, P. A. (1939) 'A Synthesis of the Principle of Acceleration and the Multiplier', *Journal of Political Economy*, XLVII, 786–97.

Samuelson, P. A. (1968) 'What Classical and Neoclassical Monetary Theory Really Was', *Canadian Journal of Economics*, I, 1–15.

Sargent, T. J. and Wallace, N. (1975) ' "Rational" Expectations, the Optimal Monetary Instrument, and the Optimal Money Supply Rule', *Journal of Political Economy*, LXXXIII, 241–53.

Sauvy, A. (1967) *Histoire Economique de la France entre les Deux Guerres* (4 vols), Vol. II *1931–39* (Paris: Fayard).

Schumpeter, J. (1939) *Business Cycles*, 2 vols (New York: McGraw-Hill).

Shackle, G. L. S. (1967) *The Years of High Theory: Invention and Tradition in Economic Thought 1926–1939* (Cambridge: Cambridge UP).

Shiller, R. (1978) 'Rational Expectations and the Dynamic Structure of Macroeconomic Models: a Critical Review', *Journal of Monetary Economics*, IV, 1–44.

Skidelsky, R. (1967) *Politicians and the Slump* (London: Macmillan).

Stedman Jones, G. (1971) *Outcast London* (London: Oxford UP).

Stein, H. (1969) *The Fiscal Revolution in America* (Chicago: Chicago UP).

Stein, J. L. (ed.) (1976) *Monetarism* (Oxford: North-Holland).

Stigler, G. (1946) *Production and Distribution Theories* (New York: Macmillan).

Svennilson, I. (1954) *Growth and Stagnation in the European Economy* (Geneva: UN Economic Commission for Europe).

Teeters, N. H. (1965) 'Estimates of the Full Employment Surplus, 1955–64', *Review of Economics and Statistics*, XLVII, 309–21.

Temin, P. (1976) *Did Monetary Forces Cause the Great Depression?* (New York: Norton).

Thomas, B. (1937) *Monetary Policy and Crises: a Study of the Swedish Experience* (London: Routledge).

Tobin, J. (1965) 'The Monetary Interpretation of History', *American Economic Review*, LV, 464–85.

Tobin, J. (1972) 'Inflation and Unemployment', *American Economic Review*, LXII, 1–18.

United Nations (1953) *Economic Survey of Europe since the War* (Geneva: UN Economic Commission for Europe).

United Nations (1964) *Economic Survey of Europe in 1961. Part II: Some Factors in Economic Growth in Europe during the 1950s* (Geneva: UN Economic Commission for Europe).

United Nations (1982) *Economic Survey of Europe in 1981* (New York: United Nations).

United States Department of Commerce (1975) *Historical Statistics of the United States: Colonial Times to 1970* (Washington: Bureau of the Census).

Wallich, H. C. (1955) *Mainsprings of the German Revival* (New Haven: Yale UP).

Ward, T. S. and R. R. Neild (1978) *The Measurement and Reform of Budgetary Policy* (London: Heinemann).

Wecter, D. (1948) *The Age of the Great Depression 1929–41* (New York: McGraw-Hill).

Index

Boston Public Library

WEST ROXBURY
BRANCH LIBRARY